TRANSFORMING A UNIONIZED PLANT

*Leadership Lessons for
a Divided World*

Thomas C. Tuttle

To Ross, Roger, Arnie, Bill, Stew, Bobby, Mo, Dave and Sten Åke and the other men and women who dedicated their work lives to the transformation of Hagerstown Powertrain.

To Jay Jacobs, Len Elenowitz and Rudy Lamone for establishing the Maryland Center for Productivity and Quality of Working Life at the University of Maryland.

To Judy, for her love and support.

CONTENTS

LIST OF TABLES

LIST OF FIGURES

APPENDICES

CHAPTER 1

Introduction and Background

In June 1991, Ross Rhoads, General Manager of the Mack Hagerstown Powertrain Plant, hosted a meeting in his office involving Bill Nutter, Shop Chairman of UAW Local 171 and Dr. Tom Tuttle, Director of the University of Maryland Center for Quality and Productivity (UMCQP).[1] Tuttle had been introduced to Rhoads a few months earlier at an Executive Development Program conducted by the University of Maryland College of Business and Management. Since Rhoads had become General Manager in 1986, Mack's Corporate leaders had been at war with the UAW and the company was enduring financial turmoil that threatened the future of the Company as well as the Hagerstown plant. A major component manufactured at the plant, the rear axle or carrier, was being outsourced from Hagerstown. This action would reduce the number of jobs by over 1000. This job loss in Hagerstown, in the western Maryland region that had, over the last decade, already experienced significant manufacturing job loss alarmed the Governor of Maryland, William Donald Schaefer.

[1] At the time of this meeting the UMCQP was called the Maryland Center for Productivity and Quality of Working Life. At the time of the Center's founding in 1977, a major emphasis of the Center's purpose was to promote union and management collaboration. "Quality of Working Life" was a phrase that aligned with the purpose of labor unions until the phrase was co-opted by companies as a label applied to so-called, non-union "breakaway plants" built by a number of companies in the Southern part of the U.S.

Fearing the loss of the entire plant, Governor Schaefer dispatched his Secretary of Economic Development, Randy Evans, to France to meet with the Chairman of Renault, which was in the process of acquiring Mack. Evans delivered an offer of assistance from the State of Maryland to save the Hagerstown Plant. Part of the package offered to Renault and Mack from the State of Maryland included, in addition to financial incentives, consulting and training assistance from the UMCQP which was directed by Tuttle.

The First Encounter

Launching a quality and productivity improvement process could not be done by management alone. It had to be a joint effort involving plant management and the United Auto Workers who represented the manufacturing work force. The purpose of this initial meeting was to determine if the UAW would be willing to enter into a joint union management improvement process to save the plant. In this meeting, the essence of the dialog was this exchange between Ross Rhoads and Bill Nutter:

> **Ross:** *"Bill, is the UAW willing to participate in a joint union—management employee involvement process to save this plant?"*
>
> **Bill N.:** *"If the University of Maryland is involved in guiding us, we are in. But if this is just more Mack Bullshit, forget it!"*

Overview of the Book

The story I will tell began that day in 1991. This story ends in 2007, when Roger Johnston, Vice-President of Manufacturing, left Hagerstown. The key message of the story is that the efforts of a relatively small group of business and union leaders in Hagerstown, Maryland, supported by their community, their families, the University of Maryland, and the State of

Maryland, rose above their individual self-interest to work jointly to save a plant that was on the verge of being closed by its owners. Furthermore, these key individuals, by showing their ability to work together toward common aims, convinced two major corporations to invest over $400 million over this period to modernize the facility, bring new products to be produced in Hagerstown and assure the security of the jobs of over 1200 employees and the economic well-being of their families.

The success story created by these men and women lives on 15 years later with a plant that now employs over 2000 employees and serves as the headquarters and major engineering and production center for Volvo's North American Powertrain division. And the carrier production that was outsourced in the late 1980's, has returned to Hagerstown. The plant also produces most of the engines and many of the transmissions for Volvo and Mack branded trucks sold in North America.

This importance of this story is much larger than the accomplishments just in Hagerstown. Communities all over this nation are struggling to adjust to the impacts of new global ownership, new technology, globalization of workforces and products, changing regulation, and the impact of climate change. On top of that has been the impact of the global pandemic on workplaces and supply chains, political discord, and the impact of protests against racial injustice and inequality. As this story will point out, efforts by politicians, education organizations and local community leaders are a part of the story, and their support is necessary. But in the end, operating a successful global business comes down to decisions made by union and management leaders in the international, national, and local organizations themselves to determine whether businesses are viable and competitive. Doing so, requires leaders to take advantage of the assistance offered them to grow, learn and be able to change their behavior in order to survive and thrive.

This story provides lessons learned with respect to adapting successfully to the needs for collaboration and change. Whether the challenge is new customer requirements, changing employee perceptions and needs, the impact of globalization, climate change, new ownership, new products, new technology, operating in a pandemic or all the above, there are lessons to be learned from the Hagerstown experience.

The story will be presented in 6 Chapters. Chapter 1 sets the stage and provides some context for the key story that began in 1991. It also addresses some of the key issues in the trucking industry and history of both Mack Trucks and the Hagerstown plant. Chapter 2 covers the period from when Ross Rhoads became the General Manager of the Hagerstown plant from 1986 -1998. It will focus primarily on the period from 1991 – 1998. Chapter 3 addresses another stormy period in the plant's history following Ross's departure as GM. During this period from 1998 – January 1999 the plant was led by Olivier Vidal, a young General Manager from France. It represented a major shift in the management style from that established by Ross Rhoads, which was to work jointly with the UAW. Olivier's mandate was to enable Renault to obtain a return on their investment in Mack and Hagerstown. The goal was appropriate, but the methods backfired. Chapters 4 and 5 address two phases in the period from 1999-2007 and involved the transition from Renault to Volvo ownership. Roger Johnston arrived in 1999 as the new General Manager with the challenges to improve relationships with the UAW that had "gone south" under Olivier and to increase engine production to 200 engines per day. Chapter 5 focuses on the roll-out of a new product and culture that would eventually be spread into the entire plant. Chapter 6 addresses key principles and major lessons learned from this 16-year period in the Hagerstown plant's history that have relevance for any manufacturing or business organization today. The lessons learned are relevant for all levels of management, for union officials, and for government and policy makers in the economic development field. The story also has important relevance for the relationships between higher education organizations and businesses specifically in terms of how education organizations can promote private sector economic growth and competitiveness as "third party" facilitators of business-labor collaboration.

Background of Mack Trucks and the Hagerstown Plant

Mack was founded by the five Mack brothers, Augustus, William, Joseph, Charles, and Jack. They were second generation Americans who were sons of German immigrants and were raised on a farm near Scranton, Pennsylvania. The most adventurous of the brothers was Jack who ran away from home at age 14 and worked on a variety of jobs and eventually became a stationary engineer on steam engines. He spent time in the U.S, in the Panama Canal Zone and spent time at sea on ocean vessels. These travels not only allowed a young man who never finished high school to become quite proficient in the steam engine technology which was the principal technology used to power vessels of all types in the late 1800's. In Europe, crude efforts were underway to experiment with self-propelled vehicles. Jack Mack, either through knowledge of these efforts or simply his vision and imagination realized that the days of the horse and wagon were numbered. He returned to the U.S. and together with his brother Augustus bought a small wagon building firm in Brooklyn, New York. Their first Mack motor vehicle, launched in 1900 following 8 years of experimentation, was a self-propelled wagon, actually a bus, which was the first successful bus built in the U.S. It was used to carry tourists through Prospect Park in Brooklyn.

Following this successful beginning, the company grew and began to offer not only buses but also introduced a line of heavy-duty trucks. By the summer of 1911, Mack had 825 employees and produced almost 600 units per year. By 1911, the Mack Brothers Motor Car Company was one of the largest producers of heavy-duty trucks in the U.S. Under Jack Mack's leadership the company established its reputation as the premier heavy-duty truck in America due to its quality, dependability, and durability. Mack Trucks views Jack Mack as its founder.

As is often the case as companies grow, the need for more capital and the need for a different style of management led Mack to seek external investment. The price of that investment was that Mack was merged with two other truck makers by J.P Morgan, their investment banker, to form the International Motor Company. Shortly after the merger, Jack Mack and three of his brothers disassociated themselves from the merged company.

The International Motor Company merged Mack with the Sauer Motor Company and the Hewitt Motor Company. Later, the International Motor Company dropped Sauer and Hewitt and became Mack Trucks, Inc. In this evolution, Mack became the brand due to the reputation established by Jack Mack for quality, dependability, and durability. The merger also brought engineering talent to the company. Edward R. Hewitt was the grandson of Peter Cooper who is credited with building the first American steam locomotive. Hewitt became chief engineer of the new company and designed the AB Mack first produced in 1914. This was said to be the first truck in the U.S. that did not look like a wagon. Hewitt was followed as Chief Engineer by Alfred F. Masury who designed a truck that eventually gave the Mack Brand its status as an American Icon. This was the AC Mack that gained its prominence in World War 1, particularly for its performance in France used by the U.S. Corps of Engineers serving with the U.S. Expeditionary Forces. "Rugged, dependable, and tenacious, it took incredible abuse – the roughest possible terrain, continuous operation, inexperienced drivers, and gross overloading – and came back for more. It had all the qualities of a Bulldog; and with its blunt, snub-nosed hood it looked like a Bulldog- and it became the "Bulldog Mack" to the British Tommies and the American Doughboys. The name stuck and by the end of the war the Bulldog had been registered as Mack's corporate signal, remaining in use ever since. This was the beginning of the Bulldog, and of Mack's famous slogan "Performance Counts."[2]

Following the war, throughout the 1920's, Mack's reputation as the premier truck maker was well established and the phrase "Built like a Mack Truck" was built into the national lexicon. While the AC model continued to be produced there was significant innovation going on under the sheet metal exterior. Innovations such as vibration dampening by a shock insulator patented by Mack became standard through the industry. From 1919 to 1927 Mack engineers were granted more than 270 patents. By the end of 1927 production had risen from 5.000 units in 1919 to over 7500. Sales had more than doubled from $22 million to $55 million.

This success was credited to the technical leadership of the engineering team as well as the talent and spirit of teamwork that prevailed throughout the Mack organization. The Bulldog was a source of pride and it helped unite the workforce. Success in the marketplace was also because in many parts of the country there had been a "good roads" movement that created decent inter-city roads. While railroads were the major power

---

[2] Zenon C. R. Hansen, *The Legend of the Bulldog,* Address given at the 268th Franklin Birthday Dinner of the Newcomen Society of North America held at the Franklin Institute, Philadelphia, Pennsylvania, January 16, 1974.

in the transportation industry, emphasis was being placed on speed in transportation of raw materials as well as finished goods. Only the motor truck could offer, direct, point-to-point delivery from origin to destination. "Best of all, product could be moved at the convenience of the shipper and his customer rather than at the convenience of the railroad."[3]

Mack like most companies struggled during the Depression of the 1930's. By 1932, it had taken a 75% reduction in domestic sales. However, the company was fortunate that it was led by a CEO, AJ Brosseau, who stuck to the core values of the company. "He realized that cutting quality, introducing cheaper models, and curtailing factory branch operations would, in the long-run, be self-defeating... Mack kept faith with its own tradition and its customers; maintained the high quality of the Mack product; and offered a noncompeting line of light-duty trucks through its branches."[4]

One of the significant developments in the late 30's was Mack's introduction of the automotive diesel engine. It had begun research on automotive diesels as early as 1928. In the early 30's both Cummins and Mercedes-Benz diesel were installed in Mack chassis as research endeavors and were tested thoroughly. However, Mack management was committed to developing and launching its own Mack components. However, by 1938 when the Mack Diesel was launched, Mack became the first truck manufacturer to produce its own diesel engine.

The 1940's were largely consumed with war production. The company made an enormous contribution to the effort as it had done in World War 1. Much of its production was for the British military and it included a six-wheeler as a tank transporter for British General Montgomery's North African Campaign. After the Japanese strike on Pearl Harbor, almost all its production went to the war effort. Before the war ended over 30,000 heavy duty trucks were produced for the military and its Allies. This effort clearly established Mack as a global brand.

---

[3] Ibid, p 16.
[4] Zenon C. R. Hansen, *The Legend of the Bulldog,* Address given at the 268th Franklin Birthday Dinner of the Newcomen Society of North America held at the Franklin Institute, Philadelphia, Pennsylvania, January 16, 1974, p.9

For the next decade and into the early 60's Mack prospered. However, during the 50's a closed end investment company had acquired enough Mack stock that it was able to take control of the company. These "outsiders" provided badly needed capital as the post war production was ramping up.

> *". . . as the outsiders gained complete control of it—that's where the trouble started. At times, it seemed as if Mack was playing musical chairs with its CEO's, all of whom were finance oriented, with no experience in the truck industry. The results were almost disastrous. Veteran executives with years of experience were fired or retired, and replaced with still more outsiders, isolating management from operations. Seeking to show a paper profit, management allowed facilities to deteriorate, maintenance was deferred; and badly needed machine tools and quality control equipment were not purchased. The decision to cease production of buses (1960) was undoubtedly correct . . . But other management decisions were almost beyond belief. The obsolete engine and transmission factory in Plainfield, New Jersey, was kept in service too long; then suddenly scrapped in favor of a new facility in Hagerstown, Maryland—a location selected based on a consulting firm's recommendation. This move cost Mack over $17 million in startup costs alone; and the new plant proved to be a millstone around the company's neck. The Mack executive offices, which had been moved from New York City to Plainfield in the mid-50's, were again moved to Montvale, New Jersey. And while this move may have been ideally suited to elegant suburban living for executives, it further isolated management from operations . . . and from customers! One of our top engineering executives recalls that in those days he spent almost 75% of his time on the road between Montvale, Allentown, and Hagerstown. Labor relations were practically non-existent, and repeated work stoppages and strikes had become almost routine.*
>
> *By 1964, Mack's vaunted product had begun to deteriorate, even as had the facilities in which it was produced; and the company was experiencing declining market penetration, sales, and earnings along with still-soaring production costs. Between*

1959 and 1964, Mack lost approximately one-third of its share
of the market and earnings had declined from $15.8 million
to $3.4 million. A proposed merger with Chrysler might have
saved the company, but perhaps predictably this proposal was
denied by the Justice Department. Many of us in the industry
were convinced that it was only a matter of time before Mack
ceased to exist."[5]

The quoted sections above are quite significant in understanding the history of the Hagerstown plant. These comments made by Zenon C.R. Hansen are the thoughts of a seasoned truck industry executive who was about to become CEO of Mack Trucks as of January 7, 1965. Obviously, his bias is that of an operations-oriented CEO. However, his insights regarding prior management's decision making clearly demonstrate how the previous management by the financially oriented leaders totally divorced Mack Trucks from its founding values and what the Bulldog had come to represent. It also clearly demonstrated what forsaking these values did to the company in terms of profitability. Anyone who claims that "values-based management" is a soft, fuzzy idea only must look at the roller coaster history of Mack Trucks from its founding in 1900 until 1965 when its very survival was uncertain. It was adherence to the founding values of Jack Mack that had allowed the company to become a national icon. When leaders strayed from those values in seeking short term profitability, the company lost money and lost its way.

A lesson that can be learned from this early history is one that repeated itself again in the 1980s. As a capital-intensive business, heavy truck manufacturing tends to be a very cyclic business. It is seriously impacted by business cycles, and regulatory changes also create additional cyclic pressures that are independent of the business cycle ups and downs. Particularly with respect to environmental regulation, there tends to be accelerated buying of trucks just before a new environmental standard will be released. The market tends to "cool off" for as much as a year or more until customers are convinced that the product changes required by the new regulation have been fully tested. When the negative regulatory impact on the truck

---

[5] Zenon C. R. Hansen, *The Legend of the Bulldog,* Address given at the 268th Franklin Birthday Dinner of the Newcomen Society of North America held at the Franklin Institute, Philadelphia, Pennsylvania, January 16, 1974.

purchasing cycle coincides with a decline in the larger economic business cycle, truck manufacturers can be severely stressed. If the company is not sufficiently capitalized to weather these cycles, the low points can lead to the need to seek external investment which can bring other threats to the business as Hansen's comments vividly describe.

When Mack's survival was at stake in 1965, the company was fortunate to be able to bring in an experienced operationally oriented truck industry executive who appreciated the values that had made the "Bulldog" a national Icon. Hansen described the situation he moved into as a great challenge that he could not resist.

> *"Quite frankly, I accepted the Presidency of Mack Trucks because it was the most tremendous challenge that had ever been offered to me! Here was an opportunity to put many of my ideas into effect, and to rebuild a very individual truck company back to the leader of industry it had been before. Many well-informed individuals advised me that I was taking over a sinking ship, that Mack was too far gone to save, that Mack would either go under or be absorbed by one of our competitors. But I thought they were wrong. Mack still had a great name, a great product, and above all it had the people. All that was needed was leadership."* [6]

What Hansen might have also said was that what Mack needed was leadership that shared the values that had made Mack a great company in the first place. One of the ways in which Hansen exhibited these values was to begin his term in office by holding meetings with union representatives and to "lay the cornerstone of a highly successful labor relations program—so successful, in fact that Mack has not had a strike for the succeeding 9 years. (i.e., the 9 years from 1965 until the date of Hansen's speech in 1974).[7]

As CEO Hansen stated that there were so many serious problems that he had to "triage" the problems and tackle them one at a time. He had

---

[6] Zenon C. R. Hansen, *The Legend of the Bulldog*, Address given at the 268th Franklin Birthday Dinner of the Newcomen Society of North America held at the Franklin Institute, Philadelphia, Pennsylvania, January 16, 1974, p.32.

[7] Ibid, p.33-34.

initially worked on employee morale, next was the financial condition of the company, need to increase production, modernizing production tools, dealing with deferred plant maintenance and finally coordination and communication. After returning the executive offices to Allentown to reconnect management and operations more effectively he turned his attention to Hagerstown. Here is how Hansen described his approach to the site that built engines and transmissions.

> *"Concerning the Hagerstown facility, I received several proposals to the effect that the plant should be sold, and that engine and transmission production be moved to Allentown. In terms of centralization, this was an attractive idea, particularly so in light of the fact that the productivity of the Hagerstown plant left a lot to be desired. But our investment in that plant was so enormous that the cost of replacing it could not be contemplated. So, we decided to keep Hagerstown in operation and make it more productive. We commenced a modernization and retooling program; corrected some basic flaws in design; and as production costs dropped, productivity began to increase.*
>
> *. . . In retrospect the most important decision I had to make in 1965 was whether to put the new Maxidyne Diesel engine into production. Conceived as the successor to the Thermodyne, a prototype that had already been built when I arrived at Mack, I was amazed. Designed by Walter M. May and his associate Winton Pelizzoni, this engine produced essentially constant horsepower over a wide operating range instead of the typically narrow operating range common to other Diesels. And this constant horsepower feature enabled Mack engineers to use a simple, uncomplicated five-speed transmission as opposed to the complex 10, 13 and 15 speed transmissions offered by competition. To be offered as a complete powertrain, the Maxidyne engine and the Maxitorque transmission offered a 65% reduction in highway shifting: more usable horsepower and torque than any other comparable powertrain, greatly increased service life and substantial fuel economy. Yet, former*

management had been reluctant to put it into production . . .
So we went ahead with production of the Maxidyne, which
was introduced in late 1966, and it enjoyed almost immediate
acceptance. It has since been described as the greatest
breakthrough in Diesel technology in 15 years. (By 1974) 90%
of Mack's production is powered by Maxidyne/Maxitorque
powertrains."[8]

This breakthrough was helpful for Hagerstown since the engines and
transmissions were built in the Hagerstown plant. Two years into Hansen's
tenure as CEO, Mack achieved record levels of performance in terms of
production, sales, and earnings. But despite that, by the end of 1966 the
need for additional capital returned. In essence, the company was a victim
of its own success. Hansen described the issue as follows:

"Our own success had put us in a financial bind—the more
trucks we built and sold, the greater the need for capital- and
with a common equity capitalization of only $134 million,
Mack's borrowing power was severely limited. At the same time,
our outstanding earnings in 1966 had made us a prime target
for a takeover, and I was greatly concerned that we might be
taken over by a conglomerate whose best interests might not
coincide with ours."[9]

After fighting off several takeover attempts, discussions with a New York Bank
led Hansen, who had just been named President and Chairman of the Board,
to talks with the Signal Oil and Gas Company. In his new role, Hansen
negotiated a takeover of the company by Signal that would provide the
capital required but that would assure that Mack would retain autonomy. In
addition, the agreement would not permit any other truck manufacturer to be
brought into the merged company that would be called the Signal Companies.
Mack thus became an affiliate of Signal Companies in September of 1967.

---

[8] Zenon C. R. Hansen, *The Legend of the Bulldog*, Address given at the 268th Franklin
Birthday Dinner of the Newcomen Society of North America held at the Franklin
Institute, Philadelphia, Pennsylvania, January 16, 1974, p. 36-37.
[9] Ibid, p.38

Commenting on this relationship in 1974, two years after Hansen retired in January 1972, he stated that the relationship has remained successful because:

> *"Mack insisted on maintaining its autonomy, and Signal has subscribed to that philosophy. Since the merger, much has been made of the financial backing which Signal provided for us. But while Signal did provide us with substantial capital, the really significant value has been that: Mack has been associated with a high-grade organization which has honored all its commitments."[10]*

Decision to Build the Mack Hagerstown Powertrain Plant.

As Zenon Hansen pointed out above, the story of the Mack Hagerstown Plant began in 1959 when Mack Trucks leaders in its Allentown, Pa. headquarters began looking for a place to build a modern alternative to its engine, transmission and carrier plant in Plainfield, New Jersey. The company leaders settled on a 280-acre location in Hagerstown, Maryland to build a $45 million, 1-million square foot manufacturing plant. The plant produced its first Mack engine in the new facility in 1961.

Some of the employees for the new plant transferred from the Plainfield, New Jersey Mack facility that was closed. The company also recruited machinists throughout the region from Pennsylvania and Maryland. According to Jim Stewart, who was hired in 1962 from the Frick Plant in Waynesboro, Pa. "anyone who had any machining experience was in demand. "[11] Initially, only about 200 people moved down from the Plainfield Plant. Another relatively large group of employees were hired from the Fairchild Aircraft Company in Hagerstown that was downsizing and they, like the Plainfield transferees, had been members of a UAW local. Another group of former union members, from the United Steelworkers Union, moved down from the Pittsburgh area. Virtually all these people

---

[10] Zenon C. R. Hansen, *The Legend of the Bulldog,* Address given at the 268th Franklin Birthday Dinner of the Newcomen Society of North America held at the Franklin Institute, Philadelphia, Pennsylvania, January 16, 1974. p.10

[11] Jim Stewart, 2020, personal interview.

who came from other plants came from the experience of either a plant closing or downsizing and brought with them the scars and suspicions of management created by the painful experience of seeing your job disappear.

Employees at the Plainfield plant had been represented by the United Auto Workers. When the Hagerstown Plant opened in 1961 there was no union representation. However, when the UAW launched an organizing campaign in the plant, Mack management had agreed, prior to the move, not to oppose a union organizing campaign. In July 1962, UAW Local 171 was chartered to represent the manufacturing employees in the new plant.

Other than the former union members from Fairchild, the ex-Plainfield and ex-Pittsburgh area employees referred to the local people hired from Hagerstown as "the farmers." Jim Stewart, who was from Hagerstown described this early experience of how he became a union member. Although he had worked in a machining job for 6 months following his high school graduation, he did not feel ready to consider himself a "machinist." He was probably more comfortable considering himself as one of the "farmers."

> *"I was green as grass. I had just turned 19 in December before I was hired in April. When I went in there, we had an assistant foreman who came up and said 'I'm going to tell you something. I want you to tell me when you have to go to the bathroom, and you are not going to eat around your machine." I said 'What?' He repeated "I want you to tell me when you have to go to the bathroom and you can't eat your lunch here, I don't want anyone eating anything in this department." At this point I was not sure that I even wanted a job where I was confined into a building anyway. So, I thought it was a little strange that I had to tell someone when I had to go to the bathroom, and I could not eat anything down in my department. It was not long after that when someone came by and said "I want to give you a sign-up card because we are trying to get the UAW in here. These cards are to show interest in getting a Union." I did not know anything about unions. However, I must have had a little "hair up my butt" over having to get permission to go to*

*the bathroom. So, I said yes, I will sign the card and while you
are at it, give me some more of those cards and I will get some
of these guys around here that I work with to sign them as well.
And I did.*"[12]

Little did that assistant foreman know that his "autocratic" orientation to this new employee would be quite persuasive in convincing this 19-year-old to sign a union card. He also would not have imagined that this new employee would, 23 years later, become the President of the UAW Local Union 171.

Even though he had to ask permission to go to the bathroom, gaining a 42% increase in his hourly wage from his previous entry level job seemed like a good decision to Jim as well as to many of the "Hagerstown farmers" who chose to work at the plant. For many of the people recruited to this new plant in Hagerstown, the financial benefits were the major incentive. However, for many, if not most, of the employees the Mack bulldog reputation, earned during World War 1, was also a major source of pride. The phrase "built like a Mack truck" was a badge of honor to those who were the truck builders.

Until 1967, Mack was an independent company. Following the merger with Signal Oil & Gas Company, Mack became an affiliate of the Signal Companies as Zenon Hansen described above. This was a happy and beneficial marriage. However, by 1979 things began to change. In 1979, Signal Corporation sold 10% of Mack to Renault, the French government owned auto and truck maker. Renault's primary interest in Mack at that time was to gain access to Mack's truck sales network consisting of approximately 300 sales offices across the country to sell Renault's mid-sized diesel trucks. In 1982, Renault increased its ownership to 20%, and in 1983 it was announced that Renault would pay $100 million to more than double its stake in Mack and take over management of Mack. From the end of 1973 to the end of 1982 Mack's sales had increased from $880 Million to $1.29 billion. However, in 1982 it lost $32.3 million. Mack's losses were a major reason that Signal was eager to divest the company as

---

[12] Jim Stewart, 2020, personal interview.

it was undergoing restructuring following its acquisition by Wheelabrator-Fry, Inc.[13]

The difficulties for Mack really began in 1980 when the Motor Carrier Act of 1980 partially de-regulated the trucking industry. This act led to many non-union trucking companies to enter the market. For trucking industry customers, it led to lower shipping costs. For unionized trucking company employees, the entry of non-union workers into the industry dramatically reduced wages. For truck manufacturers like Mack, it led to a dramatic reduction in retail sales of trucks that bottomed out in the mid-80's.

In 1980, Mack also promoted John B. Curcio to be President following four years as Executive CEO. Curcio was the second CEO to follow Zenon Hansen. Also in 1980, Ronald Reagan was elected President of the U.S. and he was well known for his strong stance in favor of de-regulation as he stated that "Government is not the solution to our problems, Government is the problem." Upon becoming CEO of Mack, facing the financial realities accelerated by trucking deregulation and and realizing that Mack again lacked the capital to compete successfully in the de-regulated trucking environment, Curcio looked for a partner. Renault, which already owned 20% of Mack was a logical potential partner to pursue. At that point, Renault agreed to increase its stake in Mack from 20% to 44.6%. Curcio commented at the time "They came to the party in 1983 when nobody else loved us."[14]

Like most investors, Renault was impatient to see a return on their investment in Mack. When the market forecast for heavy duty truck sales predicted improvement for 1985, Renault wanted to take advantage of an improved retail market. However, Renault's hopes for an improved financial return hit another major hurdle.

When the contract with the UAW expired in 1984, bargaining began on a new contract on August 13. Negotiations broke down in October and on October 22, the UAW went on strike at all the Mack plants including

---

[13] Barmash, Isadore, *New York Times*, Section D, p.1, June 3, 1983.

[14] Shope, Dan, Renault's buyout of Mack puts bite back in the bulldog, *The Morning Call*, October 2, 1990.

Hagerstown. The main issues were job security and economics. [15] David Smith, President of Hagerstown's UAW Local 171 described the situation as follows: "a company proposal to provide job retraining funds and establish a union-company committee to develop a job security plan were not acceptable…Job security does not lie in retraining workers, but rather in keeping jobs in Hagerstown and other Mack locations."[16]

On October 28, 1984, the strike related layoffs spread to the Canadian plant of Mack Trucks. The 9200 striking U.S. workers created a lack of parts for the assembly plant in Oakville, Ontario which was forced to lay off 30 additional workers that were added to 416 already on furlough. The next day, a tentative contract to end the strike was reached. Mack workers returned to work pending ratification of the contract agreement. On November 13, the announcement was made that 87% of the voting membership in Mack plants in Allentown and Macungie Pennsylvania, and Hagerstown, Maryland along with a distribution center in Bridgewater, New Jersey accepted the agreement.

The three-year contract was viewed by the UAW as meeting its key goals. Bill Casstevens, a UAW vice-president and one of the negotiators said: "We achieved our primary goals of winning solid economic gains, stemming the tide of plant closings and restoring the eight paid-days-off per year that Mack workers sacrificed in 1982."[17] This agreement also provided some additional improvements in the company benefits for pension, health care and insurance coverage. While the Mack employees, could celebrate a short-term victory, the "war" had just really begun.

The 1980s, within Mack Trucks, was characterized by a war between management and the UAW. This situation at Mack in many ways exemplified the climate in the nation with respect to union-management relationships following Ronald Reagan's inauguration in January 1981. On August 3, the nation's air traffic controllers, complaining about pay, job

---

[15] AP, Around the Nation; 9,200 auto workers strike Mack plants, *New York Times*, October 22, 1984.

[16] *UPI Archives*, Mack strike in second day, October 22, 1984.

[17] *New York Times*, Employees at Mack Trucks Ratify New 3-Year Contract, November 13, 1984.

stress resulting from long hours and poor working conditions, and a basic lack of recognition for what they were expected to do went on strike. That same day, President Reagan declared the strike illegal and threatened to fire any controller who did not return to work in 48 hours. In addition, the President of the Professional Air Traffic Controllers Association (PATCO) was found in contempt by a Federal Judge and was fined $1000 per day. On August 5, Reagan carried out his threat and began firing the 11,359 air-traffic controllers who had not returned to work. As if to rub salt into their wounds, Reagan issued a lifetime ban on rehiring any striking worker by the Federal Aviation Administration. The FAA then began accepting applications for new workers and on October 22, the Federal Labor Relations Authority decertified PATCO.[18]

The decade of the 80's in the U.S, reacting to the firing of air traffic controllers by Reagan, saw "union-busting" legitimized by the President. This was an action that exemplified a broader philosophic shift taking place at the time that has been labeled "Neoliberalism." Margaret Thatcher was its advocate in the United Kingdom and Ronald Reagan championed it in the U.S. Some describe it as "a set of economic ideas and policies designed to liberate the private sector from the shackles of government."[19]

Simon Sinek describes the impact on CEO's as follows:

> ". . . Though I am certain Reagan never intended it as such, some eager CEOs interpreted his actions as permission for them to do the same. There was now a precedent for protecting commerce before protecting people. And so, for the first time ever, the social conventions that had restrained many a CEO from doing something that many may have wished they could in the past were instantly gone.

---

[18] History.com, This day in history, August 5,1981: Ronald Reagan fires 11,359 air-traffic controllers.

[19] Les Leopold, How strikebreaking hurt innovation, May 19, 2014, an introduction to the book: *Leaders Eat Last: Why Some Teams Pull Together and Others Don't* by Simon Sinek.

With the tacit approval from on high, the practice of laying off people in mass numbers to balance the books started to happen with greater frequency . . . It's like parents putting the care of the car before the care of their child. It can rip apart the very fabric of the family. Such a redefining of the modern leader wreaks the same havoc on relationships in our companies (or even our society) as it does in our families.

. . .This new leadership priority rattles the very foundation upon which trust, and cooperation are built. This has nothing to do with restricting a free market economy. This has to do with forgetting that people-living, breathing people, those who will play a greater role in our ability to innovate, make progress and beat our competition- are now no longer viewed as our most valuable asset as we aim to compete with the numbers. If anything, prioritizing performance over people undermines the free market economy."[20]

There seems to be no question that the actions of Ronald Reagan had an impact on decisions by Mack leaders.

". . . The Reagan changes had a strong impact in the Lehigh Valley, too. Seeing a Reagan-appointed National Labor Relations Board, Mack Trucks, Inc. attempted to skirt a contract with the United Auto Workers Union in the mid-80s and replace it's Allentown manufacturing facility with a non-union plant in South Carolina. There was no strike, and no replacement of boycotting workers. There was simply a highly publicized demand for concessions by Mack, rejections from the UAW and jobs moved to Winnsboro, South Carolina. The UAW sought legal action, and eventually won transfer rights for displaced workers and the right to represent the new Southern

---

[20] Simon Sinek, *Leaders Eat Last: Why Some Teams Pull Together and Others Don't*, 2014, Portfolio/Penguin.

plant. Mack went into a financial tailspin and did not pull out until this year (1994). "[21]

While there was no strike in the tumultuous period from 1985-1989 the "war between Mack and the UAW" left plenty of scars on people in Hagerstown.

A very vivid view of the toll the uncertainty and anger produced on the employees in Hagerstown can be illustrated by the story Jim Stewart, President of the UAW Local 171 told about one of his members.

> *"He was the nicest guy in the world. He was working down in the department where Bobby Mangini was the General Foreman. Somebody said something about him talking about bringing a gun in there.*[22] *Bobby Mangini went nuts. He went up and got security and took him up to the locker room, parading him through the shop and used bolt cutters to open his locker to find there was no gun there… They took him to industrial relations and gave him the third degree and told him all this stuff and then he went home. He had one house payment to go before his house was paid off. He was so upset about losing his job and with people in the plant talking about losing their benefits, and their pension, and they had just laid off 1100 people. He went home and stabbed his wife to death. He then sat in a chair and stabbed or cut himself 13 times. They found him in the chair, but he lived. They charged him with murdering his wife. To show you the kind of person he was before this workplace trauma hit him, his wife's family all came to his defense. They said he has been so upset about losing his job and not being able to make that final house payment he was not responsible for*

---

[21] Dan Shope, Replay of some Mack history seen in UAW-Caterpillar strife reporter's notebook: Labor Law, July 18, 1994, *The Morning Call.*

[22] Jim Stewart explained that back in the 70's and 80's it was not that uncommon for guys to bring guns into the plant despite the fact that the plant had a policy against this practice. It wasn't like today that if you thought about bringing a gun in the plant, they would shackle you and lock you up. I've brought guns in the shop. Back then, it was not that big of a deal.

what he did. The court sent him to a mental hospital for over a year. When he got out of there, they found him not guilty of murder. Families supported him, and he came back to work. That was a hard thing for him to do but that was part of the therapy. He needed to come back in there and he worked for a while and then he retired. It destroyed his life.[23]

This is an extreme example of how this Mack Headquarters organized union busting strategy impacted the shop floor. There were a lot of scars. A lot of people hated to come to work. This was the environment that the new General Manager, Ross Rhoads entered when he was named General Manager of the Mack Trucks Hagerstown Powertrain Plant in 1986.

---

[23] Jim Stewart, Personal interview, April 21, 2020.

CHAPTER 2

The Ross Rhoads
Period—Breaking from the Past

Ross Rhoads became General Manager of the Mack Hagerstown Plant in 1986 during the period when Mack Headquarters and the UAW International Headquarters were at war. He remained General Manager until 1998. Between 1986 and 1998 he had five different direct bosses and the company had 5 different Presidents.

The plan to outsource rear axle manufacturing (also referred to as the "carriers") and 3 miscellaneous manufacturing operations from Hagerstown was well underway as well as the layoffs of 1100 employees who had been involved in these operations. The company had announced its plan to close an old truck assembly plant in Allentown, Pennsylvania, and open a new non-union plant in South Carolina. The Top Union person and the Mack CEO were in open warfare and the "word on the street" was that Mack was trying to bust the UAW like Ronald Reagan had done with the Air Traffic Controllers. It would be hard to imagine a more challenging situation for the new General Manager in Hagerstown.

Ross was born in New Orleans. His childhood was challenging. His first four years of elementary school found him in a different school every year—as his family moved from Pennsylvania to California.

"My dad was an engineer, and he was transferred to all these places. During the war he was the only engineer at an oil refinery in New Orleans. That kept him out of the Army. After the war he bought into a construction company in Pennsylvania. It was a road construction company. It did not take him long to figure out that you had to be paying off politicians to be doing road work in Pennsylvania and he did not like that. So, he went to work for a company that built refineries and chemical plants and they jumped at him because he had the hands-on experience. That is when we moved to California. So, 4th grade through high school I was in California."[24]

Ross finished high school in California but did not want to go to college. He stated that he had always hated school and attributed part of his feelings to the fact that he had moved from school to school. However, those moving experiences *"enabled me to make quick adjustments wherever I went to make friends and find trouble."[25]*

After high school, Ross was on his own for a while in California after his dad was transferred to Summit, New Jersey.

"In New Jersey, my dad happened to live next door to an executive VP of Mack. In conversations, he (my dad) was telling this guy (Mack VP) that I have a son in California, bumming around—trying to hold a job and live. The Mack VP said, "bring him back-I'll find a job for him.'. . . So, I go to work for Mack. It was an engine plant that later was moved to Hagerstown.

I loved the job. It was a non-union salaried job in engineering. I tested engines. I was a student engineer. You collect and record all the data while an engine was in the test cell. Later I moved into engineering development trying to improve fuel economy and gain more horsepower.

[24] Ross Rhoads, personal interview, October 29, 2019.
[25] Ibid.

> *Then, I became a supervisor of engineers. Then they sent me to California for a year when the V-8 production was moved. I was pretty much the expert on it, so they sent me out there to get the production started and work out the bugs. After a year there, I was not happy, so they brought me back to Hagerstown for 5 years. The guy who had hired me to go to California, that I thought I had disappointed, opened a re-manufacturing center in Harrisburg, Pa. It was not doing well and the guy they brought in to manage it wanted out, so he came after me again and asked me to run this little operation in Harrisburg. So, I went up there and I loved it. I had 25 or so people, and the first thing I did was lay off 8 or 10 of them because we did not have any business. A few years later we were building 15 or 20 engines a day with 250 people. We opened a second building in North Carolina. All of a sudden, everybody in the Company knew who I was. I found my niche. They told me that in a couple of years, I would be the first choice to be the next GM in Hagerstown if you keep doing what you have been doing."[26]*

Ross's rise through the company was based on his performance. When asked if not having a college degree was a handicap for him, he responded:

> *"I took courses, I never got a degree. It seemed that I had some common sense that some coming out of college did not have. If you could not get it out of a slide rule or a computer, they (the degreed engineers) did not know what to do. Looking back, it seems that my background required me to adjust to new situations and new people and it served me well."[27]*

At the time Ross became GM of Hagerstown, the battle was raging between the UAW and Mack. The UAW believed that the company wanted to break the union. So, what did the leaders of the UAW think when Ross

---

[26] Ross Rhoads, personal interview, October 29, 2019.
[27] Ibid

was brought in as GM. He was somewhat known for his previous time in the Engineering Division in Hagerstown and for his reputation at the re-manufacturing center. When Jim Stewart, who was President of UAW Local 171- the local that represented the manufacturing workers in Hagerstown- was asked whether they thought that Ross was brought in by Mack CEO John Curcio to break the union in Hagerstown Jim stated:

> *"I did not know Ross much in Engineering and Research (E&R). Ross's reputation was that he was very anti-union when he was at E&R and when he was at the Re-manufacturing Center. Let's just say that Ross was not waving a UAW flag (to be polite)"[28]*

When asked specifically if he thought Ross was brought in to support this union busting strategy Jim stated:

> *"I expect so. They brought Ross in when they took Jack Costa (Ross's predecessor as GM) up to World Headquarters. He would have fit the plan at the time with his reputation. However, when he came in, he was sort of low-key because all of the shots were being called from World Headquarters.[29]*

As an example of how all the shots were being called from Allentown, and how they made it more difficult for Ross to change the culture in Hagerstown, he told this story.

> *"At one point in an effort to change the culture in the mid-80's they (Mack Hq.) were going to have one company newspaper and it was going to come out of Allentown. Hagerstown had its own little newspaper. It was printed once a month and it was done by workers who volunteered their time (although it was during paid work time.) but we had to disband that. We could no longer print our own newsletter. Those kinds of things just isolate you.*

---

[28] Jim Stewart, personal interview, April 21, 2020.
[29] Jim Stewart, personal interview, April 21, 2020.

It is not good for morale and Headquarters did not understand that. People in Allentown calling those shots just did not understand that. Our newsletter was not about company policy, it was about the local news, sports, what an employee is doing with Little League or serving on the school board. The chairman of the Board of county commissioners was a Mack employee. One of the school board employees was a Mack employee. Our people were leaders of the community. And there are a half a dozen little towns around like Greencastle where people were involved with their communities besides working at Mack. The powers that be did not recognize that.[30]

This story illustrates the way that Ross understood and appreciated, on a human level, the concerns of the people in the Hagerstown plant. He also understood and was able to relate to the employees on issues that were important to them. He saw his employees as people not just as workers. This empathy would serve Ross well later as our story unfolds.

Another story Ross shared illustrates how he could also empathize with customers and think about problems not just from a manufacturing perspective. His experience in testing engines and in interacting with engineers in his previous job gave him valuable insight with respect to how engineering staff looked at the world. Obviously, his bosses recognized this as one of his strengths that was valuable for a general manager.

"Probably the reason I got the job in Re-Manufacturing is because my last job in Hagerstown was in Engineering. People in service engineering would come to my department to talk about field problems. Other engineers would just ignore it thinking that it was a manufacturing problem. They thought that people (in manufacturing) didn't tighten the bolt right. It wasn't because the gasket had not been sized right or wasn't designed right. So, I

---

[30] Ross Rhoads, Personal Interview, October 29, 2019

> *got the reputation for being somebody in engineering that someone from the field could come and talk to."[31]*

Ross described his mandate when he came to Hagerstown as very simple:

> *"The signals I was getting from my boss were to 'fix it'. Give me 100 engines per day. "[32]*

In the discussion with Ross, there was no hint that he was given any mandate to try to break the union. He seemed to have adopted a "problem solver" view that, in order to fix Hagerstown and deliver the 100 engines per day that the assembly plants needed, he had to reduce the friction between the union and management.

He described the situation he inherited in this manner:

> *"The decision had already been made that we were going to outsource rear axle (aka "Carrier") production. All of those machines were being taken out of the plant. In the late 80's we were being forced to come out with a new engine to meet new emission requirements. This involved spending 100 million dollars on new equipment and machines to produce the new engine. So, that provided a sure thing that Mack would stay in Hagerstown for engines if nothing else. There were pressures from the union, pressures from Allentown, there were pressures to get this 100-million-dollar investment done because by the first of the year any new engine built had to comply with the new laws on emissions. "[33]*

Early on, a situation arose that seemed possibly to be a symptom of the friction between the union and management. Ross took advantage of this situation as an opportunity to begin a dialog with union leaders.

---

[31] Ross Rhoads, Personal Interview, October 29, 2019.
[32] Ibid
[33] Ibid

*"We had 4 bomb threats. I had not been there very long
when the first one occurred. The first one, the state police
said 'This one is for real. The caller said all the right
things.' So, they sent a couple of troopers and a dog into
the plant. They came back and said that the dog is burned
out because of all the oils and fumes. The dog has no nose
left. They asked do we know what we are looking for, and
I said, 'not really'. They said, 'if there is something about
the size of a deck of cards that, if placed in the right spot,
such as the powerhouse or computer room, it could bring
this plant down for months.' That was the first one."[34]*

Those events impacted the union as much as they affected Ross. They
said we cannot put up with this. So, at that point we started sitting down
together and Bill Nutter, the UAW Shop Chairman and Jim Stewart the
UAW President at that time were willing to talk. As it turned out, they had
a lot more to talk about than just bomb threats.

By the middle of 1989, the tsunami of bad news was becoming public
knowledge. The difficult start-up at Winnsboro, the flawed introduction
of the new engine to meet 1988 emission standards, the war between Mack
and the UAW and a decline in customer demand all converged to cause
Mack to announce a second quarter financial loss as truck sales plunged
by 1/3 compared with the same period in 1988. [35] In April 1989, the
employees in Winnsboro, voted for representation by the UAW by a vote
of 453 of the 867 votes cast for a slim majority of 52%. The combination
of the financial losses and the loss of the union election led Mack to replace
its CEO John Curcio. In June 1989, Ralph Reins was named President of
Mack and Chairman, five months later.

The second quarter results ballooned into a record loss for the year. For
1989, Mack reported losses of 185.4 million compared with a profit of 31.8
million for 1988. Revenues for 1989 fell to 1.75 billion from 2.1 billion in

---

[34]   Ibid
[35]   Bradsher, Keith, Mack Trucks expects loss for 2nd quarter, *New York Times*, June 23,
      1989, Section D, page 3.

1988, a decline of 16.7 percent. [36] In the 4th Quarter 1989 alone, Mack lost $79.5 million compared to a profit of $13.8 in 1988. In announcing the results, the new chairman and chief executive Ralph Reims said that Mack had cut costs and he predicted that the losses would be less in 1990. [37]

A truck industry analyst from Deutsche Bank Capital Corporation, Frank J. Prezelski, stated that:

> *"Most of Mack's problems have been self-inflicted. They've done just about everything wrong they could have done in the last couple of years. Mack spent $60 million and five years developing a new long-haul truck, the CH600, but introduced it last spring before all the bugs had been worked out... The truck's engine did not become available until September and proved too expensive to produce."[38]*

Jim Stewart provided insight, from his UAW perspective inside the Hagerstown plant, regarding what was going on in Mack across the organization.

> *"They only hired people in Winnsboro who were anti-union. They did not have to know how to build a truck. We fought and fought through arbitration to get people to transfer down there – but everyone who went to work in that Winnsboro plant – they had to have one point of view that was that the union was the worst thing in the world for anybody. You did not have to have experience. The result was they could not build a truck that was ready to put on the road that would satisfy a customer – to keep it humming up and down the highway. They had these fields and fields of trucks that were built but were missing parts, that did not have the right parts – it was a nightmare. The result is that the warranty on those*

---

[36] Bradsher, Keith, Mack Trucks has a record loss, New York Times, February 17, 1990, Section 1, page 35.

[37] Ibid.

[38] Ibid

trucks was so bad that those loyal Mack customers were approached by Freightliner offering to 'give' them trucks. Literally, they were giving them trucks. If you switch to Freightliner, we will give you 10 trucks for no money to try them out."[39]

Jim also pointed fingers not only at Winnsboro but also at Hagerstown as well, since Hagerstown was the only powertrain facility in Mack Trucks. In 1988, it seemed that the signals from Allentown to the Hagerstown plant before Curcio was fired were to give us 100 engines per day, without equal concern for quality. Based on what the work force in Hagerstown had experienced following the strike in 1984, and especially since the war between Mack and the UAW heated up since 1987, the morale was very low and not conducive to producing quality products. Jim described that situation:

"From the time I went to work for Mack in Hagerstown until I became President of Local 171, I was always around the people that I knew and grew up with. When you were President of that local union you better be able and willing to sit down and cry with a guy whose wife just ran off with his bankroll and his kids while he was sitting there and shaking like a leaf. You were a counselor, as well as being President of a local union. But you knew everybody. You got to the point that you had a sense of what was going on. The sense you had in there at this time is that "This is over." ...Not only were they considering shutting down, but if they did that, they would have liquidated Mack Trucks. It would not have been able to exist."[40]

As Chairman, Ralph Reins, seemed to have a far different vision for the company than John Curcio. In November 1989, in a letter to distributors, Reins stated:

---

[39] Jim Stewart, personal interview, April 21, 2020.
[40] Jim Stewart, Personal Interview, April 21, 2020.

"The bulldog is not going the way of the dinosaur...We are going to restore his pride, but not his arrogance."[41]

He "called a truce" with the UAW officially ending the war that existed with Curcio as President and Chairman. In February,1990, Reins published a public letter outlining his call for Mack to change. In his letter he outlined the urgency for change and pointed out how hard, but necessary, change was for Mack.

"As a result of globalization, the entire Lehigh Valley is experiencing a rough road in its desire to increase growth and nurture prosperity. Our businesses must undergo some severe cultural changes in their new marketplace, and the changes must be rapid in order to survive. Ten years ago, change could have been more gradual, but that is not the case in today's competitive environment.

Business and industry in the Lehigh Valley must come to the realization that things cannot go on as usual, and that what was good for business 20 years ago is not necessarily good for business today. To be solid performers in the global business game, we must elevate our standards and fully understand the criticalness of today's product as it relates to cost, value and design.

So, what do we do to prepare properly for this globalization process? Success will not be easy. Unfortunately, people perceive of companies like Mack as American institutions. The truth is that even institutions are vulnerable in today's competition.......
Change is a very great and powerful discipline, and companies that deny change is necessary will certainly suffer. For both Mack and the Lehigh Valley to be healthy in the 90's, we must adopt a whole quality attitude and view change as an opportunity to advance and improve. To nurture a quality attitude, which is nothing more than a commitment to improving everything we do, management must encourage and allow people to use

---

[41] Ralph E. Reins, President and CEO Mack Trucks Inc. Letters: Manufacturing, *The Morning Call*, February 25, 1990.

> *their capabilities to the fullest. Quality is something that must pervade an entire organization, not just touch isolated pockets within the company. Quality, and the change it brings about, does something very important- it breeds success. That, in turn will provide more growth and opportunity, as well as a real future for a company and its employees.*[42]

This message in 1990, for a company with acres of partially finished trucks sitting in an open field outside its new manufacturing plant in Winnsboro, S. C. due to poor quality and missing parts, would seem to be the right message. However, after Reims returned from a visit to France to meet with the owners of Mack, where they talked about RVI's vision for the company, Reims was not happy with the new "marching orders" and resigned in October 1990. His 12-month tenure was the shortest in the company's history.[43]

The clash of philosophies that led Reins to resign was a preview of what was to come. While no one knows for sure what Reins had in mind for Mack, it appears that he was an advocate for the type of Total Quality revolution that was being widely adopted by leading firms in the United States. Firms such as Motorola, Xerox, Corning Glass and many others who had lost market share to Japan were attempting to learn from firms like Toyota, Canon and other leading Japanese firms. These firms were turning to Quality gurus such as W. Edwards Deming, Joseph Juran and Philip Crosby who were leading firms to rethink traditional management practices driven by a focus primarily on cost and productivity. They advocated a "Quality First" philosophy that argued that quality and cost do not trade off against each other. They emphasized a model that says that by putting quality first it is possible to achieve quality improvements that will simultaneously also drive costs and schedule/delivery. If this was the view held by Reins, he may have perceived the view of the new 100% owners of Mack to be pushing a more traditional management view that emphasized costs and productivity more than quality. Certainly, based on what came

---

[42] Ralph E. Reins, President and CEO Mack Trucks Inc. Letters: Manufacturing, *The Morning Call*, February 25, 1990.

[43] Ibid.

later, the RVI approach focused on reducing costs as they attempted to rapidly show a return on their substantial investment in Mack Trucks.

On October 2, 1990 a headline in *The Morning Call*, the local newspaper in Allentown, stated *"Renault's Buyout of Mack Puts Bite Back in the Bulldog."* While people in Allentown, the site of Mack's World Headquarters were celebrating, the politicians in Maryland were alarmed at that fact that Renault's purchase of controlling interest in Mack could put the Hagerstown plant at risk. The article stated:

> *"With Mack facing losses exceeding $180 million for the second consecutive year and fearing that banks would force the company into bankruptcy, Renault decided to take charge. In a deal worth $107 million RVI (Renault Vehicles Industriels, the truck making division of Renault), invested $107 million to buy the 55.5% of Mack's shares it did not already own. Mack's chairman Ralph Reins stated earlier that: "In no way should the offer from RVI cause any Mack employee to think our difficulties are behind us."[44]*

William Donald Schaefer was Governor of Maryland from January 21, 1987 to January 18, 1995. Because he had been a long time Mayor of the City of Baltimore, it was important for him to expand his support beyond the city to Western Maryland and the Eastern Shore. Shortly after becoming Governor in 1987, he became alarmed by the "war" between Mack and the UAW and even more alarmed with the company's decision to shut down the plant in Allentown. Schaefer had a great fear that the plant in Hagerstown would also become a candidate for shutdown since they were already outsourcing jobs from Hagerstown. This is what let him to join forces with the Governor of Pennsylvania to intervene in the dispute between the UAW and Mack in 1987 and seek the involvement of William Usery as a mediator.

When Governor Schaefer learned that Renault's Truck Division, RVI, had assumed full control of Mack in 1990, his concern for the fate of

---

[44] Shope, Dan, "Renault's Buyout of Mack Puts Bite Back in the Bulldog", *The Morning Call*, October 2, 1990.

Hagerstown surfaced again. He feared that the "red ink" that had gushed from Mack in the last year would cause the new owners to close its power train plant in Hagerstown that employed over a thousand Marylanders. Politically, he was especially concerned because Mack was part of a region of the State that had had already been hit hard in recent years with plant closures in Cumberland, Maryland, a city west of Hagerstown. This fear led Governor Schaefer to dispatch his Secretary of Economic Development, Randy Evans, to France to meet with the Chairman of RVI. Evans arrived in France as a way to show the State of Maryland's support for the Hagerstown plant and to explore ways that the State of Maryland could assist Renault in its effort to improve the competitiveness of the powertrain operation.

Two of the key elements of the package offered to Renault by Secretary Evans were training assistance funds and consulting support from the University of Maryland's Center for Quality and Productivity (UMCQP)[45]. The Center had, in the past, worked closely with the Maryland Department of Economic and Employment Development on a number of programs including conducting manufacturing productivity assessments and conducting training for firms seeking registration of their Quality Management programs to the International Quality Standard (ISO-9000).

It was this initiative from the Maryland Department of Economic Development that led to the meeting described at the beginning of Chapter 1. Following Randy Evans meeting with the Chairman of Renault in Paris, I, as Director of the UMCQP was asked to meet with Mack's General Manager Ross Rhoads and the UAW Local 171 Shop Chairman, Bill Nutter to pursue the possibility of a joint union-management Total

---

[45] The UMCQP was created in 1978 as a joint initiative of the Maryland Department of Economic Development and the University of Maryland's College of Business and Management. The focus of the Center was to assist in the retention and growth of Maryland businesses through accelerating improvement of productivity and quality of working life. A major focus of the Center's work was improvement of union-management relationships and creating joint union-management improvement initiatives. The Center was guided by an external Board of Advisors drawn from business, organized labor, education, state government and professional associations. The Center received approximately 10% of its funding from the University, the other 90% was from revenue derived from fees obtained for services it provided to Maryland organizations.

Quality Management Initiative that would be facilitated by the UMCQP as a third-party neutral. Ross hosted the meeting in his office. When Ross posed the question to Bill Nutter of whether the UAW would be willing to participate in such an initiative, Bill's response was very candid as was quoted in Chapter 1. He made it clear that after what the Union had experienced since 1984, that their participation was contingent on the involvement of the University of Maryland staff as third-party facilitators. As Bill said, *"if this is just more Mack bull-shit, we are not interested."*

Following that meeting, on June 3, 1991 the UMCQP submitted its proposal jointly to Ross and Bill. The proposal organized the implementation of the Total Quality Process in 3 phases. Phase 1 was the planning phase and it consisted of 12 tasks. Phase 2 was the implementation phase and it was comprised of 5 tasks. Phase 3 focused on making Total Quality a Way of Life for Hagerstown and from a consulting perspective it involved one task.

Although Reins was Chairman for only 12 months, his efforts to create a truce with the UAW was a step in the right direction. One of the legacies of his tenure was the creation of an agreement with the UAW to pursue a collaborative effort with the union that they referred to as the UAW/Mack Employee Involvement Process (EIP). The brochure describing the EIP defines its purpose as "a committed effort on the part of the union and the company to work together to improve the quality of employee work life and, as a result, improve the strength of the company. It further describes the EIP as employee run under the guidance of a joint steering committee comprised of local union leaders and facility management.[46]

While Mack and the UAW developed the EIP Guidelines at the Headquarters level, the process was not mandated across the corporation. It was left up to each facility to develop a process consistent with the guidelines but customized to their needs. In discussions with the Hagerstown plant, the UMCQP provided a comparison of Total Quality and Employee Involvement (Table 1). This was a generic comparison, not specifically focused on a comparison with the Mack EIP. However, across U.S. industry in 1990 there were many variations of Employee Involvement initiatives. Many of these had evolved from the Quality Circles programs that began

---

[46] UAW/Mack Employee Involvement Process brochure, May 1990.

to be established in the late 1970's modeled after the Japanese Quality initiatives that were credited with enabling Japan to successfully capture many US markets for automobiles, copiers, and other consumer products.

From this consultant's perspective, the situation in Hagerstown could not have been more fertile for the implementation of a Total Quality Initiative. As the lead consultant, I was not totally aware at that time of just how fertile the situation was. However, some years before the beginning of the process in Hagerstown, I was in a conference listening to a presentation from a senior executive from Motorola. Motorola was one of the first US companies to pursue a comprehensive Total Quality process. I remember his answer to a question from the audience that asked, "What do you think was the major factor contributing to the success of Motorola with Total Quality." Without hesitation, the speaker stated, "It was the recognition that survival was at stake!".

TABLE 1 – COMPARISON OF TOTAL QUALITY VS. EMPLOYEE INVOLVEMENT[47]		
DIMENSION	**TOTAL QUALITY**	**EMPLOYEE INVOLVEMENT**
1. Who is involved	Everyone	Members of teams
2. Link to business	Strategically driven	Cost and QWL focused
3. Sr. Management role	Active	Passive
4. Union role	Partner	Observer-partner
5. Teams	Management and non mgt.	Mostly non-mgt
6. Business info sharing	High	Low – moderate
7. Training	High	Moderate
8. Power sharing	Mid -high	Low
9. Rewards/recognition	High	Moderate – high
10. Customer focus	High	Low
11. Impact on management process	High	Low
12. Potential payoff	High	Low – moderate

[47] UMCQP, July 1990.

13. Time frame	Long term – 3-5 yrs. +	Mid-term – 1-3 years +
14. Improvement focus	Process focus	Problem focus

In preparation for this book, I asked Jim Stewart, the former UAW Local 171 President to reflect on his view in 1990 of the situation at Mack and why he and Bill Nutter committed to participate in the Total Quality Process. Jim's response echoed the message from Motorola when he said:

> *It was not a matter of something better, it was a matter of survival. It got to the point that you had to survive. You can live to fight another day if you are there. If you are not there you cannot fight…you have to survive. The chances of survival at that point of time looked very slim because of all the things that had happened. It had gotten very bad. The only way that anything would change would be if someone was directing management that this had to be done. Not that this is management's game plan, it had to be someone else's game plan. That is where you (the third-party facilitator – UMCQP) came in.*[48]

Jim's comments were very profound with respect to why a third party is essential to this process. Our role as the facilitator was not to tell management and the union what to do. We could give advice and suggestions, but our role was to pose questions that were essential to secure their survival and success and be a "forcing function" to make them answer those questions. When an organization is facing survival, everything seems urgent. However, there are many things that are important for survival that do not seem urgent at a particular moment in time. The facilitator's job is to create and guide a process that will be rigorously followed that forces these important but not urgent questions and issues on to the agenda of a group of very busy people.

---

[48] Jim Stewart, personal interview, April 21, 2020.

Planning Phase

Table 2 lists the 3 phases proposed by the UMCQP for implementing the Total Quality Process and the tasks in each phase. Phase one of the implementation initiative began with an orientation to the Senior Management and the Union Leadership. The purposes of this orientation Task 1-1 were to 1. Develop a shared understanding in the UAW and plant management of the basic principles and elements of a Total Quality Process. 2. A second key purpose was to enable management and union leaders discover and understand the major behavior changes on their part that would be required for them to effectively lead the process. This task involved a series of sessions over several months.

Task 1.2 calls for the UMCQP to conduct a comprehensive quality and productivity assessment of the Hagerstown plant. This assessment involved a combination of interviews, surveys, and observation of plant operations. The key purpose of these assessments was to (1) provide feedback to the plant union and management leadership of strengths and opportunities for improvement and (2) to provide content that would allow the UMCQP to tailor the content of the Total Quality training to relevant issues in the plant.

Tasks 1.3 through 1.12 consisted of the formation of the joint management – union steering committee followed by work that had to be done by this committee to define the content and develop the materials to train all members of the plant community with respect to the Total Quality process. The original members of the Steering committee are listed in Table 3.

Table 2 – Phases and Tasks Proposed for Total Quality Process Implementation	
	Phase One - Planning Phase
Task Number	Task Definition
1.1	Senior Management and Union Leadership Orientation
1.2	Conduct Quality and Productivity Assessment

1.3	Form Total Quality Joint Management-Union Steering committee
1.4	Develop Vision/Mission Statement for the Plant
1.5	Develop Policies – Quality, Suggestion, and Communication/Recognition Policies
1.6	Develop Baseline Performance Measures
1.7	Quality Improvement Model Selection/Definition
1.8	Begin Initial Quality Improvement Projects
1.9	Quality Leadership Action Plan Development
1.10	Training Material Development
1.11	Senior Management/Union Leadership Training
1.12	Revise Training Material
	Phase 2 – Implementation
2.1	Select and Train In-House Trainers
2.2	Task 2 Quality Improvement Team Formation
2.3	Team Facilitator Training
2.4	Quality Improvement Team Plan for Addressing Quality Leadership Action Areas
2.5	Corrective Action Team Formation
	Phase 3 – Total Quality As A Way of Life
3.1	Conduct Periodic Implementation Progress Reviews

Table 3 Steering committee Members – 1991		
Management Members	**Name**	**Title**
	Ross Rhoads	General Manager
	Pete Banyard	Manager, Mfg. Engineering
	Steve Heffner	Chief Engineer
	Bob Mangini	Superintendent Engine Mach.
	Tom Kriner	Manager, Quality Assurance

	Dan Stoner	Transmission Section Supv.
	Dan Dawson	Supervisor, Human Resources
	Kevin Burgess	Manager, Human Resources
UAW Members	Jim Williams	President, UAW Local 171
	Jim Stewart (Joined in mtg 5)	VP, UAW Local 171
	Bill Nutter	Shop Chairmen Local 171
	Becky Smith	President UAW Local
	Billy Rhodes	Committeeman
	Steve Hess	Committeeman
	Frank Schleigh (replaced by Gene Nunamaker in mtg. 8)	Chairman
	Bobby Lewis	Chairman

The Steering committee met regularly (at least bi-weekly) beginning in late September 1991. Ground rules were established for the meetings, and the initial meetings focused on reviewing the results of the assessments conducted by the UMCQP and orienting the Steering committee members to the fundamental elements of the Total Quality Process. Based on the assessment data, three working Steering committee teams were established. One focused on how Hagerstown would begin to implement Employee Involvement, another focused on developing the plant-wide training program and a third focused on development of a mission/vision and quality policy for the plant.

A regular part of each Steering committee meeting included reports from the three teams that had been established as a major part of how the Steering committee did its work. As an example, Table 4 provides the results of the team set up to develop a Mission/Vision and Quality Policy for the plant.

By April 1992, the Steering committee teams continued to make progress. The training team led by Pete Banyard developed a plan for training all members of the plant population in groups of 25 -30. The group decided that training sessions would be kicked off and ended with comments from

Ross Rhoads and the Union President Jim Stewart. Training would consist of 20 hours delivered in 5 4-hour blocks. This would require approximately 40 weeks of training to cover the entire organization. All manufacturing management and union employees were expected to attend training however, the training was introduced as voluntary. To the extent possible, managers and their employees would be trained together.

The training committee solicited volunteers to serve as trainers. Both management and hourly employees were invited to apply. These individuals were given an orientation to the trainer role and those who volunteered were given train-the-trainer training that covered "stand-up skills", facilitation skills and teambuilding skills as well as training in delivering the specific content contained in the training notebook.

The UMCQP consulting team produced a script for the training. In addition, the script incorporated videos produced by external suppliers as well as a Mack specific video developed by Mack headquarters based on a script developed by the UMCQP. This video focused on the purpose of the Total Quality Strategy for Hagerstown and included Mack specific content. Most of the live video was shot in the Hagerstown plant and included interviews with key Hagerstown management and union employees.

The Total Quality Involvement Committee (formerly the Employee Involvement Committee) arranged benchmarking visits by the Steering committee members to businesses in the region that were deemed exemplary in some aspects of their Total Quality implementation. Visits were made to Marada, a parts supplier to the automotive industry, Corning Glass, and Pangborn.

Table 4 – Vision/Mission and Quality Policy
HAGERSTOWN EMPLOYEE'S MISSION
To Supply Mack customers worldwide with engines and transmissions that will ensure complete satisfaction.

Vision

To develop an organization that every employee is proud of and committed to. To have our Hagerstown Operation recognized as the leader in our industry, in providing engines and transmissions enabling us to provide a fair return to RVI and job security for ourselves.

Quality Policy

We are dedicated to:

- engineer, manufacture, and deliver quality products that exceed our customer's expectations;
- openly communicate to build trust and eliminate barriers;
- maintain a safe, healthy and efficient workplace that ensures a quality of life for all employees;
- provide the training necessary to perform and secure our jobs while understanding, utilizing and improving our Hagerstown Operation;
- provide an environment where continuous improvement is both recognized and expected, where individual dignity is respected, and personal involvement is encouraged.

In addition to the Steering committee team activity, meetings focused both on the implementation process as well as the business results Mack needed to focus on. One of the activities of the Committee was to define and gain consensus of the management and union on the Key Result Areas that were critical for the plant. Table 5 lists the top 4 priority Key Result Areas that would serve as the dimensions of performance that were the focus the TQ process.

Table 5	
Final Key Result Areas – Mack Hagerstown	
Priority	**Definition**
1. Safety	Establish a work environment and work practices that promote occupational health and freedom from injuries.
2. Quality	Produce products that meet customer expectations and increase the speed of implementation of new ideas and techniques.

3. Cost	Increase productivity and reduce costs through inventory reduction, total productive maintenance, reduction of overtime, etc.
4. Positive Employee Attitudes	Take actions to create a positive employee perspective through communications, employee involvement, training and recognition of performance.

In the April 3, 1992 Steering committee meeting, Ross Rhoads reported on a recent visit by his bosses from Mack and RVI. This report provided an example of the pressure that Ross was under from the parent organizations and clearly depicted the challenge that the plant had to meet. They provided a list of goals that the plant had to meet or else face closure for lack of competitiveness. The goals focused on Safety, Staffing levels, Inventory levels, Productivity, Receiving inspection results and Absenteeism. On safety, Hagerstown was performing worse than the previous year in terms of incident rates and severity and were far below benchmark levels in the machining industry. In terms of staffing – ratio of direct to indirect employees- the goal is one indirect for each two direct employees. On that ratio, the recall of employees from layoff will enable them to meet goal level performance. With respect to inventory levels Hagerstown is at 22 days and needs to be at 15 days or lower by the end of 1992. Ross pointed out that RVI did not think in 1990 that the management team at Hagerstown could improve fast enough and they were on the verge of bringing in a new team from RVI. However, they changed their mind and believe that once they (RVI) provide the training and direction that the Hagerstown management team could get it done.

With respect to productivity, one of the key metrics for the plant was manhours per unit of production – engines or transmissions. Another metric is "direct runners" that is the percentage of engines and transmissions that come off the assembly line and do not require rework. The current level of direct runner performance in 1992 was 70% for engines, and the goal is 85%.

The fact that RVI set a goal of 85% for direct runners is an example of how they were "stuck" in traditional management thinking. From the total quality perspective, one could ask when the goal is that 85% direct runners, that means that there is also a "goal" of having 15% that require rework. The cynic might ask, "how will I decide which of the engines going down the line should I choose to need rework?" The only goal that is acceptable in the total quality framework is 100% direct runners. If the current level of performance is less than 100%, then the goal should be set in terms of the rate of improvement to move from current performance toward perfection. Changing from the traditional management view to the total quality perspective is an example of what this culture shift is about.

The message from Ross's presentation to the Steering committee is that employees in Hagerstown have demonstrated that they are capable of improvement. However, the message from RVI is also that continued improvements are urgent in order for the plant to survive. Basically, survival is up to the management and employees of Hagerstown to create their own future. This became one of the key messages to employees in the Total Quality Training.

The training material for the 20-hour program was organized into 5 modules: 1. Why Total Quality at Mack Hagerstown? 2. What is the Mack Hagerstown Total Quality Process?; 3. Total Quality Process Implementation; 4. The Quality Improvement Process Methodology; and 5. The Problem Solving Process Methodology. Modules 4 and 5 were the key methodologies used by Quality Improvement Teams and Quality Action Teams to drive performance improvement.

Table 6 Summarizes the 6 core principles of the Total Quality Process for Hagerstown and also lists the 10 key elements of the culture change that the process involves.

Ross, in a presentation made several years later, reflected back on this period as the training was being rolled out. He said: ***"When we reached the point of developing the TQ training program and selecting trainers from our workforce, we wanted two trainers per class, one union and one management. To our surprise we had more volunteers than we needed, and they were all good. So, we ended up with three trainers per class. For me this was the biggest eye opener and most rewarding event to that point.***

We found experienced trainers everywhere. Outside of Mack they taught Sunday school, sports, scouting, prepared people for hunting licenses, taught classes at local schools. One was a minister. And we gained respect when we made them all trainers rather than cutting some out. "[49]

Ross, in this same presentation, continued to discuss the training more specifically.

"Initially, the union insisted that attending the training be voluntary and we agreed to that. Before it was over more than 80% of our employees attended. Training sessions were

Table 6	
Core Principles of Total Quality for Hagerstown	
The Total Quality Process for Hagerstown involves a major paradigm shift	
From	**To**
1. Primary Focus on Cost and Schedule	Primary Focus on Quality and Cost/Schedule
2. Focus on Internal Standards	Focus on Customer Requirements
3. Focus on Fixing Problems	Focus on Preventing Problems
4. Management by Experience and Intuition	Management by Facts and Data
5. Stepwise Improvement of Performance	Continuous Rapid Improvement
6. Focus on Employee Individual Self Interest	Focus on Mutual Respect for All Employees

---

[49] Ross Rhoads, Notes from his presentation to the U.S. Conference Board Performance Excellence Council, Wednesday October 16, 2002.

The Total Quality Process is Enabled by a Culture Change with Respect to 10 Quality Leadership Action Areas	
Quality Leadership Action Area (QLAA)	**QLAA Definition**
1. Sustained Commitment	Commitment to the Total Quality Process
2. Communication	Signal commitment to TQP through both the methods and messages of communication
3. Quality Teams	Teams are the vehicle to implement the TQP
4. Identification of Opportunities/Problems	View problems as opportunities to improve
5. Problem Resolution	Avoid firefighting by eliminating chronic problems permanently
6. Visible Performance Measurement	Measurement system that provides employees with regular visible performance feedback.
7. Development of People	Ongoing development to improve skills
8. Recognition	Recognize those who live the TQ principles
9. Celebration of Milestones	Have celebrations linked to achievement of performance milestones
10. Quality Goals	Achievable

Monday-Friday, half day starting in the morning. The Presidents of the two Unions and I would greet each class with an explanation of what they were there for. Classes were mixed – union and non-union. On Friday, the Union Presidents and I would go back and answer questions and listen to comments. The major messages we were trying to deliver were:

- *Customer defines quality*
- *Why we need to change*
- *Key principles define our philosophy*
- *Build in the internal customer-supplier perspective*
- *Introduce the improvement methodology*
- *Company is showing a personal interest in people*

- *Making it voluntary shows trust in people.*

Early on, a pattern of responses from the trainees emerged:

- *About Wednesday of the training, it started to make sense.*
- *I've been here 30 years and I never realized . . . .*
- *I'd never been in the shop, didn't realize some of their problems.*
- *Never been in the office, didn't realize some of their problems.*
- *Never knew why I did what I do.*
- *Finally met the person I'd been cussing.*
- *I had never met a Plant Manager.*

Out of almost 1100 people, I bet we did not get 10 complaints. It was the most productive thing we had ever done."[50]

Jim Stewart, President of UAW Local 171 also reflected on the training process. Here is how he answered the question regarding "What are the major factors that led to the improvements between 1991 and 1994?" Jim's first response to the question dealt with the need to build trust.

"The things that led to the improvements were simple. Up until that time there was no one in that plant that did not think that they were going to lose their job simply because of what management had done and how we had performed. How they had gone to Winnsboro, shut down plant 5C in Allentown, the whole 9 yards. Talk about outsourcing the work-the carriers, the transmission, the miscellaneous machining. And they did outsource the carrier and miscellaneous machining that was 1100 jobs.

When the University of Maryland came on board, the union sat down with Ross and said here is the deal. It was

---

[50] Ibid.

> *Tom (Tuttle) who told Ross and the union that there is only one way this works. You have got to be honest; you have to be "up-front", and you have got to include each other in decisions and not "back-door" anyone. Management has to be honest and upfront with the union and the union has to be honest and upfront with the Company. You might not like what you hear, but you have got to be honest and that is the way you have to operate. That was the main factor in making the thing work. If the top guy in the company was calling the shots and everyone in management had to live up to the shots he would call or the process he was going to put in regardless that would not work. If it did not work that way, then you were just blowing smoke "[51]*

Jim then shifted gears and talked about the Total Quality training process:

> *"When we went into the training sessions, in the kickoff meeting (when the Plant Manager and 2 union presidents made opening comments for each 5-day training session), I told them you have every right to say "screw this whole mess" because they have lied to us, they have told us this, they have told us that, and they have done everything in their power for me not to trust them. And you have every right not to. But we can take that position, or we can say 'Hey look- if we are going to salvage everything, salvage our pension, salvage our health benefits, salvage our job then we have got to do something different. That is where things started to turn around. There were a lot of people that didn't do it, but there were a lot of eager people that knew that was the way we had to go. I think that is what started the improvement process."[52]*

There is no doubt that the straight talk from the Union Leaders and from Ross, the Plant Manager, gave the training sessions the type of support from

---

[51] Jim Stewart, personal interview, April 27, 2020.
[52] Ibid.

the top of the organization that elevated the importance of the sessions in the eyes of participants. In addition to that, the Total Quality Steering committee had discussions of other ways to signal to the members of the plant population that this "program" was different. We discussed the types of actions that could send that message. Jim Stewart spoke of what was done and the impact on the people.

> *"One of the key things was that when we started this process, foremen had reserved parking places. They had numbered spots right up front. If you pulled into a foreman's parking spot and if you did not go out and move your car, they reprimanded you. They would also tow your car away. They towed one guy's car away one time before all of this (Total Quality Process) started. The other thing was they (foremen) all wore white shirts and they all had red badges. We (the Union) had white or blue badges. When we (the Steering committee) sat down and did this (TQ) process, one of the first things we did was to get rid of the reserved parking spaces for foremen. We sent the message 'we are all in this together. We are all going to be working together- one does not have the advantage over the other - we are all in this to save this plant here in Hagerstown'. They also took away the red badges and white shirts. They eliminated the symbols that said, "I am the boss, and you are the other guy." That was a main thing psychologically, in my mind, that helped to get this thing going."*[53]

Jim wanted to make it clear that the idea to take away parking spaces, white shirts and red badges was not the Union's idea. Actually, this was an idea brought to the Steering committee by the University of Maryland from their research on factors that contributed to Total Quality implementation success from other firms. While the UMCQP, as facilitators of the process did not dictate actions, we did serve to "tee up" ideas for the Steering committee to discuss and consider. The reason for these actions was to

---

[53] Jim Stewart, personal interview, April 27, 2020.

signal unambiguously to the plant population that top management of the plant supported the Total Quality Initiative.

For both the Plant Manager and the Union Leadership, embarking on the Total Quality Initiative required a "leap of faith'. They had to go out on a limb to embark on something that they could not be absolutely certain of its ultimate success. One of the key elements of the leap of faith was not only whether the ideas being trained and implemented would lead to improved performance of the plant, but also for both the union and plant management was whether they were out on this limb together. Could they trust each other to stay the course and follow through on the commitment to make this initiative a success? One of the factors that assisted in enabling management and the union to take this "leap of faith" was that they both believed that "survival was at stake" and they had few alternatives. However, other companies in a similar situation made other choices rather than to choose to collaborate. It is to the great credit of the Hagerstown leaders that they chose to take the "leap" together.

In the interview with Jim Stewart, I asked him what convinced him that the Plant Manager - Ross Rhoads - would follow through about seeing the union as a trusted partner in this initiative. I asked this question, because Jim had implied that when Ross was brought in as Plant Manager the general union view, based on what was known about Ross, was that he was "anti-union." The specific question posed to Jim was: "Was there any point in time when Ross was GM that you changed your view of him as an anti-union person?"

The decision by Ross to take people off the job for 20 hours of training was what convinced Jim that he could trust Ross. What Jim saw in this decision by Ross was that he took a personal risk of his reputation and his job, at a time when he was being pushed very hard by Renault and the Mack corporate leadership to improve productivity and quality in Hagerstown. He saw this as Ross investing in the members of the UAW and trusting them to take the actions necessary to save their jobs and the Hagerstown Plant.

The relationship forged between Ross and the two UAW local Presidents[54] was a major contributor to the success of the Total Quality Process. By having Ross and the two union Presidents kick off and end approximately 40 5-day training sessions, they spent a lot of time together preparing for their "remarks" and in listening to the feedback from trainers and trainees. Their understanding and respect for each other spilled over from the training sessions to overall policy making in the plant. Everything was not always smooth, but the strength of this relationship at the top of the Hagerstown organization was very powerful in propelling the change that prevented a decision by Renault (RVI) to close the plant.

Jim Stewart "pulled back the curtain" regarding what was happening behind the scenes as he and Ross worked through their respective roles in leading the Total Quality effort.

> *"I sat down with Ross many times – just the two of us. I would make it a point as President of the local union to walk around the plant. As President, I could just sit in my office (at the union hall) and never go into the plant if I wanted to do that. Or I could go into the plant and talk to the people that I knew for 27 years at that point in time. I could walk through the plant and get a feel for what was going on. I knew the players. There were some guys that you would never convince. There were other guys that would say 'I'm scared to death that I'm going to lose my job.' There were other guys that were the doom and gloom merchants. They would say 'that no good University of Maryland bunch is not going to help us' and they would go on and on especially if they could get a little crowd around them.*
>
> *When I sat with Ross, I said if we are really going to do this and go in front of these people here is what we have to do. We have to make these people believe, and you*

---

[54] The Hagerstown Plant had two local UAW unions. Local 171 was by far the largest and covered hourly manufacturing jobs. The second UAW local covered hourly administrative positions in other departments.

have got to make me believe, that this is sincere. Because these guys have got scars upon scars and attitudes upon attitudes. They deserve to have the negative attitudes. They don't deserve the scars, but they deserve to have the negative attitudes because you have not been upfront with them, and you have not been truthful with them. You've been in here trying to eliminate the UAW, you've been in here telling them they are not going to have a retirement, they are not going to have benefits, they are not going to have a job. And then all of a sudden you are now saying we want to be buddies. It doesn't work that way! It just doesn't work that way.

So, we would sit down and before we went into the first session there are a couple of things that you will have to agree to, and you will have to agree to them in front of everyone. The main thing is that if your managers- the foremen on the shop floor, the general foremen on the shop floor and the superintendent on the shop floor – every guy on the shop floor with a badge that says I am a Mack manager- he has to be a part of this thing (i.e., the Total Quality Process). He can't just be a part of it in the meetings and go out on the shop floor and say, 'Aw, this is bullshit.' We are not going to do that. He's got to be a part of everything we are going to talk about and if he is not, you are going to have to tell these people they are going to have to get another job. He is going to have to find employment other than in Mack Trucks. He needs to fill out a resume and go look for another job because he will not be a part of this program that we are going to do to save everyone's job.

Ross agreed to do that. It surprised me that he did. And he did it at every one of the sessions!"[55]

---

[55] Jim Stewart, personal interview, April 21, 2020.

Jim also shared the message that he delivered to the participants at the beginning of the training sessions:

> *"I would start the meeting out and say I appreciate every one of you coming to the session. I know what you are thinking right now. You are thinking that this will be the biggest bunch of B.S. that I have ever sat through. And I hope you are wrong. Let me explain something to you and it is very simple. Unemployment in the State of Maryland pays $400 per week. And it does not matter if you have a blue shirt on or a white shirt on. When this plant shuts down, you are going to be in that line. You might be in that line in front of Jim Stewart or behind Ross Rhoads. I don't know where you are going to be in that line, but you are going to be in that line somewhere. Because the destiny of this place is not good. You know it and I know it. The market share is gone. We've lost orders out the kazoo. We've got Winnsboro down there with trucks they cannot get to run unless something happens, we have all invested many of our years and it will have all been in vain. I am not asking you to bow down and kiss the ring of anyone in management but if improvement doesn't happen, we are kidding ourselves to believe that we are going to be here forever. Because it is not going to happen. But it is going to take time. I'm not saying you will be done after 20 hours of training and that you are going to be a loyal employee. For it is hard for me to imagine ever that you can be a loyal employee for what you have gone through. Because you have got the scars."[56]*

As the lead consultant from the UMCQP, I believe that the third-party role played by the University of Maryland was also essential in creating a process that enabled this relationship building between Ross and Jim to occur. Jim Stewart spoke of the role the UMCQP played as the third-party consultants when he pointed out:

---

[56] Ibid

"It was good when you were there that the company has someone that they had to answer to (for Total Quality). It was easy for them to go to Allentown (Company Hq) or meet with their superiors and come out of that meeting and set things that needed to be done (in order to advance the Total Quality Process) on the back burner for a while because of the numbers (the performance numbers that Ross's bosses from RVI had used in their threat to close the plant unless performance on productivity and quality improved.). That was frustrating, but it was part of life, I guess."[57]

However, the success of this phase of the Hagerstown story was led by two strong leaders – primarily Ross and Jim Stewart- as well as their respective teams of management and union committeemen. They put aside their individual egos and personal self-interest and worked jointly toward the greater good of the plant, the employees and the larger Hagerstown community.

The roll out of the training program took roughly two years.

Ross echoed Jim's comments that:

"There were weeks when we made progress and there were weeks when we just shadow boxed with each other. But, overall, as we went through these first two years, more and more people started seeing the potential upside. We were gathering momentum."[58]

In addition to the training, there were a number of other changes going on in the plant. One of the most significant was a major change in the management structure in the plant. Ross described this change:

"We formed business teams to manage our two products – engines and transmissions- and abandoned the old

---

[57] Ibid
[58] Ross Rhoads, Presentation to the U.S. Conference Board Council on Quality, 2002

> *organization of departments based on "discipline."*[59]
> *Support people were now assigned to a business team.*
> *Just as the union feared getting too close to management,*
> *support people feared reporting to production. They*
> *were losing their independence and their ability to*
> *walk away from problems and their authority without*
> *responsibility."*[60]

This was a very significant change. By creating the two business teams, the engine team manager and the transmission team managers were able to really focus the priorities of their people and align their work and improvement efforts on the key performance targets. This also made it possible for these managers to align support functions e.g. maintenance, materials, quality, manufacturing engineering, etc. as well as the team structures, e.g. Total Quality involvement teams, on these performance targets. It is hard to overestimate what a change this was for the Hagerstown plant, and it was a major step in the right direction.

In an article for the ***Hagerstown Herald Mail***, following the very successful year for Mack in 1994, business writer Terry Headlee described the impact of the changes that resulted from the Total Quality Process in Hagerstown.

> *"The changes began in 1991 after the company saw the results of*
> *a plantwide survey of employees. It was clear that something had*
> *to change......When company officials finally asked employees*
> *what was wrong in the survey they were stunned by the answer.*
> *'The end result was people said this was the most mismanaged,*
> *screwed up place I ever worked in', said Jim Stewart, president*
> *of United Auto Workers Local 171, which represents most of the*
> *Hagerstown plant's employees. But it wasn't just union workers*
> *griping. Managers also complained. It became very clear that*
> *attitudes had to change if Mack Trucks and its 1,275 jobs,*
> *among the best paying in Washington County at an average*
> *$20 per hour- were to survive.*

---

[59] "Disciplines" refers to manufacturing support functions such as quality, safety, materials, maintenance, industrial engineering, etc.

[60] Ross Rhoads, Presentation to the U.S. Conference Board Council on Quality, 2002.

The answer was found in total quality management.

Dozens of teams were formed with union workers and managers sitting down together to find answers to problems. 'They're letting us make the decisions, which makes the guy on the floor feel like he's part of the company and in turn he is going to do a better job' said Robert Mills, a set-up operator in the finish gear grinding department.[61]

The article also presented other examples of how the formerly hostile union-management relationship had changed and how both shop floor employees and managers were behaving differently.

"When Mack Trucks asked two union workers to fly to Chicago to buy a new machine last May, David Perkins didn't quite believe his ears. 'I honestly thought it was a joke' he said. A machine repairman, Perkins had reason to be skeptical. Managers had always bought machinery before, even though union workers knew more about how they worked."

"Five years ago, we picked the machine and told them to live with it." said Plant Manager Ross Rhoads. But Perkins and Ron Hutzell, an electrician, soon found themselves in Chicago picking out a new lathe turret. When they returned to Hagerstown, they made their recommendation to managers, who signed off on the deal. It marked the first-time union workers were ever chosen to buy a new machine on their own."

"In some departments, union workers given the power to buy new tools are forcing vendors to make competitive deals. Rhoads said the company never emphasized competition before; deals were more likely to be made with managers over expensive lunches. Since March, Department 110, the cylinder block machining department has closed 23 different tool deals saving the company $211, 485 said Ray Johnson, a union steward and machine operator."

---

[61] Headlee, Terry, Mack: The next generation, **The Herald Mail**, 1994.

"When Mack officials talked about buying a special machine to wash metal chips out of engine blocks, an employee said he could do the job by tapping into a three-inch water line running over his workstation. It worked. Mack saved nearly $1 million."

"Workers in one transmission department have adopted a "cell concept" perfected by their French counterparts in which the same worker is trained on five different machines. In the past, five different employees worked on five different machines to turn a rough casting into a finished gear. Now one worker does it all."

'With one worker doing everything, there's less room for error and when you make a mistake you catch it right away' said gear-cutter Gary Eichelberger. 'The main thing is quality. You control your product right in the cell.'

"Selling the idea (Total Quality Management) was the hard part. Union workers were skeptical that Rhoads was serious when he said employees would have more say in daily decisions.

Still, roughly 90 percent of the workers signed up for a voluntary 20-hour TQM seminar during a two-year period. And Rhoads backed up his promises. Some symbolic gestures were made. The executive cafeteria and manager's parking lot close to the front door were closed. Management titles, long a symbol of power were changes. Supervisors are now 'team leaders' or 'advisors'. Also, many engineers now work on the floor, rather than out of their offices, speeding up the time to fix problems.

But probably one of the biggest changes is that any union worker in the plant can shut down a line any time that he believes that quality is being compromised. It used to be a supervisor would say, 'that's OK' just keep going. Today a union worker can override his boss, said Rhoads. Even he can't override the worker – the final decision is left up to engineers. "

"There is still much to do, say Rhoads and the union leaders. Not every department has a team and not all suggestions worked out. 'We're not living in a perfect world...but there have been some major, major accomplishments' said Bill Rhodes, who is a union committeeman and sits on the plant's Total Quality Steering committee. "

(Plant Manager Ross) Rhoads agrees there is work to be done but said at least most everyone is now working together. "When you all believe in the same thing, you all start speaking the same language and you all start pulling in the same way" Rhoads said. "Fortunately for us, we found that out before it was too late."[62]

The improvements cited in the previous article demonstrate that the training, the organizational changes associated with the shift from a departmental focus to business teams, and the culture change emphasis between 1991 and 1994 led to an improved organizational climate and tangible results.

The Hagerstown plant that had struggled with quality problems in the late 1980s celebrated the news when 4 years later they shipped 21 V-8 engines to their parent organization in France. Renault inspectors, wearing white gloves, examined the engines carefully for defects. They were unable to find a single oil leak, speck of rust, or even a paint run on any of the engines. It never hurts for your parent organization to experience the quality of your product as your customer.

There were significant improvements in most of the key performance indicators for Mack in Hagerstown. The improvements from a baseline of 1991 to 1994 are summarized in Table 7. These performance changes demonstrate very tangible business results from the organizational and culture changes described above.

---

[62] Headlee, Terry, Mack: The next generation, ***The Herald Mail***, 1994.

Table 7	
Total Quality Performance Improvements – 1991 – 1994	
Performance Indicator	**% Improvement**
Days' supply of inventory	66%
Inventory – Millions of Dollars	50%
Inventory Turnover	195%
E7 Engine Quality	83%
E7 Engine Productivity	32%
E9 Engine Quality	81%
E9 Engine Productivity	20%
T200 Transmission Quality	92%
Lost Days per 100 Workers	91%
Lost Time Cases per 100 Workers	54%

These improvements were well timed as the heavy-duty truck market grew significantly in 1994. These results in Hagerstown contributed significantly to the ability of Mack to improve its market share to over 11%, its highest market share since 1990. In addition, Mack returned to solid profitability in 1994.

The significant turnaround in the Hagerstown plant drew recognition in the local press and beyond. Based on these results, the plant applied for and won the U.S. Senate Productivity Award for Maryland in 1994. This award utilized the same criteria as the nation's highest accolade for business, the Malcolm Baldrige National Award for Performance Excellence. Mack completed a rigorous application that was reviewed by a team of examiners and the plant was then subjected to a site visit by the examiner team to validate the performance results claimed in the application. This award was given to the plant by Maryland's U.S. Senators Paul Sarbanes and Barbara Mikulski. In addition, in 1995 the plant became ISO9002 certified. This certification recognizes the existence and continual improvement of a rigorous quality management system.

Following the receipt of the Senate Productivity Award, there was a period of stabilization and strain in Hagerstown. On the one hand, the plant had worked very hard to change the culture and improve performance. It is fair to say that these improvements had been able to, at least for a time, take away the threat that RVI would close the Hagerstown plant. However, leaders of the plant, in retrospect, agree that a level of complacency set in. The business teams were functioning, but the ability of these teams to operate cross functionally was easier on paper than in practice. It was difficult for the support groups to leave their disciplinary perspective behind and totally embrace their role as members of a cross functional engine business team rather than a maintenance department or a materials department. These new roles required new skills in terms of communication and advocacy of the importance of their function with peers who were competing with them for limited resources.

In addition to the learning and adjustment going on in the Business Teams, former "Supervisors, Foremen and General Foremen" were trying to get used to the roles of Team Leader or Advisors. These new roles required them to earn their influence through discussion, negotiation, and expertise rather than exercise "formal" power due to their position in the traditional organizational structure. In the same vein, union committeemen assumed new responsibilities as proactive advocates for improvements rather than the more passive role of "policing" the union contract and writing grievances when supervisors failed to follow the rules. These new roles required "old dogs" to "learn new tricks."

Despite the pains of change, the transformation that had taken place between 1991 and 1994 planted a number of "seeds" that would, in future years, take the plant to new levels of achievement and help assure the plant's future into the next two decades. An example of a "seed" that was planted resulted from a decision by Ross to "walk the Total Quality talk" by empowering two UAW members to make a decision that had always previously been made by management. This was the decision regarding the purchase of a new metal working machine described earlier in the article in **The Herald Mail** newspaper. Little did Ross Rhoads know when he chose two hourly employees to go to Chicago to purchase a new turret lathe that one of those employees would play a very significant role in the continuing future leadership of the plant after Ross had retired. We need to detour from the main story to share some details about how the ground had been prepared to help one of these "seeds" sprout.

It is not possible to trace how all these "seeds" planted during this period grew to maturity. However, the story of David Perkins illustrates many of the key elements of the Hagerstown transformation and how the ground had been made more fertile to allow a future union leader to develop. Dave's family had moved around the country as his father pursued a variety of jobs as a truck mechanic. Dave worked with him as a helper and gained a significant mechanical aptitude that he would put to use at Mack. After high school he began working for Mack in Hagerstown in July, 1973. He joined the workforce as an assembler in the carrier department that was outsourced in in late 80's. After a short time as an assembler, Dave became bored and looked for a greater challenge despite the fact that he initially loved the money and the fact that it was the easiest job in the world. He said: ***"every two minutes I had to do two minutes' worth of work, and I can do this for the rest of my life."***[63]

However, his mechanical background led him to seek to become a skilled trades apprentice. This experience demonstrated a trait that would show up a number of times in his career trajectory toward significant leadership positions. It also taught Dave a lesson about the value of the union. The personal trait was that Dave was totally determined to overcome obstacles to his development and career growth. He viewed "setbacks" simply as "challenges to be overcome." The lesson learned about the union is a bit more complicated.

His application to become an apprentice was turned down. While disappointed, he did not give up the aspiration. A month and a half after he learned he was not chosen, a union official from the skilled trades department contacted him and asked if he was still interested in the apprenticeship. David picks up the story here:

> ***"I said yes. Are they going to start another one? He (the union official) said there have been some mistakes. We just wanted to find out if you were still interested. Long story***

---

[63] David Perkins, telephone interview, July 26, 2021.

short, part of the screening procedure for skilled trades was a written test as well as an interview by maintenance management. You got points for work experience, test results and 25% was based on the interview. Some of the questions they asked were 'What religion are you? This was because at that time the top management of Mack was totally into the Boy Scouts and the Roman Catholic Church. The union came in and pointed out that besides this being an illegal screening process, they had gotten rid of the management interview in the previous union contract. But the company still used it. So, when they threw the interview out, I qualified for skilled trades. But it took a year and a half to settle this. What I learned about the union was that I was paying union dues to make sure things were running fair and equitably.[64]

The apprenticeship program Dave completed was not the typical union conducted apprenticeship because he missed the "regular" program due to the errors in his screening process. As a result, his apprenticeship program consisted of taking several courses at the local Community College. This enabled him to realize that he really enjoyed the courses and enabled him to realize he could succeed academically in a higher education environment. So, following the apprenticeship program he continued to take courses that allowed him to receive an Associates Degree from the Community College. He was the first in his family to obtain any higher education degree.

Dave continued to work as a skilled tradesman and loved the work. But then the downturn hit in the late 1980's when Mack was losing money at a very high rate. During this period, the Mack-UAW war was raging and the decision by Mack Hq. to outsource the carrier production from Hagerstown was an especially cruel blow to David. He described the situation he faced and his feelings:

"When I started in Hagerstown, I worked on the Carrier Assembly Line.... Then as a skilled tradesman, we were unhooking machinery so it could be hauled out and taken

---

[64] David Perkins, telephone interview, July 26, 2021.

to the Dana facility to be operated where the outsourced work would be done. It was quite a time to see my friends that I had worked with on that assembly line being laid off while, as a "skillie", I stayed. Had I not switched to skilled trades, I too would have been laid off. So, I'm in here unhooking machines, so they can be hauled off to a place that was replacing my friends. It was a very emotional time. There were tensions everywhere…. That was one of the few times in my life that I hated to go to work. So, I would go back in there and say, "who will be laid off today?" Are they going to lay off any "skillies.?" Are they going to lay off any more people that I know? It actually changed the outlook of the entire workforce. You still had the people from Plainfield who thought this was the beginning of the end – just as it happened in Plainfield when the plant was closed and moved to Hagerstown. Bottom line, in 1991, I was laid off."[65]

While this experience left him with some scars, it also presented Dave with an opportunity that helped prepare him for what came later in his career. He continues the story:

"Fortunately for me, I ended up getting a job at General Motors in Baltimore as a skilled trades person. That kind of changed my perspective. I worked in the paint shop. There were two of us and it was "hands off". We had a boss, and he would tell us at the beginning of the week what needed to be done for the week or we could just pull the assignments off the computer if he was tied up doing something. We were basically a two-person, "self-directed work team." I've never been happier because it was self-directed. It was not formal – but we also got personal recognition. When the boss was on vacation, the guy who replaced him said when he came back "I never saw Marv and Dave." The boss asked, "Did the work get done?" He answered, "yes but I never saw them." He said, "You

---

[65] Ibid

don't need to see them as long as the work gets done." It was my first foray into a self-directed work team. It was unofficial and only done by this one boss. So, when I was recalled to Mack, it was a very difficult decision (to leave this position that I really liked). I had been at GM for three years and loved every minute of it, but the pension took me back to Mack.

I came back to Hagerstown in late 1994. They called 6 skillies back, all at the same time, and they threw us into this team. This team was for preventive maintenance on the gear cutting side. We were all coming back from layoff. And we were looking at each other and the management person was Larry Schoop. He kept telling us he wanted us to run this team. I remember my friend Gary Miller, who had gone to the apprenticeship program with me asking "Do you believe any of this?" I said, "Gary let's believe them until they prove us wrong."

The team elected me as their spokesperson. It was not team leader it was team spokesperson. I was the spokesperson in terms of talking with management. So, we sat down and determined how our performance should be judged. Initially, they wanted to charge how many hours we put into PM (as the performance measure.) I thought that was really not the best measure of our performance. So, we decided that a better measure would be how many daily corrective maintenance requests we got for the 100 machines we were given to service for preventive maintenance.

They did the numbers and they found that that for 1994 it was about 2000 maintenance requests for these 100 machines. We started the PM program and Larry Schoop gave us free rein. We reported to him, but he told us we set the schedule and we do it however we want. It was the most work that any "skillie" had to do and that is why many people did not want the job. That is why he took people that just came back from layoff. There are no breaks on PM. It is not like you finish a job and then wait for a call for the next job. The guys on the team really got into it. By 1995, we went from 2000 to 1500 corrective maintenance requests (for our 100 machines) and in 1996 it dropped to less than 1000.

However, Larry Schoop was pulled out of the program, and we were given a different leader. We saw the "handwriting on the wall" that this was coming to an end very shortly. They started doing things like – we got off at 3:30 and by 3:00 most of the skill tradesmen were in the shower room. We stayed on the job until 3:15 and then we cleaned up because we had our own PM stuff. High level management people would stop by and just say "Hey how are you doing." We knew that it was not an accident, they are checking up on us.

I had really bought into this "autonomous maintenance concept and the team concept because to me it was my General Motors experience on steroids compared to what I was used to at Mack before I was laid off. Then the roof came crashing down on us. "[66]

In addition to the new status quo that all were trying to adjust to, the market for trucks softened in late 1995 and 1996 and this led RVI to push much harder for continued performance improvements to sustain profitability in a truck market that was growing slowly or actually declining.

There was a recognition among the plant leaders that there were essentially two parallel organizations in existence in Hagerstown. There was the Total Quality Organization with Business Teams, Quality Leadership Teams and Quality Action Teams that were working hard to make the new culture a way of life in Hagerstown. Then there was also the old traditional functional organization with old habits and ways of thinking that resisted change.

[66] David Perkins, personal interview, July 26, 2021.

This dichotomy led to results and performance improvements stagnating. With the market softening, RVI pushed harder for cost reduction and more engines out of the door per day and this ignited the strong tendency to revert back to the old traditional management approaches. The TQ culture was operating side by side with the "real business." As General Manager, Ross Rhoads was caught between these two realities.

Jim Stewart describes what happened as Ross Rhoads was feeling tremendous pressure to improve the performance that had stagnated. He reacted with great surprise and disappointment when he discovered what had happened:

> *"Ross went out and got this group of people to come in and "swarm" the shop floor- every department- they just brought these people in to take a look at the plant and come up with suggestions regarding what to do. He (Ross) did not come to the union to talk about it. That all happened without our knowledge that it was going to happen. That was a big setback. Ross realized it "after the fact." Before the week was over, they got these people out of there, but it undercut our efforts to tell the people on the floor that you have got to trust these people(management) and they need to trust us (the UAW leadership). We will work with them as long as we can trust them. That was part of our pitch. As long as we can depend on what they say as being factual and there is a trust built between us, we can change this. We can turn it around. But when that happened, that one incident that went on for about a week before they got them out of there, was not good on the shop floor as far as attitudes. If you walked down there, they said 'We told you so, you can't trust the no-good so and so's.' That was a drawback."[67]*

David Perkins shared a perspective from the shop floor that illustrated the tension and fear that existed during this period with the additional pressure for results from RVI and from the consultants that were brought in to cut

---

[67] Jim Stewart, telephone interview, April 27, 2020.

short term costs. As the spokesperson for the Preventive Maintenance Team (PM) he received an invitation to what he called the "Inquisition." He was called to meet with a group of Managers who were feeling the performance pressure and who were investigating the cause of a recent machine break down. Here is how Dave described that meeting:

> *"They (the managers around the table) started the meeting by saying "We are not here to criticize; we just need to understand what is going on. Your team PM'ed this machine 2.5 or 3 weeks ago and it broke down last night." I had my book with me so I said, "Can you tell me which machine it was?" They said it was 5829 – a Barber Coleman Gear Cutter (this is not the actual number). So, I opened my book and found that we definitely had PM'ed the machine 3 weeks earlier. And we sent the report to (and he named the three managers who received the report.) We found an inordinate amount of shavings in the gear box, we listed it as level 1 critical, in need of immediate repair. I asked what broke down on it? They said the "gearbox" went down on it. I said is there anything else. They said there is nothing else. Two weeks later, I was moved out of the transmission division and sent to the engine division where I had never worked. And they disbanded the self-managing PM team and put it all under management supervision."[68]*

As the interviewer of David Perkins, I was puzzled by the incident he described. So, I asked Dave to help me understand what I should take away from this story. Did they shut down the PM team because they were not happy with its performance? Or did they perceive the PM team as a threat to management because the managers who received the PM team's report that the machine needed immediate repair (which was not the job of the PM team to perform) did not follow up on their recommendation? Which was it?

---

[68] David Perkins, telephone interview, July 26, 2021.

Perkins responded: ***"Honestly, I think there was a lot
of trepidation, not just in skilled trades but also in
management. So here was a team that was not tied to
management, and it threatened a lot of management
people (basically by telling the truth.) When you PM a
machine you cannot fix everything that needs to be fixed
at that time. If we found something that needed to be
fixed, we would send a report out that it is supposed to
be fixed by another maintenance group whenever the
department management can afford to shut the machine
down. Because a lot of times, we would have a machine
for 3 days and some of these repair jobs might take a
week. So, we came up with a form and started sending
these forms out and we ranked the issues we found from
level 1 "critical" to level 4 "that can wait until the next
PM."*[69]**

David continued the story that sheds some light on the impact of the
external Industrial Engineering Consultants brought in by Ross who were
nosing around the plant trying to find opportunities for improvement, or
as some skeptics might say, trying to find ways of justifying their existence
and their fee:

***"They even had one of these consultants with us (the PM
Team). I remember an incident in which an electrician
was wiring up a motor. Instead of looking at the diagrams
(which required you to run up to the Maintenance office
to get) the electrician just hooked it up. In that situation,
it will either run the right way or the opposite. If it is
wrong, you just need to turn off the switch and turn
the leads around, button it up and put it away. The
consultant wrote down that the electrician wired the***

[69] This situation meant that managers must frequently make judgements between keeping
a machine running to meet production goals or to take it out of production for repair
in order to avoid a major shutdown that would have an even greater impact on meeting
production goals. In the situation described here with the production pressures and
concern that the owner could shut the plant down if goals were not met, these were
very difficult decisions.

*motor the wrong way and had to rewire it. If he had left
the workplace, gone to the maintenance office, searched
for the print, it could have taken him as much as two
hours. As it was, it took 10 minutes, and no harm was
done. That is how we did some things on the "fly." These
engineers were just there presumably to save money but
instead, they added costs."*[70]

The disappointing experience with the external consultants was initiated unilaterally by Ross under pressure for results that he was feeling from his RVI bosses in Allentown and in France. Following this experience, everyone in Hagerstown, including Ross, realized that this had been a mistake. Unfortunately, the fact that it was launched without warning or consultation with the UAW, meant that a great deal of the trust that had been built up over several years between Ross and the UAW was damaged. As the previous quote from Jim Stewart pointed out, it not only reduced trust between Ross and the UAW leadership, it also seriously impacted the trust between the union members and their UAW leadership because they assumed, wrongly of course, that their leadership had been involved in the decision to hire the consultants or at least allowed it to happen. The only saving grace was that despite that, the fear that RVI could possibly close the plant tended to force management and the UAW to at least "paper over" their differences with regard to the consultants and seek a way to respond to the bigger external threat.

Because of the past success the plant enjoyed with the Total Quality process, even though it was incompletely implemented, both management and the union leadership chose to revisit the joint improvement initiative that had produced improvements between 1991 and 1994. Ross and Jim Stewart invited the UMCQP to a meeting to discuss implementation of a possible new version of the Total Quality initiative.[71] The UMCQP prepared a new proposal and planning began on a new initiative to move beyond the

[70] David Perkins, telephone interview, July 26, 2021.
[71] The University of Maryland Center for Quality and Productivity (UMCQP) had not been on-site in the plant for approximately a year or more during which the company was rolling out the Total Quality Training and pursuing the teams and other improvement activities. It was the Center's intention not to remain on site permanently but to help the company become self-sufficient. This call to submit a new proposal was

parallel realities that existed between the new Total Quality culture that had led to significant performance improvements between 1991 and 1994 and "the old management style." The old habits were difficult to abandon as pressure from the new owners kept being increased month by month.

Pressure on the Hagerstown leadership was increased in two ways. First, the goal for the Hagerstown plant for engines was now to move toward producing 200 engines per day. This level of production was twice the level Hagerstown produced when Ross became General Manager. Two hundred engines per day seemed to everyone in the plant to be quite a "stretch" goal. Second, RVI had assigned a young French engineer to the newly created position of Assistant General Manager. This was done in two Mack plants, so Hagerstown was not singled out. Jim Stewart pointed out that after Michel Gigou replaced Pierre Jocou as CEO of Mack in December 1996, RVI began bringing more people in leadership positions from France to the U.S.

I asked Ross to talk about this move by RVI.

> *"The President of the Company at that time was a Frenchman- Michel Gigou. The President called me and said about Olivier (the Assistant General Manager to be) I'm getting tired of negotiating with him to come over and if you say so, I will take him off the list. I responded – I will take all the help I can get (thinking that was the right thing to say under the circumstances). But I could see the handwriting on the wall. So, Olivier, the young French engineer, came over as my assistant for a year. (At the end of the year) I was promoted out of there. How did the relationship go? It was testy. I tried to tell him everything – but I probably told him too many old stories. I tried to give him all the background – why things were the way they were- how we got there. Sometimes, what it will take to change. But then, we seemed to get along fairly well. But my direct boss – another Frenchman, was*

a recognition that for various reasons the "train" had gotten off the track and corrective action by the "third party" was again needed.

Andre Morel. Andre is the one who brought Olivier over to Hagerstown. He and I had trouble- I knew I was short-lived with him."[72]

During this time, development work continued on the new training program that was called *"Creating the Future Through Total Quality Planning."* The focus on planning was chosen for a number of reasons. First of all, the shop floor people in manufacturing had historically been given very little information about the planning process within Mack and the Hagerstown Plant. So, in order to enable shop floor people to better align their daily work with the desired direction of the business, it was important for them to have a basic understanding of the planning process and the plans and expectations for the plant.

This program came to be called, in plant jargon, "TQ-2." This label provoked some interesting comments from shop floor people when they were told that the plant is beginning to develop and roll-out "TQ-2". One especially insightful plant worker, Tommy Muma asked "Why are you doing TQ-2 when you haven't finished TQ-1 yet?" In fact, Tommy was quite correct. All the elements that were included in the training for TQ-1 had not been fully implemented. Even with the partial implementation, enough had been implemented to significantly change the culture of the plant and produce significant performance improvements between 1991 and 1994.

Part of the reason that TQ-1 was not fully implemented was the fact that for management there was always a tension between changing behaviors and attitudes in line with the TQ principles and values on one hand versus the pressure they were under to "make the numbers." Total Quality implementation always requires a "leap of faith" that the changes will produce results. This is always a challenge in making significant cultural change in an organization as there are no guarantees that the changes will pay off. In a situation like that faced by Hagerstown, with a very demanding owner pushing for major performance improvement, the risk of not "making the numbers" could be that RVI would move the engine and transmission production elsewhere. In part, the inability to convince some managers

---

[72] Telephone interview with Roger Johnston, September 23, 2019.

and many plant employees to "trust the process" and take the "leap of faith" must be acknowledged as a weakness of the original Total Quality Training. As the lead consultant on the initial training implementation, it was clear that despite our efforts to customize the training and "load" real world Mack examples into the training – the training was coming across as "consultant driven training content" even though delivered by in-plant trainers.

In the process utilized to develop TQ-2, significant changes in the training development process were implemented. The major change was that a training development team was formed comprised of managers and union leaders in the plant. Rather than depend on the trainees to assume the burden of integrating the key concepts of the training into their daily work as was largely done with TQ-1, in TQ-2 there was a much stronger effort to achieve the integration of Total Quality concepts into the training content so it was much more visible to trainees how they needed to apply the concepts in their daily work and how the application would have payoff in terms of improved results.

From a consultant perspective, it is a fair question to ask, why was this not done with TQ-1? The answer is that it could not have been done with TQ-1 for a number of reasons. First, the plant willingness to commit to having a team of key employees spend a day a week in training development activities over several months when they were in a survival mode, probably was not there. Second, the degree of knowledge by the in-plant staff to make the content integration was not present in 1991-92. This knowledge was considerably advanced by 1995 so that the capability of the key staff to participate knowledgeably in the training development effort was "light-years" beyond what existed in 1992.

Despite the fact that Ross Rhoads, saw the need for and initiated the planning for the TQ-2 training designed to move the plant to the next level, Ross was not able to follow through on implementing his "TQ-2" commitment. At the end of the year after he arrived, Olivier Vidal was promoted to General Manager replacing Ross.

In Chapter 3, we will review the short-lived tenure of Olivier Vidal who was brought-in from France to enable RVI to see 200 engines per day produced by the Hagerstown plant. Chapter 3 does not describe a success story although there were many lessons learned under Olivier's leadership. However, in Chapter 4 we will have the chance to reflect back on the true legacy of what was achieved during Ross Rhoad's leadership in partnership with the UAW under Jim Stewart's leadership as President of UAW Local 171. Chapter 4 will focus on the achievements of the Hagerstown Plant under the leadership of Olivier's successor, Roger Johnston, also in partnership with the UAW.

How can we assess the achievements of Ross Rhoads during his time as General Manager in a very demanding period in the history of the Hagerstown Plant? In my interview with Roger Johnston, which forms the basis for much of Chapter 4, we talked about Ross and the work Ross did in conjunction with the UAW in Hagerstown. Roger had a window to Hagerstown because at that time he was in Allentown at Mack World Headquarters and one of his responsibilities was to manage capital projects that supported the various plant improvement strategies. In the interview, Roger referred often to the work that Ross had done with the UAW and the plant and how that built a foundation for what he had to do and how he needed to manage. Roger's words say it best:

> *"Ross took the plant from the farm to the city, and once they have seen the city, you are not going to get them back on the farm. Ross had in the 90's elevated the relationships to a different level of involvement and responsibility.... At that time (Roger's view from Allentown), if you had asked me, I might have said that Ross was too close with the Union. But the Total Quality Process that Ross had begun in Hagerstown was ahead of the curve. Allentown eventually launched a process, but it was later than what was being done in Hagerstown. I became impressed with what Ross and Hagerstown were doing and that came to influence my way of looking at plant management approaches."*[73]

---

[73] Telephone interview with Roger Johnston, September 23, 2019.

Roger lauded the legacy of Ross Rhoads's work in partnership with Bill Nutter and Jim Stewart of the UAW. We will never know for sure, however, it is quite likely, given the situation and pressures on Hagerstown during Ross's tenure, if he had not had the courage to pursue the course of action described in this chapter, the Hagerstown plant would not exist today. From the perspective of the State of Maryland, Ross was placed in a situation where there was considerable fear on the part of the Governor of Maryland and the Secretary of Economic and Employment Development that over 1200 jobs in Western Maryland were at risk. Because of Ross's leadership and his decision to develop a partnership with the United Auto Workers, not only were those jobs not lost, the plant was put on a footing that helped enable it to attract over 400 million dollars in investment by two separate owners who assured its future into the next two decades.

Chapter 3

Building a Bridge to the Future – the Olivier Vidal Period (1996-1998)

Olivier Vidal came to Hagerstown as a bright, young, ambitious manufacturing engineer. He was originally from Brest, France a major port city on the West Coast of France. Brest was historically linked to the sea by its location and by the fact that it was the location of the French nation's Naval Academy. In essence, Brest was to France what Annapolis is to the US with respect to its role in training naval officers, many of whom advanced to the top ranks in the French Navy. Olivier's father was or had been a Naval Admiral. Brest's strategic location as a major port city led to it playing a key role in World War II. Like most of France, Brest was occupied by Germans and Italians from 1940 until the Allied Invasion in 1944. During the war Brest was an important German U-Boat naval base. The city also housed shipyards that were repairing German warships. In the planning for the Allied invasion of Normandy, Brest became a key target of Allied bombing, as it was needed as a key port through which to resupply Allied troops who landed on the beaches of Normandy just to the north of Brest. The result of the bombing was that virtually all of the city was destroyed. The citizens of Brest paid a heavy price during this struggle, and many were homeless and destitute as a result. Most of these civilian casualties were the result of Allied bombing and artillery strikes not German attacks.

As the son of a French naval Admiral, Olivier had been taught this history and came to the U.S. with an acute awareness of what the US and its Allies had done to his home city. As a manufacturing engineer, schooled in college and by his work at Renault in advanced manufacturing methods that he viewed as world class, he saw his mission as bringing that knowledge to a rural, somewhat archaic, manufacturing plant in Hagerstown, Maryland.

It is fair to say, that Olivier assumed his role as GM of manufacturing with a bit of an "attitude." In part, because there was a need to continue the transformation of the manufacturing operation that had been initiated by Ross Rhoads. In addition, his "marching orders" from his bosses in Renault were to increase the capability of the plant to produce 200 engines per day. While some of these improvements were to come through capital investment, the major changes to be made were improvements in the manufacturing process and the human systems. As a technical person, Olivier knew quite well what was required to do this from a manufacturing engineering perspective. However, his ability to engage the workforce to buy-in to the changes that were necessary was limited. His view of the "people" strategy was revealed by "off the record comments" in which he described his challenge as improving the work ethic of the workforce. It would be appropriate for a new leader to say that part of his challenge is to improve the "work behavior" of the workforce. However, to say that you want to improve the "work ethic" carries a very different connotation and an "air of superiority" with respect to culture. That did not play well in Hagerstown.

Prior to Olivier coming to the plant, Renault replaced Pierre Jacou as CEO of Mack Trucks with Michelle Gigou. Gigou brought in Andre Morel as VP of manufacturing, and it was Morel who brought Olivier Vidal to Hagerstown. Gigou, recognized the importance of the union-management relationship that Ross Rhoads and Jim Stewart had built in the plant. Therefore, after Olivier was GM, whenever Gigou would visit the plant, he would let Jim know and ask the union president to accompany him on a plant tour.

As part of the relationship Jim had built with Ross Rhoads, he would often go up to the plant manager's office by himself to talk with Ross and ask, "how orders are going and just to chat." Jim described how he attempted to maintain that relationship with Olivier:

> *"..I would go up and try to do the same thing with Olivier (that I had done with Ross.) But it got back to the philosophy of Total Quality-you have got to be honest and up front with the union about everything you are doing in that plant. The union has to be a partner with you. I did not want to be a manager- I had the opportunity to be a manager but I had no interest in that. But I represented the people, so I needed to know what was going on in the operation. I would sit down with Olivier, and he would do things that were contrary with what we were doing out on the floor. I told him, Olivier, you are a smart guy. And he was, he could go into an area where there is a problem and where the structure of the plant did not allow the management to go in there and solve a problem. He could go in there and in a very short time come back out and tell you what the problem was and how it needed to be addressed. ..He was a pretty sharp guy when it came to the plant. But he did not have any skills with people."[74]*

Jim shared several anecdotes to illustrate his view of the reasons why Olivier had struggled. One of them was a description of a private meeting with Olivier when Jim was trying to help him understand that to achieve his goals for the plant there needed to be a two-way relationship with the work force and the union. The "my way or the highway" approach was not the way for Olivier to achieve his objectives for the plant. Jim also had the capability to put his message in a very graphic context.

> *"One day I said Olivier I want you to do me a favor. I want you to go home this evening and I want you to spit in your wife's face. And then I want you to beat the living snot out of her." Olivier looked at me like I was some kind of idiot. Bend down and kick her two or three times. Then say, 'Hey Honey, let's go to bed.' See how you*

---

[74] Jim Stewart interview, April 27, 2020.

> ***make out with her. It is the same thing down on the shop floor. You can't go down on that floor and spit in people's face, and smack them in the face and then do whatever you want to and then say, now I need you to do 110%. It doesn't work that way. It is human nature. He could not grasp that. When he spoke, he wanted people jumping. He would say 'Jimmy, don't tell me that, don't tell me that.' I said it is true, you are a smart guy, but you don't know how to work with people. He did not want to hear it."[75]***

While Jim was having private conversations such as this with Olivier, the training program described as TQ-2 was being rolled out. Everyone in manufacturing was being trained by trainers who were both union and supervisory staff. Each five half-day training sessions was kicked off by Olivier and Jim Stewart and the two of them also appeared at the end of the weeklong training session for a wrap up. As with the first round of Total Quality training, the process was presented as a joint union & management training process and that the Total Quality process was a joint initiative to continue to improve the competitiveness of the Hagerstown plant.

The training content included five modules. (1) a refresher on the philosophy of Total Quality, (2) an introduction to the planning process used by Mack Trucks, discussion of the planning vocabulary, and an overview of the types of plans that impacted the manufacturing operation e.g., the annual business plan, a six-year rolling business plan and the Hoshin Plan that aligns the corporation around a very "few" breakthrough objectives. For example, the focus for the six-year plan included generating 200 million in capital, developing a new engine for 1998, evolving the transmission product, etc. The plan stated that the new engine – the E-7- is expected to be piloted by the end of 1996, and the ramp-up to full production would take place beginning in the second quarter of 1997 with full production slated to begin in 1998. The training also addressed the relationship between the manufacturing plan and the plans of other units located in Hagerstown – purchasing, engineering and human resources. Table 8 presents the 1996 objectives for these various units.

---

[75] Ibid

Table 8
Departmental Objectives for 1996

Organizational Unit	1996 Objectives
Engineering	New Product Development
	Improved Quality of Existing Products
	Accelerated Product Cost Reduction
	Reduce Time to Market for New Products
Manufacturing	Improve Product Quality
	Improve Process Capability
	Reduce Inventory
	Increase Safety
	Reduce Product Cost
Purchasing	Reduce the Supplier Base
	Improve Supplier Capability and Performance
	Improve the Cost of Purchased Goods
	Improve Support to the Manufacturing Shop Floor
Human Resource Plan	Benefits Cost Reduction
	Enhanced Capability of People
	Improved Mack-UAW Relationship
	Reduce the Cost of HR Administrative Processes

(3) The training also included a description of the roles of the Total Quality Steering committee and the Quality Leadership Team, and the more specific performance metrics for each of the functional areas. (4) The training focus then shifted to the rationale for these performance targets in terms of the requirements of customers, regulatory bodies, investors and employees. The intent of the training was to enable the members of the workforce who were being trained to understand the rationale behind the goals and objectives that were developed for the plant. (5) The final module focused on creating understanding among trainees of how the

work they did on a daily basis contributed to the overall mission and goals of the plant. Ultimately, since the survival of the plant was always at stake, the training was designed to help people better understand how they can contribute to their future job security through aligning their daily work with the goals of the plant.

The philosophy underlying the training was based on the view that most people are rational, and they want to do a good job. If the employees are given the information that enables them to make good decisions regarding how to allocate their time and their efforts, most people will do so. If plant floor workers have the same information that managers have, they will not only understand the decisions made by management, but when they can participate in decision making, they will be able to align their decision with actions that will help create job security. When they have choices to make, they will make choices that deliver value to customers and to the business. This philosophy builds on the partnership between the union and management built into the original Total Quality training and is a way of showing respect for the intelligence and the decision-making capability of the front-line workers.

Training not only provides information and increases employee capability. It also creates expectations for what they will be required to do and how they will be treated in the workplace. If those expectations are not fulfilled in the workplace, employees become frustrated and disappointed. The TQ-2 training did help employees have a better understanding of the business and the competitive environment. However, it also developed expectations that they would have greater involvement in decision making. Unfortunately, due to the management style promoted by senior management in the plant, those expectations were not met when employees returned to their jobs.

Why did that happen? Jim Stewart shared some light on this question. He describes some situations in which the actions of the senior management team did not align with what employees were being told in the training program about how the partnership will work.

> *"....with the Total Quality Initiative and with the guidance obtained from the University of Maryland*

the parties (union and management) had truly created an atmosphere in there of working together. One of the principles of the process was that both parties had to be involved in decision making. Whether you liked it or not you had to be honest enough to say what you were going to do so that there would be no surprises. Just like the guys who came in from the consulting organization with the clip boards on the shop floor – (When Ross Rhoads a year or so earlier made a unilateral decision to bring in a consulting organization to conduct time and motion studies on the shop floor as a cost saving strategy) that was a surprise. That set the relationship back temporarily. We hoped that with Olivier that we could return to that working philosophy of "no-surprises."

One day I went down to the Central Office – a conference room on the shop floor level that they called the Taj Mahal. At the time I walked in there, Olivier was in there with a secretary and a group of the top shop floor managers. They were in the conference room with the door halfway open. Without even thinking it was some sort of private meeting that I should not be involved in – since up until this time I had been involved in most everything. So, I just walked in. It was like I caught 15 people stealing candy out of the grocery store. They stopped, they started fumbling over their words. It was so obvious that they did not want me to know what they were doing, or what was going on in that room. I said, 'What's going on fellows?' They started making excuses and Olivier was standing in front of them. He was instructing them or whatever. I knew at that point in time that something was happening, but I did not know what.

I left the room and about a week later, I came to work one morning and on the engine assembly line they had put up a counter. For every engine that went through the line, the counter showed how many had gone down the line that day. I would walk down there two or three times a week just saying good morning and looked at the counter and it said 118. They were so proud that 118 had gone through there and that was just the daylight shift. They were pushing to get 200 engines per day out of there. Those guys were really into it and that was good. That was our future.

The following week, I get called by my committeeman, Roy Tressler, to come down there. He called me and said, 'You need to come down here. Olivier came down here and took three people out of the first 10 operations on the A engine assembly line. The foreman was in on it, the Superintendent was in on it. Olivier did a new line balance and they eliminated three of the first 10 people on the A line.' Any time they did a line balance, they would come down there and they would give Roy Tressler, the union committeeman there, the opportunity to sit down and "tweak" it. If one guy had too much to do in the time allowed, they would say someone needed to go over and pick up the slack on another operation to make these spacings even. When they did a line balance like that, Roy would say 'Hey, go back to the way you were doing it and we will get back to you in a couple of hours or by tomorrow and see if we can get this squared away.' The line balance went with the schedule. So as the schedule changes, it is not unusual that this happens. But when Olivier came down there and took out 3 of the first 10 people and just eliminated them and said 'you 7 can do what those 10' did...' Roy went down and told those three people to go back to work the way we had been with the 10 and said he would work with it and see what we could do. Olivier wanted to fire Roy on the spot! He took him to Human Resources, and he was going to fire him. I went down there, and we got it worked out, but that was the start of it with Olivier."[76]

---

[76] Jim Stewart interview, April 27, 2020.

In fairness to Olivier, he was under tremendous pressure to both increase production and to reduce costs of engine production. Unfortunately, he chose to act unilaterally, rather than work within the philosophy of the joint process to involve the union in working with him to find a way to achieve the goals in a collaborative fashion. The impact of this unilateral action was that it basically triggered a "war" between Olivier and Jim Stewart. Olivier was determined to meet the production target by whatever means necessary. Jim Stewart as President of the union was equally determined to maintain the union members role in the joint decision-making process.

After the battle over the line balance, production went from 118 per day on the A-engine assembly line to 56 per day. A year later, they got it back to 100. And when they got it up to 100, Olivier got pizza for everybody. In Jim's words: *"that was the start of the Olivier-Jim Stewart war. You could not talk to the guy. It was his way or get out of my way."*[77]

The battleground of the war shifted from Hagerstown to Mack Headquarters in Allentown, Pa. Jim and the local union presidents from other Mack plants were invited to a monthly meeting with the senior management at the Mack Corporate Headquarters. After one of these meetings, Andre Morel, VP of Manufacturing who was the executive who brought Olivier to Hagerstown from France, walked over to Jim and said, "How are you doing Jim?" Jim described what happened then:

> *"I said, I need to talk with you. He asked, 'What do you need to talk about?' I said I need to talk with you about the guy you put in Hagerstown to replace Ross Rhoads. I said, he is destroying everything. If one of our guys goes on a machine and runs 6-8 thousand dollars of scrap, you want to fire him. You know an engine coming down the line is a $10,000 unit. You've got a plant manager down there that has cost you millions of dollars and you are patting him on the back." 'What are you talking about?', he asked. "I'm telling you and I can explain it all to you. And you should know- you are the VP of Manufacturing. He's costing you millions of dollars."*

---

[77] Jim Stewart interview, April 27, 2020.

Morel said, 'He's in the building, I'll go get him.' I said that's fine, you go get him. He came down and we sat there and talked. I said Olivier, you went down on that line when we were up to 118 per day. (Following your unilateral actions, it dropped to 56) A year later, you bought pizza for the plant because they got back up to 100. It took a year to get back to 100 from 56. At $10,000 per unit, 8 hours per day, 6 days per week you tell me what you cost this company in revenue because of what you did down there when we were supposed to be working together. Olivier said 'Jimmy, I can't believe you Jimmy.' I said you did it, you know you did it. Morel acted as though he did not know anything about it.

Several months later, in one of the monthly meetings that Mack President, Michel Gigou, had with all local union presidents and their shop chairmen in Allentown, Jim had another chance to air his concerns. At the end of each of the monthly meetings that involved the President, his marketing, warranty, sales and his other staff members he would turn to each of the union presidents and ask now what is going on in your facility. When he came to the Hagerstown plant he asked 'Now, what is going on in Hagerstown Jimmy?'

I would tell him we were going great. We improved productivity, we improved lost time on injuries, absenteeism was down, all the numbers that you care about that mean dollars – we improved on all of them until you brought Olivier over here. This went on for a couple of months at the monthly meetings. One day in one of the meetings, he came across the desk at me and said, 'Jimmy you have a vendetta against Olivier'. He shouted at me and stuck his finger in my face. And I jumped up and said, 'Let me tell you something! You asked me to come up here and tell you what is going on in Hagerstown and be a part of this review. Now you want to stick your finger in my face and I'm going to tell you what. It is my last trip to Allentown – enjoy the last few minutes you've got 'Mister'. Because I'm not driving 156 miles up here for you to stick a finger in my face when I'm telling you the truth. So, let's just forget it.'

Then he apologized. 'Oh Jimmy, sometimes you have to push the envelope.'

I said 'I don't want to hear it. I came up here to tell you what is going on in Hagerstown and you don't want to hear it. If you really want to hear the honest truth don't ask Jim Stewart anymore. Go outside and get yourself another consulting company and interview everyone on that floor in Hagerstown. From the guy that sweeps the floor to the head engineer and plant manager. Ask them what they think is going on between the union and company and put it in a questionnaire. I said this is my last trip up here. I'm not coming back up here every month for this circus!'

So, we left, and about a week later I get calls from the plant manager's office and the Human Resource Office. Jim Leigh, the human resource manager was in charge of distributing the surveys.[78]

The company took Jim's advice and chose a consulting firm to conduct a plant-wide survey of managers and employees in Hagerstown. Even the process of survey distribution became contentious. This disagreement was a symptom of the dysfunctional atmosphere in the plant not only between the union and management but within management as well. Olivier instructed the Human Resources department to put every management person's survey in an envelope with their name on the envelope and a number on each survey. Olivier then personally distributed the surveys to managers.

---

[78] Jim Stewart interview, April 27, 2020.

Jim Stewart described what happened then:

"I started getting phone calls at my house from engineers, supervisors and others who wore "white shirts" (the former symbol for people who were not union members.) They said 'You don't think I am going to fill this out and hand it back with my serial number on the back that allows me to be identified by name. They will be gathering data on me, and I will be gone. I can't tell the truth'.

I went to the Human Resources Department and said forget the survey. We are not going to be a part of it anymore. We can't be a part of anything that allows individuals to be identified by name with their responses. The managers can't fill it out honestly because they think Olivier will get rid of them tomorrow if he thinks they are against him.

So, they scrapped it. After Allentown was informed that we were not going to participate, I get a call from the HR office in Allentown. He asked, "What is going on down there?" So, I told him. He said tear up all the surveys, we will send new ones down there. You- Jim- can hand them out. Jim responded that he did not want to hand them out, but he just wanted the surveys to be anonymous. They made that change and administered the surveys.

A few weeks later, the consultant held a survey-feedback session for the plant leadership. The data was broken down for union respondents and management respondents. The major findings from the union group were that the company and particularly the plant manager gave no consideration for the union's position. The approach was "my way or the highway."

When discussing the findings from the management group there was agreement with the union's view that the

plant manager did not consider the union position. But among the management group the results said that the plant manager did not listen to other people's views and the feeling that it was "my way or the highway" was felt even more strongly than it was expressed by the union respondents.

Two or three weeks later, it was announced that Olivier would be leaving Hagerstown.[79]

The events in 1998 included the following:

- March 12 letter from the UAW Local 171 to Olivier Vidal commencing local negotiations in order to obtain "*additional flexibility regarding work practices and work rules*" and announcing that the UAW suspended participation in the Total Quality Process".[80]
- July 1998 – Management launched the "Bell to Bell" Policy that stated workers must: "*clock in before the start of the shift and report to work area, or area designated by supervision, on time ready to work. Remain in the work area doing job assignment e.g., producing as many pieces as possible. Leave and return from breaks and lunch on time. Work up to the bell and clock out for T/A purposes at the end of shift. Clocking in and out must be in assigned work area.*"[81]
- July 16, University of Maryland Center for Quality and Productivity submits proposal to Olivier Vidal and UAW Local 171 to launch a new process to respond to the situation characterized as follows:
  - … Over the past few months there have been differences of opinion at the plant between management and union leadership regarding the improvements needed and the approaches required to make these improvements. This has coincided with management changes at the plant, which has led to some personalization of the differences. That is to say that the size of the "gap" between where the plant is

---

[79] Jim Stewart interview, April 27, 2020.
[80] Ibid
[81] Mack memo, "Bell to Bell", 20 July 1998.

currently operating and where it needs to be is not shared by management and the union leadership. Furthermore, the union leadership apparently believes that some of the approaches being taken to close the gap by management are actually "widening the gap" due to the style of implementation. This proposal provides a methodology to narrow these differences and help accelerate the plant's efforts to improve its competitive position."[82]

- Union letter responding to the "Bell to Bell" policy that stated: *"In the March 12 Letter we were hopeful that after negotiations we could, together, get back to that productive, successful process (i.e. the Joint Total Quality Process that was the most successful and productive venture in both of our histories – we achieved profitability, market share, quality in the product, reduced cost, job security, positive attitudes, high morale and as workplace employees enjoyed) but upper management, without question has made a decision to go back to the old traditional way of management "I'm the boss"- reprimands – threats- "managing by fear and intimidation". Our contract is clear:*
    - *We subscribe to the concept of a fair day's work for a fair day's pay*
    - *Quality must be a priority*
    - *We will abide by the Current Contract:*
        - *Skilled trades must do skilled trades work **only**;*
        - *Machining classifications – must do work in their classification **only**;*
        - *Assemblers – must work within their job description **only**; and*
        - *Indirect classifications – must work within their job description **only**.*

- *Again, Local 171 is willing to be a part of a process where both parties are **committed** and **stay committed**. That process must*

---

[82] Proposal Letter from Thomas C. Tuttle, Director of The UMCQP to Olivier Vidal and James Stewart, July 16, 1998

benefit Mack, Mack products, our customers, maintain mutual respect and insure integrity in the workplace. "[83]

The proposal letter from the UMCQP to Olivier and Jim followed a phone call and a meeting in Hagerstown in which they shared the difficulties that they were having and requested that the UMCQP re-engage with the company to attempt to help restore the positive relationship between the union and management.

In describing this situation that existed in July, 1998 when I was interviewing Jim Stewart for this book, I said to Jim that this must have been about the time that I got the phone call saying that the "train is off the track." Jim laughed and said, "The train was off the track, brother, I will tell you that.!"[84]

- October 1, 1998 - A letter from the Shop Committee of the UAW Local 171 to members stated:

  "As you are aware, the profitable partnership enjoyed by Mack Hagerstown has been damaged to the point of near disrepair.

  The October issue of "Powertrain" (the local newsletter published by the Hagerstown plant Human Resources Department) has an article from the desk of Olivier Vidal. Mr. Vidal states "The plant is also in the process of succeeding with another challenge – to put in place more flexibility in our organization by implementing new work rules and changing longstanding work practices."

  In the recently negotiated contract the Union provided the Company the flexibility needed to be both competitive and flexible. We did not then, or will we now, relinquish the long-standing practices in our workplace. Any changes or modifications to these practices must be accomplished by a proper two-party process.

---

[83] Letter to Members of UAW Local 171, September 14, 1998.
[84] Jim Stewart interview, April 27, 2020.

These practices are just and fair for both parties and have provided for us a direction in which we can enter into a very profitable future. [85]

- In November 1998, the Powertrain Press carried a message to the plant from Olivier.

  "This month I want to underline two events.

  _First, I congratulate the plant for the financial results of September. The plant had its best performance of the year......
  And equally important, safety and quality indicators are on target. So even if the plant is far from reaching its year-to-date financial commitment, September's improved performance is encouraging. I believe this achievement is due in part to implementation of the new flexible work rules and for that I thank each of you._

  The second event is the signing of the Mack and Cummins partnership agreement. I heard questions from the floor about a threat for Hagerstown. Cummins will supply engines outside the core of our business – the E-Tech. It will allow Mack to offer trucks that our company does not offer today. The partnership is an opportunity because it will increase our market share.

  The E-Tech engine will remain the Mack engine like the T200 – the vocational Mack transmission. But together we have to take care of our core products in an environment that is changing and is more and more worldwide open. We have our future in our hands if we are able to implement breakthroughs in the efficiency of our operations, increase the productivity of our cells and departments, decrease tool expenses improve the quality of our products, work better between departments and involve all our employees. These are the keys of our future.

  To involve our employees a survey was released to half of the plant. This survey will be studied by both management and

---

[85] Letter to UAW Local 171 Members from the Shop Committee, October1, 1998.

union leadership in order to improve our partnership and the implementation of continuous improvements for our customers. We look forward to the positive changes resulting from our employees input to this survey."[86]

The survey Olivier referred to was the one that Jim Stewart described above. It turned out that despite Olivier's optimism regarding use of the results, the survey results contributed significantly to his demise.

In writing this Chapter, it was not possible to interview Olivier to understand his perspective more fully on his mission, and his assessment of the challenges and accomplishments during his time in Hagerstown since Olivier had long-since moved on to his new job in Spain. However, we can gather some insight into his views and perspective from interview notes done in 1998. I interviewed Olivier after the University of Maryland was called back into the plant for the third time to assist the plant union and management leadership in re-establishing an advanced Total Quality Process after the "war" between the UAW and Olivier had led the union to pull-out of the initiative.

Following the survey discussed above, the University of Maryland team conducted a series of interviews with management and union leaderships in an effort to diagnose the issues that had led to the negative comments shared in the survey and to gain some insight into the most effective way forward.

The interview with Olivier at this time, (August 1998) provided significant insight into Olivier's view of the plant. When asked what he considered the major strengths of the organization he listed the following: experienced manpower, a lot of reactivity skills and the ability to react quickly to short term problems, a lot of involvement from management people, good technical expertise. On the flip side, he was asked "what do you consider to be the major roadblocks that you or your people face in doing their job?" Olivier said, it is an old workforce. The workforce has been spoiled by management by awarding too much overtime and by long standing practices that are bad. They have developed bad habits that are authorized

---

[86] Powertrain Press, November 1998, p.1.

by management. There is also a lack of planning – for example there is no plan to rebuild the older machines. Management on the floor has not been backed by top management – there has been weak management. The machines are old and not enough capital has been committed to modernize and maintain the equipment. Work rates have been based on practices from the 50's and 70's and the work rates are not sufficient to be globally competitive. There is not enough flexibility in the work force and the union leadership is focused on the past. It lacks a global picture, and it is fighting the battles of the 70's.

When asked to describe a situation that made him feel especially proud to work for Mack Hagerstown, Olivier listed a number of items that he viewed as accomplishments. He stated that he was proud that they have been able to make progress toward getting to 200 engines a day which was only a dream 2 years ago when he arrived. He credits a stronger management team focused on results and action plans and a management system that can deploy targets to the supervisory level is in place. He said that there have been changes in the work ethic of a minority of the workforce and the major problems are on the table – some of them have been solved. There has been better planning regarding what maintenance should focus on during the plant shutdown period. The amount of capital invested has doubled and the relationships between production, maintenance and engineering are better aligned to achieve performance targets. He also felt that there have been improvements in the willingness of management to put problems on the table, and he sees more trust between the management team and the plant staff. The assembly line is more efficient and organization on the shop floor has been improved. The PM (preventive maintenance) program has been improved and there has been an improvement in the hours per unit in the cylinder head and crankshaft departments.

When asked to reflect on his major disappointments he pointed out that the process of generating the improvements was done without the formal involvement of the people – because we stopped the employee involvement in teams. He also was disappointed that we did not put into place a living training program.

Olivier was asked to envision a ladder with 100 rungs where a score of 100 would be truly world class. What would a truly world class organization look like? He stated that "it must involve its people – true involvement-where the people have to work and participate on improving the process." In this statement, Olivier reveals a part of his world view that tended to be problematic in terms of his relationships with the Union and the employees in Hagerstown. When he says that in a world class organization people "have to" work and participate on improving the process it connotes a top down "control" oriented workplace. A truly world class organization would be better described in terms of people who "choose" to participate on improving their process and "have the information, knowledge and skills" to do so.

When asked to describe what Hagerstown must do to assure its future and convince RVI (Renault Vehicules Internationale) to locate the production of the next diesel engine in Hagerstown, Olivier was quite specific in describing the challenge. He said it must achieve world class financial performance levels, involve its employees and realize the game is global not just Washington County. The company must have good data systems accessible to all people on the shop floor, high visibility of plant performance, regular information meetings, not town hall style but meetings on the shop floor – stop the line to discuss issues and get feedback. Information on the bulletin boards would be current and of interest. Performance wise, the plant must meet hours per unit targets, respect the budget, make the plant clean and well arranged, parts arranged efficiently and maintain quality and delivery.

It was in the December 1998 *Powertrain Press* newsletter that Olivier sent his farewell message to the plant workforce.

> *"At the end of the year, I will leave Mack to go back to Europe as the quality and service executive of a joint venture between the bus activities of Renault and Fiat, the Italian car and truck maker.*
>
> *I want to thank you for the welcome you gave to me and my family in this community. These two years in Hagerstown will*

really count as some of the best years of our family story. I want also to thank you for what we have accomplished together. Two years ago, the plant was static, its capacity stuck at 120 engines and 55 transmissions per day, its productivity steady, and its total quality management without dynamism. In addition, the work ethic of a minority of employees was not addressed.

During this time frame we had to face several challenges, a booming truck market in the US and in Europe, a new labor contract demanding productivity targets from Mack's headquarters and from our parent company.

What are the main accomplishments and what are the main changes implemented during these two years?

Three main accomplishments

- *A rate of 200 engines per day will be attained beginning next year – a level of production that we did not dare to dream one year ago.*
- *A good productivity trend in the Transmission Division*
- *A better organization of flow and of the engine assembly line*

Four main changes

- *More flexibility negotiated during the 1998 contract although this flexibility is still far from world-class manufacturing which will handicap the plant in the future if changes do not occur*
- *The same work ethic for everyone (attendance, starting and stopping work on time, respect of the breaks, etc.)*
- *A new dynamic to put in place actions to solve our key problems – with the involvement of the employees. This is how we have achieved the capacity and productivity targets.*

- *An improved spirit of cooperation between Production, Maintenance, Materials and Engineering.*
- *..Both management and union leadership after two all-day meetings in October agree that after achieving a breakthrough in quality in the early 90's, the plant now has to focus on two breakthroughs – increase our engine capacity and increase the engine and transmission productivity. This is the condition necessary for this plant to survive in the next 10 years. It will require a strong and positive leadership of both management and union. Some successes in the past will not ensure our success in the future as we enter the 21st century......*

Assessment of the Leadership of Olivier Vidal

It seems clear that Olivier served as a bridge between the past and future for Hagerstown. As a European, he brought a global perspective that had been largely lacking in Hagerstown. Olivier was widely viewed as a smart engineer who was skilled in diagnosing and resolving manufacturing production problems. He certainly "pushed the envelope" in Hagerstown and as his departure message pointed out, he had some successes.

But at best, as even he admitted, his record was mixed.

One manager in the diagnostic interviews described the situation as follows:

> *"We as managers did not have a clear sense of direction. We were afraid to speak our feelings. When middle managers tried to form teams, supervisors were not committed to goals so there was conflict. We haven't reached the ability to say we don't agree. The plant manager (Olivier) never said that the changes we needed to make would not lead to the elimination of jobs, so people were afraid to suggest or make changes. We as managers get consumed with tasks. Initially, we tried to involve people – but then under pressure for results, we resorted back to our old*

tactics. We tried to force it to happen. We got frustrated,
then we pushed. We did not communicate and sell the
outsourcing decision – (i.e., partnership with Cummins
which workers viewed as a threat). Supervisors lack the
skill to motivate without giving orders. [87]

One of the people with the most objective and balanced perspective on the Olivier Vidal period in Hagerstown was that of Olivier's successor in Hagerstown. During Olivier's time as GM in Hagerstown, Roger Johnston was in charge of the capital review process at Mack Headquarters in Allentown. In this capacity he worked with Olivier to improve the technical capability of the Hagerstown plant, as well as other Mack plants, through capital investments.

Commenting on Olivier's management style Roger stated:

"When Olivier took over, he saw his role to 'civilize'
the people in the plant..., Ross (Rhoads) had in the
90's elevated the relationships to a different level of
involvement and responsibility. Olivier took the wind out
of their sails by pushing them back to just taking orders
from management. (The) Union saw it as a lack of respect
for the people." [88]

In a following interview, Roger summarized the period with Olivier at the helm more succinctly but quite accurately. Speaking from the perspective after Roger had assumed the General Manager role he stated: ***"Prior management (i.e., Olivier) had done some things that were absolutely directionally correct, even if their approach left a lot of singed feathers."*** [89]

It was the "singed feathers" that caused the train to jump the tracks in Hagerstown and that led to Olivier's forced departure. In reflecting on this period that I have chosen to call a "bridge" period between the past

---

[87] From interview with middle manager conducted by Thomas C. Tuttle under the ground rule of confidentiality, August 1998.

[88] Personal telephone Interview with Roger Johnston, September 30, 2019.

[89] Ibid

and future of Hagerstown, it is fair to ask whether the approach taken by Olivier in Hagerstown was necessary to enable the plant to survive?

One way to answer this question is the answer that Roger Johnston gave when he was asked if Olivier's approach was necessary. Roger hedged a bit and then stated: ***"Well maybe. If Olivier had not been so rigid with the people and provoked a problem, then Roger would never have been asked by Andre (Morel) to go to Hagerstown."*[90]**

So, in one sense, Olivier created the opportunity for Roger. As you will see in Chapter 4, Roger Johnston turned out to bring the perfect set of knowledge and skills, personality, and values required to lead Hagerstown through the next phase of its journey toward world class manufacturing performance.

---

[90] Ibid

CHAPTER 4

Securing the Future for Hagerstown – The Roger Johnston Era -Phase 1

The last year of the Millennium brought both relief and uncertainty to the management and union members of the Mack Hagerstown engine and transmission plant. It brought relief from the autocratic management style of Olivier Vidal. However, it brought new uncertainty due to a lack of knowledge about the new General Manager and uncertainty regarding the ability of the plant to convince Renault that this plant should be the engine plant of the future for Mack. In addition, there were rumors afoot that negotiations had begun regarding a possible sale of the plant to a new owner.

At the end of 1998, the plant management received some informal, but positive, news from Mack President Michel Gigou following his visit in October 1998. His reaction to the visit was provided informally by a memo to Mack management from a manufacturing executive at the headquarters in Allentown. The message was that Michel supports the things that are happening in Hagerstown. The message relayed to the plant stated "*He (Michel) supports us. He does not expect us to miss shipments, but he does understand what we are doing and the time it will take to get to where we want to go. So, it is still up to us. Please continue to move in the direction you are going. Not all the people are against us. Some union members agree with the direction we are taking. They just get too much pressure from other union members; including the voted reps to not cooperate with management."[91]*

The decision regarding the new General Manager was made by Andre Morel, the same person who made the decision to send Olivier to Hagerstown. One would think that given the way things turned out with Olivier, that Andre might have been looking for a way to play it safe by sending a person with a significant amount of experience as a plant manager to replace Olivier. However, to Andre's credit, he took a risk on someone he knew but who had never run a plant before. That guy was Roger Johnston. By not playing it safe, in retrospect, we can say that Andre could not have found a person who would have been a better choice to lead Hagerstown into the future than Roger. In many ways, and perhaps Andre knew this, Roger had spent most of his life, up until this point, preparing for this challenging assignment. Roger and Andre had spent some time together when both were at Mack Headquarters in Allentown. Andre was Director of Manufacturing Engineering at the time and Roger was involved in supporting the manufacturing plants through capital investments. They had many discussions regarding manufacturing management strategy. Here is how Roger described some of those discussions:

> **"I would provide my thoughts on strategies for manufacturing and Andre would say 'Roger, it seems that you are making this decision based on your heart instead of your head.' I would respond to him by saying 'Andre, if I do not use my heart, I do not have a soul. And that is not acceptable to me."[92]**

Serendipity always plays a role in career decision making. In addition, fortunately for Hagerstown, Andre Morel must have used both his brain and his heart in choosing the right guy at the right time for the Hagerstown GM role. The people needed Roger's head and his soul following the plant's experience with Olivier Vidal especially at a time that the plant's future was still uncertain.

---

[91] Internal Memo, "Visit by Miche", from Steve Pacini, October 10, 2002.
[92] Telephone interview with Roger Johnston, September 23, 2019.

How Roger Johnston Became the Right Leader at the Right Time for the Hagerstown Plant

Roger grew up in Western Pennsylvania in Canonsburg, Pa. The town was a blue-collar factory town that had a rich and colorful ethnic mix. It was the birthplace of two famous American entertainers – Perry Como and Bobby Vinton. As a young child, Roger has memories of driving by a McGraw Edison plant and seeing people on strike walking the picket line. He remembers thinking to himself at that early age that if the people in the plant had challenges or disagreements that could cause them to shut a plant down why would you not talk through the issues and find ways to save the plant and keep it from closing. His dad was a management guy in a Continental Can plant, but Roger has no memories of his dad ever "bad-mouthing" the union members in his plant. So, he did not grow up with an anti-union bias even though his father was a member of management.

Roger graduated from high school at age 17 and started looking around for schools to continue his education. One of his fond memories of his dad who "worked all the time" was the chance to work with him on the family car. This time together contributed to Roger becoming a self-described "car-nut". When, through his college search, he found out that there was a school in Michigan that allowed you to work in a car factory and go to school at the same time, that was quite attractive. The school was the General Motors Institute. So, Roger enrolled, and his work assignment was at the Flint Truck Assembly Plant. Initially, it was the Chevrolet Flint Assembly Plant and they shifted over to trucks a year after he arrived.

The philosophy at GM at the time was that to become a contributing member of management, you had to have worked on the assembly line. For 2 1/2 years while he was also taking academic classes, Roger worked on the 55-minute line. This meant that he had one minute of work that he repeated 55 times each hour. He said:

> *"I did sheet metal, I did repair, I hung doors, I drove cars off the line, I put gas tanks in, I did windows and doors. I learned what it meant to work on the line where you had less than desirable work instructions, less than desirable*

working conditions, and less than desirable self-respect
since you were chained to that line for the full shift. It was
a very enlightening experience for me. Something I carry
with me today."[93]

In Flint even though he was working on the assembly line with UAW workers, he was not a member of the union. He was a student. However, he interacted a great deal with regular union employees who were his peers on the line as well as with the elected union committeemen who represented the line workers in union business and negotiations. Reflecting on that time Roger stated:

"I credit my time in Flint working on the line that taught
me the value of sitting down with people and talking
through issues and problems. I had a lot of discussion
there with Committeemen that were very valuable in
helping me see the value of discussion and the ability to
look at the world through their eyes.

When I was in Flint, the population of the town was just a
little under 200,000. GM employees were 80,000 of that
number. Today, Flint has less than 100,000 people- the
city has lost half of its population. 46,000 GM workers are
on strike across the whole nation. Why has this happened?
To me it is due to the fact that the company and the union
were not committed to work out their differences. They
walked away from their responsibilities and that is a
disservice to everyone involved. My thinking on that is
based on the experience that I have had. Perhaps God
sent me there (to Flint) as a 17-year-old to learn "this
is not the way you do it." I was given some motivation
and tools that enabled me to use them when I was in a
position to make a difference."[94]

---

[93] Telephone interview with Roger Johnston, September 23, 2019
[94] Telephone interview with Roger Johnston, September 23, 2019

Roger's college major was manufacturing engineering/industrial engineering. A requirement for graduation from the General Motors Institute in manufacturing engineering was to do research and write a thesis. Roger's topic for his thesis was the development of an early warning system to determine before it was implemented whether the manufacturing schedule would work. "Schedule" for an assembly line refers to the schedule of how many units would travel down the assembly line in a given period of time. Obviously, the number of units to be produced and how work was assigned to workstations would determine the number of people required to produce that many units – i.e., number of trucks, number of engines, number of transmissions, etc. The term used to describe the number of units of work and the number of people required is "line balance." Roger described the problem addressed by his thesis topic as follows:

> *"The system allowed you to determine before the fact if the schedule could be attained and how we could improve the line balance. This allowed us to go to the supervisor and tell him about that next Tuesday at 10:00 you need your utility person to help out this workstation because he will have too much work assigned. When I came to Mack, I was pleased that they had this process built into the schedule.*"[95]

Roger's time in Flint led him to learn some lessons that helped him prevent having Hagerstown become another Flint. Fortunately for Hagerstown, the experience in Flint would not allow Roger Johnston to walk away from his responsibilities to the company, the union members and their families and to the community.

Roger's Personal Development Continues in Two New Directions

Two additional aspects of Roger's development took place after leaving General Motors. Following graduation from GMI, he worked for two more years as an Industrial Engineer at General Motors. By this time, he

[95] Ibid

was ready for another learning experience. This opportunity came as a result of another auto company expanding its operations in the United States. Roger learned that Volkswagen was coming to the United States and was building a plant 40 miles from where he grew up. It was December 1976 when Roger joined the VW America launch team for the new plant. Not only did this provide Roger with the opportunity to be a part of a new manufacturing startup process, but it also gave him the opportunity to gain international experience and travel. He described that time:

> *"(I) went to Germany many times to get up to speed. (My responsibility included) process engineering and industrial engineering. (I) became a Senior Engineer and was offered the job as Manager of Manufacturing Engineering. (I) had to work on moving to the VW Golf model from the VW Rabbit model. I became fluent in German when I worked for VW and had to go talk to guys on the line."[96]*

In addition to building his cross-cultural skills, and increasing his global awareness, Roger gained maturity in another critical dimension of management effectiveness. It is a common weakness of technical people who are recent graduates from a technical discipline that they overvalue their own technical competence and undervalue the technical competence of non-college graduates who have learned much from on-the-job experience. Roger, very insightfully, describes how he fit this pattern in his early days with VW.

> *"I was involved in correcting some manufacturing process problems. We were in the early stages of knowing how best to do that by asking the people who do the work. However, as manufacturing engineers we sometimes think we know better than the people who do the work how to do this better. I completely forgot what I told myself back when I worked on the line about valuing the guy who does the work. The manufacturing engineer in me, liking to turn the wrench myself, caused me not to seek the input from*

---

[96] Telephone interview with Roger Johnston, September 23, 2019

the guy on the line. That realization and practice came later. Eventually, I threw away all that high and mighty stuff and I finally realized – Hey, I need to talk to the guy who is doing it.[97]

Immediate Challenges Facing Roger Johnston

Any General Manager assuming a new role in a different facility faces challenges. At a minimum, the new person, if coming in from outside the organization, must develop trust with the management and non-management workforce. In some cases, the new GM is also presented with the need to turn around an organization and move it in a different direction. In other cases, the need is to continue the direction but speed up the progress toward key goals and objectives. Rarely, is it the case that all is well, and the new person just is asked to stay the course and keep doing what has been done.

In Roger's case the challenges both involved a turn around with the respect to the management style as well as a need to speed up the change process. Roger described these challenges:

"For me the first area of focus was to rebuild the relationship between union and management. It was clear that the relationship between the leaders from management and the union had been damaged. That needed to be rebuilt. Another challenge was that trust needed to be rebuilt in management...There had to be faith that the people who were making decisions had their head screwed on right ...It was once there; I do believe it was. The efforts that had been there, (referring to the work led by Ross Rhoads in the early and mid 90's) which were recognized by the U.S. Senate Productivity Award, provides evidence of that. Things had been on a good track and that had been evident to me from my earlier efforts in working with Hagerstown...It was a disappointment

---

> *for me in the late 90's that things seemed to change…*
> *So a challenge was to rebuild trust in management. The*
> *third challenge was that we had a business to run.…*
> *The big demand was to hit 200 engines per day. We had*
> *never built that many. Prior management had done some*
> *things that were absolutely directionally correct even if*
> *their approach to people left a lot of singed feathers. They*
> *set the wheels in motion, but we had to deliver the goods.*
> *That was a significant challenge. When you are running*
> *three shifts, seven days, it is difficult to squeeze in extra*
> *hours."*[98]

While it is possible to view the issues Roger raised as three separate challenges, he viewed them as highly inter-related issues.

> *"We can think of it as the pieces of the "soft side" that*
> *would enable the "hard deliverables" to be accomplished.*
> *It was evident that the ability to get there (200 engines*
> *per day) was tied to having those things on the "soft*
> *side" in place. If there was a better relationship between*
> *the company and the union, if there was trust in*
> *management.… this would help us find a way to take*
> *the collective intelligence of the work force and move it,*
> *like the Queen Mary, so it could be brought to bear on*
> *the challenges of the business to deliver that many engines*
> *per day."*[99]

One of Roger's many strengths was the ability to speak in terms of principles and broad concepts and also to illustrate the concepts with very concrete and specific examples. This enabled him to communicate effectively to very diverse audiences with different frames of reference and points of view. He framed the challenge of getting to 200 engines per day in part in terms of changing the mind set of front-line workers from thinking of their job as just as a set of tasks to being a part of the larger challenge to turn the Queen Mary. To do that, it was necessary to help them understand that

[98] Telephone interview with Roger Johnston, September 23, 2019
[99] Ibid

they could, through their efforts, make a difference with respect to the larger challenge that was critical to their job security.

One of the more difficult departments in the plant to develop this mindset was the cylinder block line. In part that was due to the lay out of the cylinder block production process, the age of the machines, and the culture that had developed in this department. Roger used this example to describe the challenge:

> *"We remember that the cylinder block line was a quarter of a mile long. There was a transfer system that was aged, and sometimes a bit recalcitrant. Most of the knowledge of how to keep that series of machines running resided in the heads of the people who were there all day long. That group of people had the ability to get us there. But we were not, as an organization, yet to the point where they felt the responsibility to do that. They hadn't had to work at that level before. And the division of work concepts that existed, dictated that if a machine stopped then a maintenance person was the person to take care of that. Not the operator. That was counter to the concepts that we wanted to have in place. We did not want to diminish the maintenance crew. We wanted them to work on the things they were good at, but we wanted the operators to do the things that were most effective in getting where we needed to go. We had not yet crossed that bridge.... Instead of the role of the operators being to control the output (controlling the output being a euphemism for limiting the output – i.e., we only make so many and if we make more then someone else is going to have to do something else beyond what we are doing but don't tax me with it. (Our challenge) was to move beyond that to the view that 'we are all in the same boat. If we don't row fast or plug the hole in the bottom, we are all going down. So, let's see how we can do this together."[100]*

---

[100] Telephone interview with Roger Johnston, September 23, 2019

The process of building a culture in which most of the people in the plant believed and acted as though we are all in the same "boat" did not happen overnight. It was a process that had a number of elements. These elements, coupled with Roger's leadership and the re-creation of the joint union-management improvement process, enabled great progress to be made. In the next section we will review the challenge presented to Hagerstown and the key elements of this change process and how they contributed to the effort to create the "same boat" culture.

The Mission for the Change Process

Prior to Roger's arrival, Andre Morel, who would be Roger's boss asked for a phone call to share his expectations for the change process. In the conversation on January 7, 1999, with Dr. Tuttle who was the lead consultant from the University of Maryland, he made several points that he expected Hagerstown to address in order to increase the odds that the plant's future could be secured. The key points from this conversation were:

- Hagerstown is not at the level of the best – the plant must prove that it is at the level of the best and must prove it daily;
- The point of the change process is not to please the workers, it is to assure their future;
- In order to get to where the plant needs to be, the improvement process needs to get to the team level on the shop floor;
- The basic work unit teams have started in other plants – Winnsboro, McCungie, etc.
- In 2004, a new generation of engines will be on the market. The plan is to have 2 engine assembly plants – but components could be made anywhere. The decision of where to produce will be a rational one made in 2001 to begin tooling in 2002;
- Between now and 2001, the Hagerstown plant must prove it is at the level of the best every day;
- Roger Johnston will be the plant manager and there will be continuity of direction and purpose. Andre will be in Hagerstown 1 day per week, and he wants to stay informed and can be reached easily.

Prior to his arrival in Hagerstown, it is certain that this same message was delivered to Roger since Andre was the person who chose Roger to become the next plant manager.

Key Elements of the Partnership for the Future – The Process to Build the Culture That Would Assure the Plant's Future

The organizational change initiative launched in Hagerstown was named the "Partnership for the Future". This name carried great significance for the plant in two key ways. First, it signified the desire to re-create the partnership that had been developed between management and the UAW under Ross Rhoads and Jim Stewart's leadership. Second, the objective of the partnership was not simply to improve the working relationship within the plant, it was an essential part of the plant's effort to convince Renault that Hagerstown would be the best location to manufacture the next generation diesel engines and transmissions.

The structure of the Partnership for the Future to meet the challenges defined by Andre had five key components: (1) The Mack-UAW Guidance Team, (2) three Subteams of the Guidance Team, (3) the Values Management Process, (4) Partnership for the Future Training and (5) Assessment Tools used to measure progress and take corrective action. Each of these five components of the process are briefly described below.

1. **Mack-UAW Guidance Team** - The Guidance Team was a joint management-union leadership team chartered to guide the development and improvement of the Partnership for the Future and to meet the challenge defined by Andre. Members of the team were the key department managers who report to the General Manager, the Union President and Shop Chairman and UAW committeemen who represent Production and Maintenance. Arnie Gozora from the Mack Human Resources Department coordinated the Team and Dr. Tuttle, from the University of Maryland, served as the team facilitator, The purpose statement for the Guidance Team defined its role as:

*To develop and deploy a partnership that will allow us to become
and prove every day that we are the world's best with respect to
quality, cost, delivery and plant cleanliness.*

The charters for the Guidance Team and the three improvement sub-teams are shown in Appendix A. Creating a "team charter" became a requirement for each of the teams and sub-teams launched in the Partnership for the Future process. The purpose of the charter was to force the sponsor of a team to clearly define the purpose of the team, it expected results, its boundaries, its "customers" and its time frame for results.

The Guidance Team met on a bi-weekly basis and members who were in the building were required to attend. If a member was not in the building due to travel, annual leave, etc. the member could send a substitute if that substitute had been fully briefed on the business of the Guidance Team and was prepared to fully participate meaningfully in discussions. Minutes of the guidance team meetings were maintained and distributed to the major organizational units of the plant. The Guidance Team chartered, supported and enabled Departmental Leadership Teams, but it did not micromanage the functional departments.

2. **Guidance Team Sub-Teams** – The Guidance Team chartered and supported sub-teams as required to address key areas of focus of the Partnership for the Future. These areas of focus were chosen to address key elements of the partnership as well as key needs of the plant identified in surveys and an organizational assessment that was conducted prior to Roger Johnston's arrival. These subteams were facilitated jointly by Dr. Tuttle and Arnie Gozora. The initial subteams that were created are described below.
   - **BWU Sub-Team** – The Basic work unit (BWU) teams were improvement teams in each business unit. In previous versions of the Mack Total Quality Process there had been a number of efforts to move improvement decision making to the shop floor level through team structures. Initially, the mechanism was called Quality Action Teams (QAT). These were facilitated teams

of employees who identified a problem, analyzed causes of the problem and developed and implemented action plans to remove or mitigate the problem. While these team had some success, some were bogged down and created frustration when the teams asked for resources (e.g., maintenance support, financing, etc.) to implement their recommendations and the resources were not provided. This history led to discussions by the Guidance Team during the re-launch of the employee teams of ways to improve the functioning of the teams that would further improve their impact.

- **OME Sub-Team-** OME is an acronym that refers to Other Manufacturing Expenses. The OME team was chartered to create visibility as to the sources of OME expenses, determine their magnitude and most importantly develop and implement approaches to reduce these expenses.
- **Communication Sub-Team** – The culture assessment focus groups conducted following Olivier's departure and prior to Roger's arrival identified a major factor that impacted employee effectiveness and performance of plant units was "communication." The Communication Sub Team was chartered with the mission:

To improve communication effectiveness in the plant through assuring that the appropriate communication processes are continuously improved.

The focus was both on messages and media. Examples of the key communication messages judged essential included:
- "the gap" – the difference between where the plant performance needs to be and where it currently is;
- Translation of "the gap" into specific actionable goals at the workplace level;
- Daily production results;
- Financial data;
- Success stories of performance improvement;
- Recognition of accomplishments and service;

- Linking profit sharing check to accomplishments of the plant.

Key communication media in use in the plant, and their effectiveness ratings by the communication team members on a 5-point rating scale (1 = very ineffective and 5= very effective), are shown below:

- Departmental meetings (4.0);
- Supervisor safety training (3.25);
- Town hall meetings (3.5);
- Information boards (2.75);
- Daily "update" sheet (3.25);
- Electronic marquees at entrances (3.5);
- Electronic marquees in the plant (3.75);
- Payroll stuffers (4.0);
- New employee orientation (3.5);
- Powertrain Press newsletter (4.25); etc.

The team also conducted a rating of which media are most appropriate for which of the key messages, with the assumption that the communication media is functioning effectively.

For example, this analysis pointed out that the team members felt that the Town Hall meetings were the most appropriate medium for communications about "the gap." However, departmental meetings were the appropriate medium to communicate how to translate "the gap" into actionable workplace goals and actions. The team also rated the Powertrain Press newsletter as the most appropriate communication medium to deliver messages about success stories, recognition, and people news (i.e., retirements, obituaries, etc.)

3. **Values Management Process** - We can compare the process of building a strong, stable partnership to the process to build a house. The first step, after site selection and preparation is to build a foundation. In building a partnership the first step is to build trust between the groups of partners. Trust in a partnership is analogous to the foundation of a

building. This was especially important for Mack-Hagerstown because trust between the union and management had been largely destroyed by the previous management. Building trust is something that cannot be done quickly. It develops gradually over time as groups face different situations together.

A very important mechanism to aid in building trust and in constructing the foundation for a partnership that will last is to create a consensus regarding the values that the partnership will be based upon. The effort to create this values consensus is what we are calling the "values management process." This was a consultant facilitated process utilizing a values taxonomy developed and validated by Brian Hall and Benjamin Tonna – a psychologist and a Catholic priest.[101]

Hall and Tonna developed a measuring instrument to enable people to assess their individual values priorities with respect to 125 human values. The key steps in the values management process involved the following steps that were facilitated by Dr. Tuttle:

a. Administer the Hall-Tonna Values Management Inventory to Senior Union and Management Leadership Team members.

b. Conduct an individual values feedback meeting with each Leadership Team member to introduce them to the values framework and to assist them in interpreting their personal values survey report. This prepares each member of the Senior Leadership Team to participate fully in the values consensus session.

c. Facilitate a workshop with the members of the leadership team to develop a consensus set of values that would underpin the Partnership for the Future. The goal in creating the consensus set of values is to select from the participant's individual values a shared set of values (usually 25 to 30 out of the 125 values in the taxonomy). This process involves discussion, debate and clarification of the meaning of each of the individual values. The resulting consensus set ideally includes a sufficient number of both personal and organizational values so that each individual will

---

[101] Hall, Brian P. *Values Shift: A Guide to Personal and Organizational Transformation.* Rockport, MA: Twin Lights Publishers, 1995.

understand and experience how the consensus set overlaps each member's individual set of values. Understanding this "overlap" is necessary for the participants to feel a sense of ownership for the total consensus set of values that will serve as the values set for the union-management joint Guidance Team for the Partnership for the Future.

d. Form the set of consensus values into related clusters. Write a statement defining each values cluster. The statements are referred to as the "principles" that form the foundation for the partnership. Each principle captures the unique elements of the individual value definitions contained in the clusters formed from the total consensus values set. Some values were very basic and foundational that therefore could appear in more than one principle.

e. Translate the principles into workplace behavioral statements for the Hagerstown plant. These behavioral statements link to the consensus values and represent a translation of how living the value translates into behavior in the workplace. These statements served to guide both management and union leaders in efforts to model these behaviors in their daily work. Through this process of leadership behavior modeling, supplemented by incorporating the behavioral expectations into Partnership for the Future training, these values will be increasingly "lived" by the people in the plant. In addition, the workplace behavioral statements were incorporated into an assessment instrument – the Partnership for the Future Survey Assessment to allow the Guidance Team to measure extent to which employees saw their leaders practicing these behaviors. This survey feedback served as a feedback mechanism to management and union leaders on the extent to which they were perceived as living the values.

4. **Partnership for the Future Training-** A focused 16-hour training program was created to activate the Partnership for the Future. This training was developed by a joint management-union training development team facilitated by the consultant. The training content was selected with an eye on the challenge to the plant that had been given by Andre Morel as what it would take for the Hagerstown plant

to be chosen to produce the next generation diesel engine. The training was delivered by in-house union and management trainers who were selected and trained by the members of the joint union-management training development team. The training content consisted of 4 modules:

a. **Our successes** -This module was designed to stress the fact that past improvement initiatives in the Hagerstown plant based on the "joint union management philosophy" had produced improvements in terms of job security, job satisfaction, customer satisfaction, market share, cost improvement and productivity improvements. The plant deviated from the joint philosophy for a couple of years, but even during those two years, improvements were made that will position the plant for more rapid improvement once there is a return to the joint union management philosophy.

b. **Financial Basics of the Business** – Module two concentrated on the financial issues that drive the business. It stresses the impact of these financial realities on the plant as well as on each employee individually. It built a better understanding of the financial realities and how they impact the plant's ability to satisfy customer's and stakeholder's needs. In this way the plant could strengthen its market position and secure employee futures in a globally competitive marketplace.

c. **Meeting Customer Requirements** – Module three focused on the major forces for change in the heavy-duty truck industry and the ever increasing regulatory and customer demands. This module also focused on the values, principles and behaviors that are the foundational elements of our Partnership for the Future.

d. **Our Competitive Analysis** – Module four integrates the messages of Modules 1-3 and focused employee attention on what each Employee Work Unit (EWU) can do to improve the overall competitiveness of the Mack Engine and Transmission products. This module positioned the Employee Work Unit (EWU) as a means to harness the intelligence of the work force and focus it on meeting the needs of customers who are the ultimate judge of business success and future job security. Only through engaging all employees in the improvement efforts will the plant be able to become world-class. Becoming world-class is the only path to continued survival as an employer and as a business.

5. **Workplace/Partnership Assessment** - Once the Partnership for the Future was launched, it was necessary to periodically conduct a formal assessment of its progress. A key tool for gaining employee perceptions of the extent to which the plant population was "living the values" was the Workplace/Partnership Assessment. The 14 items in this survey were designed to focus on "my workplace" and "the overall plant and our values". This survey instrument is shown in Table 9.

Rebuilding the Relationship Between Union and Management

In Chapter 2, we pointed out that one of the reasons that the Total Quality Process was successful was that the design of the process enabled, and to some extent forced, Plant Manager and GM Ross Rhoads and Jim Stewart, President of the UAW Local No. 171 to build a close, trusting relationship. This relationship modeled the type of trust and respect that was necessary to move the plant from the confrontational past that threatened the future of the plant. With Roger Johnston now in the GM position following the confrontational two years with Olivier Vidal at the helm, everybody in the plant hoped for a change in the organizational climate. The competitive pressures from the marketplace and the performance expectations of the parent organization Renault had not gone away. In fact, they had increased. Yet the management and union leaders in the plant knew there was a different way to operate and hoped that Roger Johnston would lead them in a different direction.

	(1)	(2)	(3)	(4)	(5)
Table 9					
Workplace Partnership Assessment Survey					
Survey Items	**Strongly Disagree**	**Disagree**	**Somewhat Agree**	**Agree**	**Strongly Agree**
1. Within the last year there have been improvements in safety in my department/work area.					
2. Within the last year, improvements have been made in my department/work area in cleanliness and environmental issues (air cleanliness, noise, and waste issues).					
3. My department/work area has an effective system in place to resolve tooling, equipment or other process related problems.					
4. Information pertaining to operational performance is routinely shared in my department/work area.					
5. I take the opportunity to express my opinions and ideas about issues affecting my job.					
6. There is a good communication process in place that allows me to know what is going on in the department/work area.					
7. My contributions are noticed and recognized.					
8. I take the opportunity to make improvements in my department/work area.					
9. People in this department/ work area treat each other with dignity and respect.					

10. People within this department/ work area practice continuous improvement on a daily basis.					
11. My work group meets or exceeds departmental goals related to quality, delivery and cost on a daily basis.					
12. People in \my department/work area know how we compare to world-class performance.					

One of the first steps in creating this new direction was pre-emptively taken by Jim Stewart. "Stew" as he was known to his colleagues, and Roger did not know each other well. However, there was some history between them. During the contract negotiations in 1998, Roger worked in the Mack Headquarters in Allentown, Pa. Roger was chosen, as a management representative, to go to all of the Mack units represented under the master agreement with the UAW and make a presentation on the management position regarding some of the issues to be addressed in the upcoming contract negotiations. Roger describes how that session went in Hagerstown:

> *I came to the plant, and that was when Bill Nutter was still there as Shop Chairman and Stew was the President. I was supposed to make a presentation about changing the working times of the day. At that time, we had a paid lunch. I had done the research and found that other people out in industry did not have paid lunch and they have different break times. The paid lunch and break times had been arrived at (in Hagerstown) through negotiations before that. So as far as the union was concerned, we got it and we paid for it so get off my back. So, as one of the proposals by the company for negotiations, I had to go to each facility and make that presentation. When I came to Hagerstown, Nutter was the one that quieted the group because they were not having any part of what I was proposing for the company. It was like when one of the Conservative speakers come to*

> *a university campus and the students shout them down.*
> *They were going to shout me down. And Bill Nutter said*
> *(to his Fellow UAW members), 'Stop!' He has come here*
> *to make a presentation to us and we are going to hear*
> *what he has come to say. We don't have to agree with it,*
> *but we are going to listen to what he has to say."*[102]

Another encounter between Roger and Jim Stewart or "Stew", as he is known by his colleagues occurred in the Fall of 1998 in Wilkes-Barre, Pa. during the actual contract negotiations. Roger was part of the Central Management Group that was supporting the negotiations from the company perspective. The management leadership wanted Roger to make that same presentation again to the management and union negotiators representing all the facilities covered under the master contract between Mack and the UAW. Roger recounts that experience in his encounter with Stew:

> *"When I put the first transparency up, Stew said 'Roger,*
> *if you are going to make that same presentation again,*
> *we are not going to listen.' Then, en mass, the entire body*
> *of union committeemen (about 50) stood up and exited*
> *Stage Left. They got out of the room. I was not a happy*
> *camper, but I understand those kind of strategy things.*
> *So, I packed up my things and left the room. As I was*
> *walking back, I must have looked a little dejected and I*
> *walked by a little alcove in the lobby and there is Stew*
> *sitting there, and Roy Tressler sitting there, and a couple*
> *of other committee people. Stew says 'Roger, Roger, you*
> *are looking a little dejected. You know it is not personal*
> *and then he smiled." That was the only interface I had*
> *with Stew until I arrived in Hagerstown. It was a year*
> *later that it was announced that I would be coming as the*
> *plant manager."*[103]

---

[102] Personal Interview with Roger Johnston, March 18, 2020.
[103] Ibid.

Jim Stewart described this encounter with Roger following their walk-out during his presentation in a little more detail.

> *"I kind of felt sorry for him and then later I caught him in the hallway, and I went over and talked to him. I said, 'I don't know you from Adam, but you seem like a decent person. I'm not out here to "bust your balls" but that is not going to happen (taking away the paid lunch and paid break times.) But I understand that you got the "short straw" to present that message to the group. It was your time to come down and try to get that break time removed but as far as I'm concerned, don't take it personally. I just want you to know that I don't mean it to be personal and you should not take it personally. From that time on, Roger and I had a very good personal relationship."[104]*

The pre-emptive step taken by Jim Stewart to help Roger build trust with the workforce happened during Roger's first days in the plant in March of 1999.

> *"Stew, from day 1, took it on as his personal responsibility to introduce me to everybody. How did he know that I was the guy? How did he know that I was able to do what needed to be done? Don't ask me. I don't know why he stuck his neck out on Day 1. He and I walked around the plant and he introduced me to everyone. First shift, second shift, third shift. He said to his members, I think you will find this guy to be a change from what has most recently been here. Jim Stewart, from Day 1 had decided that he was going to trust me. I don't know why he did. But he did. And I had credibility then....And then we went to Engineering and did the same thing. They were surprised that these manufacturing guys would come over*

---

[104] Telephone interview with Jim Stewart, April 27, 2020

and introduce themselves to us. Wow! So that began the journey."[105]

Roger said several times to me during our interview that he did not know why Jim stuck his neck out to help him gain that immediate credibility with the work force. In my interview with Jim Stewart, I asked him to talk about why he decided to take Roger around the plant on Day 1 and introduce him to his members. Did he feel he was taking a risk of his reputation to do that? Here is how Jim answered that question.

> *Union officials in that plant were hands-on people. When I go down on the line, people would talk to me about all sorts of things but most about their job. That was especially true when there was a threat about their job. So, they had just gotten over this period of time (Olivier period) when they communicated a lot about their job.... With Olivier gone, it was not hard for me to walk down there and take the plant manager to key spots. We did not do it with everybody- but we went to the union official in that department, or some of the key people - and I know who they are- and I would say "Hey let me introduce you to the new plant manager. I'm sure and hoping and praying that he will be a different guy from the one we had here in the past. And we think he is. I worked with him in negotiations, and we are going to give him a shot." It means a lot, not only to Roger, but also to the people out on the floor. Because they just went through Hell!*[106]

How was Roger different? Two examples provide some insight into how he was able to show people on the shop floor how he wanted to operate. Maurice Kaiser, the UAW vice-president, was a very thoughtful man and a man of relatively "few words." "Mo" as he was called said:

---

[105] Personal interview with Roger Johnston, March 18, 2020.
[106] Telephone interview with Jim Stewart, April 27, 2020

> *"With Olivier, he told everyone what to do and you did it or else. When Roger came in, he said he wanted everyone treated with dignity and respect."[107]*

Roger illustrated those values, in a situation he encountered on the shop floor.

> *"I told people that when I knew I was coming here, I got comfortable shoes. Because I planned to be out on the shop floor all the time. I would be out there, and I would stop and talk to people. Because Stew had introduced me to people, they felt at ease to come up and talk to me. Sometimes on a Monday morning they would be yelling at me down by Department 160 – the cylinder head department. I still remember one gentleman who was 'wound up.' He must have been thinking about it all weekend. He was going to give me a piece of his mind- and he did. He was in my face early, and he was loud. And when he was done, I said 'I understand the nature of what you are talking about. I will dig into it, and I will get back to you. But, by the way, the next time you want to talk to me you can talk to me in a regular tone of voice. I will hear you just the same. You don't need to crank it up like that. That is not necessary.' And he said, 'Well, I'll try.' "*

> *……. I wanted people to understand that I'm a guy who likes to hunt, and work on cars. I'm normal and you can talk to me like the next person. Yes, I have a different job, and somebody has got to do it but that does not mean that I am better than you. I'm just different in my role."[108]*

Symbolic gestures, however small, can be powerful ways to demonstrate one's values. Roger's time with General Motors during his college experience working various jobs on the assembly line gave him an extremely valuable

---

[107] Telephone interview with Maurice Kaiser, May 6, 2020.
[108] Personal Interview with Roger Johnston, March 18, 2020

appreciation for and the ability to connect with people who work on the shop floor. Jim Stewart shared a story that showed to guys in the plant that Roger had a special appreciation for the work they did every day and he understood what they deal with in order to do their job.

"Roger had his hand's full when he assumed the job in Hagerstown. He was such a breath of fresh air after Olivier left and you had a new guy who did not say 'I'm the new guy and you have to do what I say.' Roger's way of communicating with people was to sit down and say 'Hey we have got a job to do, and we are going to try and get it done together. He did that with management, and he did it with the union. I'll give you an example of what Roger did without the union saying a word. We never had air conditioning other than in certain areas that had to have it such as the gage lab where they had to keep temperatures at a certain level in order to maintain accuracy of the gages. For the most part, the engine line had machines running 24 hours a day creating heat. Never in the 38 years that I was in there did anyone ask for relief even when the temperature got over 90 degrees. Without anyone asking for it, Roger had bottled ice water brought in and put down on the line. That seems like a small thing but to a guy working down on that line who has worked there for 25 years, and he had never seen anyone in management care about him working in the heat. He had never seen anyone care if he had cold water to drink other than drinking out of a water fountain that some guy who was chewing tobacco had just spit in. Roger took it upon himself to go down there and be considerate enough to say that every so many feet I want a bucket of ice with water bottles in it. And they can drink as much of it as they want. I got a call and they told me about that. It was so simple. It was so inexpensive. Don't you think that did not make a difference for those people that were working down on that floor. It made a huge difference![109]

[109] Telephone interview with Jim Stewart, April 27, 2020.

A few months after his arrival in Hagerstown Roger and Jim Stewart issued a joint message to the plant population. This letter, jointly drafted, was mailed to each employee in their home. This gesture was also a way for Jim and Roger to say to their employees that we are sending this to your home in hopes that you will share this message with your family. They were communicating their awareness of the fact that whether or not the plant has a future was just as important to the families of the employees as it was to the employees themselves. It was also saying to the families of employees that "We care about you. "

The full text of that message is shown in Figure 1.

> **Joint Message from Roger Johnston and Jim Stewart**
>
> *Reflecting back over the last several months we have solicited your help in assessing our present culture with surveys. Both Management and Union Employees participated in the surveys administered by Don Steele from the Performance Learning Center and by Dr. Tom Tuttle representing the University of Maryland Center for Quality and Productivity. The Performance Learning Center assessed our current culture and environment, and the University of Maryland assessed the communication needs in terms of quality and amount of communication desired. We have received the results and as we committed, we would like to share them with you.*
>
> *The results of the Performance Learning Center indicated that the management and union employees of Hagerstown show strong agreement that they want to "Be the Best" and want to work in an environment that encourages involvement, respect, and honors the integrity of its employees. This is to be accomplished by building a culture with a strong obligation to customer satisfaction and an environment that believes and supports the corporate mission and goals. The evaluations of the assessment survey clearly indicated that in order for us to secure our futures and grow our business, we need to work together to bridge the gap between the existing culture and the desired*

culture. We chose Dr. Tom Tuttle to help us bridge this gap. Dr. Tuttle recommended the formation of a Guidance Team consisting of Management and Union Officials to work together to define a plan and implement the approach to bridging this gap.

The primary approach is managing this facility utilizing the Total Quality process. Some might say, "Here we go again, we tried that before and it did not work." I understand your frustration, our organization was not structured to react to the multitude of requests or suggestions. The Total Quality Process did not fail, if anything the results consumed us. As Dr. Deming said if we meet our customer' expectations in Quality, Delivery and Cost the results will be rewarding. The efforts of all of our employees have resulted in significant cost reductions in warranty, productivity improvements and on-time delivery to our customers. Our business has grown and with that continued success we will be rewarded with a continuation of secure jobs. We are confident that the Total Quality philosophy is the approach to continue our growth.

The primary areas of focus of the Guidance Team are the formation of Basic Work Units, reducing OME costs and improving communication. Basic Work Unit Pilot teams are currently being formed in both divisions and that approach provides the perfect opportunity for us all to be involved in the process. Initially, in order to finalize the BWU process we have instituted FAST Teams (Focused Accelerated Solution Teams) to focus in on the safety, manufacturing processing and environmental needs of our operators. Most manufacturing departments have received OME training, and it again provides an opportunity to be involved in reducing our costs.

In regard to communication, we recognize our efforts in the past were not adequate. We solicited your help in the communication survey. The survey was intended to provide a baseline for measuring if our efforts in communication are improving.

The results indicated that there are opportunities to improve our methods of communication as well as the content of the message. Such opportunities consist of providing information about – how my job compares with others (competitive benchmarking), information about how we are being measured, recognition for my efforts, information on department policies and goals, information about achievements and/or failures of the organization and the extent to which people in Mack have the ability to communicate. The Guidance Team now needs to focus on each of these opportunities and develop action plans to better our communication efforts. Ultimately, the goal is to develop an effective communication mechanism that provides a daily exchange either verbal or written to increase customer satisfaction, both internal and external. Later, we intend to ask you again to participate in the survey to measure our progress in meeting your communication needs.

In the near future there will be opportunities to develop and strengthen our skills to better meet the customers' needs, in terms of financial and Total Quality training. Understanding the financial basics, relating and applying them to the customers' needs will strengthen our market position and secure our futures in this competitive market. We invite you and encourage you to participate in those training sessions to create and ensure our future in "Becoming the Best."

Roger Johnston   **Jim Stewart**

Figure 1.
Joint Letter to Employees from Roger Johnston and Jim Stewart

The Values and Principles Underlying the Union Management Partnership

This joint letter spoke of the need to bridge the gap between the present culture and the desired culture. One of the activities designed to accelerate that process was the development of a consensus set of values that would form the basic values foundation for the partnership as it addresses the major business and cultural challenges. The key steps in the process to define that set of consensus values was defined in the earlier discussion. One of the key outcomes of this process, in addition to the definition of the principles underlying the partnership, was the development of a common language that helped union and management leaders talk about values in ways that were difficult prior to this activity. We all have values that guide our decisions and behavior. However, for most of us, these values are implicit and not often addressed or discussed. The activities that the consultant led the leadership team to engage in forced them both individually and as a group to make their values explicit. Once they have been made explicit, they could be talked about openly in a more impersonal manner which made such discussions less threatening.

Table 10 lists the values that were included in the consensus set of values along with brief definitions of the values from the Hall-Tonna values taxonomy.[110] Table 11 lists the values according to the developmental Stages from the Hall-Tonna map. The Values Map represents a way to portray the entire 125 set of values into one of 8 Stages corresponding to the Hall-Tonna perspective on how these values develop over time in the process of human development. This map incorporates theoretical perspectives from a number of psychologists such as Piaget, Maslow, Rotter, Rokeach and others. While the developmental process is not rigid, and there are many different developmental paths, there is a tendency for normal development to progress from stages on the left side of the map to stages on the right side of the map. Not every person will progress through all 8 stages. Based on situations, people who have evolved to stage 5 or 6 and then encounter challenges to health, economic security or physical security may then move to earlier stages on the map until these challenges are resolved.

---

[110] Hall, Brian P. *Values Shift: A Guide to Personal and Organizational Transformation.* Rockport, MA: Twin Lights Publishers, 1995.

Table 10		
Consensus Values with Hall-Tonna Brief Definitions		
Goal Values		
Security	Creating an environment where one feels his/her most basic needs are met, such as health care benefits or salary.	
Self-Worth	Knowing that one is valued by those who know one well.	
Belief/Philosophy	Adherence to a belief system, set of principles, or established philosophy that is based on a universally accepted document which advocates the reverence for a universal order.	
Competence/Confidence	Having assurance in one's skills to achieve and make a positive contribution at work.	
Self-Actualization	Developing spiritual, psychological, physical and mental health.	
Service/Vocation	Knowing that you have skills, an occupation, or profession that is making a significant contribution.	
Faith/Risk/ Vision	Committing to the mission or plan of action based on one's values	
Human Dignity	Promoting an organizational environment where everyone is respected and has their basic needs met so they can develop their full potential.	
Knowledge/ Insight	Pursuing truth through patterned investigation and use of intuition as a basis for decision making.	
Means Values		
Economics/Profit	Establishing financial stability.	
Control/Order/ Discipline	Being disciplined and orderly according to established rules no matter how stressful circumstances are.	
Rights/Respect	Recognizing the word, accomplishments and property of others.	
Achievement/Success	Driven to complete projects and accomplish something	
Communication/ Information	Transmitting ideas and factual data between people and components of an organization.	
Duty/Obligation	Loyalty to managers, peers and the organization's customs and regulations.	
Efficiency/Planning	To do critical path planning that maximizes output and minimizes waste.	
Loyalty/Fidelity	Duty to friends and those in authority even when it is to your disadvantage.	
Ownership	Taking pride in what you own and the responsibilities you have.	
Productivity	To be energized by completing and achieving personal and group tasks and goals.	
Reason	Thinking logically and exercising reason before emotions.	
Responsibility	Being accountable and in charge of a specific area or project.	
Unity/Uniformity	Achieving efficiency, order, loyalty, and conformity to establish norms in an organization.	
Authority/Honesty	The exercise of power as straightforward expression of feelings and thoughts.	

Decision/Initiation	Starting projects and a course of action based on personal conviction, without getting others approval.	
Limitation/Acceptance	Recognizing personal inabilities as a beginning point for problem solving and growth.	
Quality/Evaluation	Appreciating objective self-appraisal. Being open to what others reflect back about oneself or team(group) and the products of one's work for personal growth and the improvement of service to others.	
Search/Meaning/Hope	Seeking to discover one's uniqueness and to make sense out of day-to-day existence.	
Sharing/Listening/Trust	Hearing another person's thoughts and feelings and expressing one's own in a climate of mutual confidence.	
Accountability/Ethics	To act on personal moral principles even when faced with pressure to do otherwise.	
Collaboration	Cooperating interdependently with personnel at all levels through appropriately delegating responsibility.	
Limitation/Celebration	Laughing at one's imperfections as a way of defining one's unique skills and abilities.	
Mission Objectives	Management of the strategic planning of an organization.	
Mutual Accountability	Maintaining a reciprocal balance of tasks and assignments with others so that all are answerable for their own areas of responsibility.	

The theory incorporates the idea that for each person or organization the concept that with respect to values there are three perspectives – Foundation, Focus and Vision. Foundational values are basic values, that are important for human survival. These values tend to move out of consciousness after they have been satisfied unless they are threatened. These include values such as Self Preservation, Food/Warmth/Shelter, Function/Physical, Security, Economics/Profit, etc. The second perspective is Focus. The Focus values are those which impact current thinking and behavior. When we say that a person is operating at a certain stage on the map it means that the central tendency of the distribution of their focus values is at that stage. The third perspective is Vision. Vision values refer to those values that a person or organization is not currently activating but they are values that the individual or organization aspires to activate. The reasons vision values are not currently activated can include lack of needed skills, abilities or knowledge, lack of opportunity, and/or lack of experience. A key assumption in the theory is that people can choose to change the stage in which they are currently focused and can move toward their vision. They do this through education, training, advancement, and/ or changing their circumstances i.e., moving to a new place, new job, etc.

As you can see from the map in Table 11, the values in the top rows of the map are labeled Goal Values while values in the lower rows are labeled Means Values. The distinction is that Goal Values refer to desired end states or outcomes while the means values are values that must be activated in order to reach the desired end state or Goal. The distinction between means and goals is important in counseling an individual or organization because if a person or an organization has a goal value but no means values in that stage of development, it will lead to frustration and the inability to achieve the desired end state represented by the Goal value.

Another key aspect of the theory is that when the mid-point of an individual's or organization's focus values moves across the line that separates stage 4 and stage 5, there is a significant shift in perspective. Individuals and organizations whose mid-point of their focus values lies in stage 4 tend to be "other directed." This means that their decision making tends to be strongly influenced by other people and what other people think of them. On the other hand, individuals and organizations whose mid-point of their focus values crosses the line into stage 5 they tend to become "inner directed." This means that their decision making tends to see life as a challenge but the challenges can be overcome through their personal initiative, learning, and their ability to create opportunities through their behavior.

Table 11 Consensus Values Arrayed in the Hall-Tonna Values Map Framework							
	Stage 1	Stage 2	Stage 3	Stage 4	Stage 5	Stage 6	Stage 7	Stage 8
Goal Values		Security	Self-Worth	Belief/Philosophy Competence/ Confidence	Self-Actualization	Faith/ Risk/ Vision		
					Service/ Vocation	Human Dignity		
						Knowledge/ Insight		

Means Values		Economics/ Profit	Control/ Order/ Discipline	Achievement/ Success	Authority/ Honesty	Accountability/ Ethics	Interdependence	
				Communication/ Information Duty/Obligation	Decision/ Initiation	Collaboration		
			Rights/ Respect	Efficiency/ Planning Loyalty/Fidelity	Limitation/ Acceptance	Limitation/ Celebration		
				Ownership Productivity Reason	Quality/ Evaluation Search/ Meaning/ Hope	Mission/ Objectives Mutual/ Accountability		
				Responsibility Unity/Uniformity	Sharing/ Listening/ Trust			

People who are "inner directed" take charge of their own life and become self-initiating. It does not mean that inner directed people don't care what others think. Their decision making is not determined by what others think. From an organizational point of view, this Stage 5 mentality is critical in enabling a plant like Mack-Hagerstown escape the old view that what happens to the plant is dependent on forces outside of the control or influence of people inside the plant. This "old" view is that the future of the plant depends on Mack Headquarters, on the factors in the heavy truck market, on competitors, etc. While all of these forces have relevance, if members of the plant population only cling to Stage 3-4 views regarding how their future will be determined, they are less likely to be willing to take actions that can help them create their own future. On the other hand, if they adopt a Stage 5-6 mentality, they feel that through their behavior they can make changes that will influence, if not determine, their own future. As we will see later in our discussion, this will become a significant issue for the Hagerstown plant.

If we examine the results of the values surveys for the Leadership Team, Union and Management, at Mack-Hagerstown the distribution of the values patterns of the 18 people on the Leadership Group is shown in Figure 2. What we see is that the distributions are very similar in the Management and Union Groups. However, both groups have a majority of their people in the Stage 4 thinking mode.

This data points out quite clearly, that the challenge facing Roger Johnston is to help move the developmental level of a majority of management and union employees to the Stage 5-6 world view. In essence, this defines the leadership challenge for Roger and joint union-management Guidance Team as it develops and implements the Partnership for the Future. Fortunately, there were people with a Stage 5 world view in both the management and the union groups. This was very important in terms of building trust and acceptance of the elements of the Partnership. Unless there were champions of the idea that we must take charge of our own future in both the management and union groups, the changes proposed could be viewed by some supervisors and some union employees as just more management propaganda. The fact that the plant had both management and union leadership in the Stage 5 level of development significantly aided the efforts to build trust and obtain "buy-in" for the needed changes in how the plant must operate.

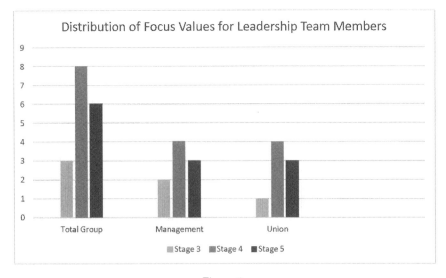

Figure 2
Distribution of Focus Values by Developmental Stage

Once a consensus was reached on the values that must be included in the set of values that would serve as the foundation values for the Partnership for the Future, the process moved to the next step. This involved sorting the individual values into a limited number of categories that would define the principles underlying the Partnership for the Future. This sorting took into account both of the content of the values and the relationships between means values and goal values. Once sorted into the categories, the principles statements were defined. These brief statements captured the essence of the values clusters. By creating these principles, it became much easier to communicate to members of the plant that had not participated in the values surveys the key ideas that the union and management leadership had chosen to serve as the values foundation of the Partnership. Figure 3 lists the 4 principles and the consensus values that were incorporated into the definition of the principles.

Mack-UAW Hagerstown
We commit to these principles and their underlying
values to enable us to "Be the Best"

- **Individual Dignity** – We will create an environment that actively supports the basic rights of each person to be respected. We will assure that each person is given the opportunity to be successful through valuing them as a person, through providing an opportunity to develop their skills, through providing timely and accurate information, and providing honest and open communication. We will honestly acknowledge our limitations, encourage and accept constructive feedback and learn from our mistakes.

(**Values included:** security, self-worth, rights/respect, competence/confidence, communication/information, self-actualization, authority/honesty, *limitation/acceptance*, sharing/listening/trust, *human dignity*, limitation/celebration).

- **Continuous Improvement** – We will actively stimulate the continuous improvement of the performance capability of all individuals and the organization. Our security comes from our ability to be the best engine and transmission plant in the world. Our design of jobs and work processes will provide meaningful work that will stimulate employee development and allow each person to see how they contribute to the mission of the plant. This requires all of us to take responsibility for and to

---

continuously improve our ability to perform. As individuals and as an organization we will continually develop and apply our knowledge and skills, using reason and logic rather than emotion, to enable us to better solve problems, increase value to customers and shareholders and gain confidence from our increased contribution. We will create structures and systems that reward people for improving their capabilities and knowledge and for sharing this knowledge to enable others to improve.

(Values included: security, economics/profit, self-worth, rights/respect, competence/ confidence, communication/information, reason, self-actualization, *search/meaning/hope*, knowledge/insight, limitation/celebration)

- **Mutual Responsibility and Collaboration** – In order to "be the best" members of the Mack-UAW team understand that their future is linked to the success of their partners in Mack, in Renault and in the customer community. This interdependence requires high levels of joint activity and mutual accountability focused on the mission of the Hagerstown plant. We will create a community that encourages initiative and risk-taking within a framework of shared values and trust developed through honest dialog and a shared purpose. We will honor our duties and obligations, be loyal to the "tradition" of Mack Trucks and the UAW and will take ownership and responsibility for the processes, tasks and relationships required to assure the continued success of the plant.

(Values included – security, economics/profit, self-worth, control/order/discipline, rights, respect, belief/philosophy, communication/information, duty/obligation, loyalty/ fidelity, ownership, responsibility, service/vocation, authority/honesty, decision/initiation, sharing/listening/trust, faith/risk/vision, accountability/ethics, collaboration, limitation/ celebration, *mission/objectives*, mutual accountability, interdependence.)

- **Performance Excellence** – The ultimate success of a business is determined by its ability to provide sustained value to customers and sustained profitability to shareholders. We will adopt, implement and improve business practices that assure continually improving processes and minimal variability in products. We will accurately appraise and evaluate our results and the processes we use to create those results and use this data to help us improve. We will minimize waste of any resource which we can control or influence, thereby minimizing our costs. By assuring alignment with the mission of the corporation and the requirements of our customers we will work to improve customer satisfaction and profitability and thereby enhance our own employment security and our ability to create a positive future for our families.

(Values included- Economics/profit, control/order/discipline, *work/labor*, achievement/success, *efficiency/planning*, productivity, reason, unity/uniformity, quality/evaluation, accountability/ethics, *mission/objectives*, mutual accountability)

* NOTE: Values that are italicized were added to the original list of consensus values to fill gaps.

Figure 3
Principles and Values Forming the Foundation of the Partnership for the Future

While the Guidance Team was focusing on implementing the elements of the Partnership Roger also had business to run. Everyday, the plant was required to meet its schedule to deliver engines to the Assembly Plants who installed the engines and transmission into new trucks. One of the key struggles the plant faced in meeting the delivery demand resulted from the fact that the production line for a major engine component, cylinder blocks, was not producing enough blocks per day. Roger was faced with a key strategic decision regarding the shortage of blocks. Here is how he described the decision he made.

> *Unfortunately, I had to make the decision at the time to go to the outside to buy blocks beyond the number that we had demonstrated that we could make which was about 160 per day. We needed more than 200 per day. So, we contracted to buy the additional ones from a company on the outside. It was very expensive, I hated to do it, but the last thing you do as a tier 1 supplier within the company was to fail to deliver the required number of products to the assembly plant. Stopping the assembly line was the taboo that you just do not break. So, we had to find a way to get that volume out. It was not going to happen without the people involvement. So, the union finally acceded to that point of view.*

> *(After the decision to outsource blocks had been made) the union came to me and said we are not happy about those blocks coming from the outside. Bobby Shoop the Shop Chairman and Maurice "Mo" Kaiser talked to me as did Andy Huffer who was a second shift committeeman. Andy believed there was another way to make this happen (bring the production back in house.) The collective effort of the union was to talk to the people and bring them together and say to them "are you willing to take all that knowledge that you have on how to control this beast (I.e., the quarter mile long block production line). I am sure they did not get a "yes answer right out of the gate, but eventually they got all the shifts in agreement that this is what they would do. And so, it was a beginning of the acceptance of taking responsibility that had been managements that, no, they should do that.*[111]

This example perfectly illustrates the point made earlier with respect to the importance of the "values shift" from external control to internal control. Some of the union leaders were people who were already operating from the internal control world view – that is," I can take charge of my life." In this case, by taking charge of the production of blocks these union leaders realized they were not only protecting the jobs of their fellow union members, they were also demonstrating that through such actions they were increasing the odds that engine production would remain in Hagerstown. So, these "enlightened" union leaders led the efforts to convince some of their colleagues who had not yet made the shift to a Stage 5 world view to move in that direction.

Roger went on to describe how that thought process might have proceeded in the heads of the union members who were being approached by their leaders to think differently.

> *Wait a minute, I know how to do that, why should I not do that. Sure, I can do that. I'll show you! There was a pride element that was there. …They had always known*

---

[111] Personal interview with Roger Johnston, March 18, 2020.

what to do. If the line stops when the bearing cap silos were not running, which limit switch is the one that needs to be "poked with a stick", was it hung up? The operators knew that. They could either make it run or not make it run. When they got busy, we got up to 225 engines per day because they knew what to do. It established that when there is a willingness and a capability it is fulfilling – and there was some money in it for them. We did not take away supervisors, but we allowed individuals within the process to have greater responsibility. There was a piece of what some would call engineering, some would call supervision, that was taken over by the operators.[112]

Roger was asked "what messages did it send when you contracted out the production of those blocks?" He responded:

The message that it sent was probably two or three-fold depending on where one stood. For me, it was a message that we are serious about this because we do not have a choice. I explained it at the time. I want us to get out the maximum we can as long as we produce them with quality. But until we know we can do it; we cannot jeopardize the ability of the company to sell trucks. We haven't a choice.

The response from Bobby (Shoop- Shop Chairman) was "can we try to get the maximum that we can get" I knew there would be a penalty if we tried to buy out the contract (from the outside block supplier). We had contracted for a quantity of blocks. I can't tell you if it was 1,000 or 2,000. And that the cost was expensive, more than it would have cost us to make them. But at least we should still be able to sell trucks. So, it sent the message that we were serious about it and (if I had been on the union side of the discussion) it probably sent the message that "I don't trust you. You don't believe I can do it." But I was

---

[112] Personal interview with Roger Johnston, March 18, 2020.

in the camp that said, "Show me!" I want to believe that you can do it. But I am sorry, until you show me that you can do it, I can't just take it on faith alone. You have to show me. And when they did show us, we came to the decision that we would buy our way out of the contract. We only got about half of the number we had contracted with the external supplier. We exceeded the volume that we thought we would need in concert with the demand that was larger than what was intended. In that way it was a win-win.

From the union point of view there were many who said you do not trust us. However, it was a challenge to them, and they said we will show you what we can do, and we will show it to you in spades! And they did. They made wonderful things happen with that equipment, they made it "sing". They made parts come through there – they found solutions. It wasn't easy. It wasn't like they just said from one day to the next "Well we will give you the number." There was a lot of hard work. It was a challenge between shifts, and then it was the competition between shifts – which shift will get to the number before the next. Wait a minute, you are leaving me in bad shape when I come in in the afternoon following your shift. It should not have been like that. I leave those buffers full, but you are not leaving them full for the next shift. What kind of deal is that? I am sure there were some spirited conversations going on between the operators and the committeemen shift by shift in terms of working out those details. But as management, we stood back and said, look let's give them some room to work here. Let's not get in their way. We want them to be able to have an effect without our interference. And it wasn't "let them fail", instead it was "let them succeed."

That worked. And that was a good beginning for the
challenges that were beyond that of getting to 200 engines
per day. [113]

Volvo AB Buys Mack and RVI

In May 2000, it was announced that AB Volvo purchased the truck
Division of Renault (RVI) which included Mack Trucks in the United
States. This purchase had been rumored for some time since Volvo's
attempt to purchase Swedish truck maker Scania was not approved by
Swedish regulators. The announcement was vague regarding plans for the
powertrain operations centered in Mack-Hagerstown. However, RVI had
developed an agreement with Nissan Diesel to build diesel engines but
that was not included in the Volvo purchase of RVI. The announcement
included the following comment:

> "Mack is one of the world's strongest brands in the industry
> and it has its own production of engines which was a very
> important factor for us. We intend to achieve further
> critical mass in the engine sector that will permit us to make
> aggressive investments that will better enable us to meet
> demands from our customers and society."[114]

However, the article also contained this line:

> *It's unknown whether individual engine lines will be merged.*[115]

While the announcement was potentially good news for Hagerstown, there
was a strong sense of "Here we go again" with respect to the uncertainty
that comes with having a new owner.

Roger Johnston described what it was like following the announcement
that Volvo had purchased Mack as part of the RVI deal.

---

[113] Personal interview with Roger Johnston, March 18, 2020.
[114] *Volvo buys Mack, Renault truck businesses*, May 1, 2000, *trucknews.com*.
[115] Ibid.

"Shortly after that time (buying out the contract for engine blocks) is when we had to confront becoming part of Volvo. This presented a whole new set of challenges. We had to satisfy the requirements thrown to us that we needed more flexibility in our contract (the local labor contract between Mack-Hagerstown and the UAW) if we were going to remain in Hagerstown and that would be the location of Powertrain. There were people who came in from real estate who assessed the site, and they wrote a report that at the time we did not know how to take it. It said that 40% of the infrastructure that was there was OK. Forty is less than 50, so at what point does it have to be before they would decide that it was better to build new somewhere else? There was implied pressure by that analysis. Later we understood that the people who wrote it were trying to say that the "bones" of the facility, or the structure or the skeleton is good. ....We had all those years of non-reinvestment (in the facility). The years that Renault had been in ownership were very difficult years. They funded almost a billion dollars, collectively, in losses for the Mack organization- not just in Hagerstown.... So, things that would normally have been done to maintain the facility were not done. Things that would have been done to upgrade the machines were not done such as upgrading controls and changing out hydraulic systems and so on. So, it was evident to Volvo that money would have to be invested. Then we had to convince the population of the plant that it was worthwhile to consider strongly modifying some of what was considered to be sanctified in the sense of things that had been negotiated year after year and things had been given and taken in order to have the work rules that they had, in order to have the time off that they had, in order to have the seniority rules that they had, in order to have the classifications that they had and in order to have the roles they had versus management. Not in addition to, but "versus" management. So, changing that had to be

given its due. That was a challenge. This was in late 2002 into 2003. So, we reopened the contract.

.......At that time, Volvo had a lot of leverage. They could have pulled the plug and gone somewhere else. And they had every intention to do that if it seemed to be the right thing. So, we had to be performing at the same time we were dealing with these challenges. We had to assure our customer- the truck plant- that they would be receiving what they needed from us and that they were satisfied with what we were sending them. That they were receiving them on time in the correct condition. We gained the "customer" Volvo. We started building engines for Volvo. We had to satisfy another customer that was used to other ways of conversing. We had to learn all of that. We always said that "we have to work on the airplane while it was flying." So, we better get good at that. "Wing walking" had become part of the job responsibility.[116]

Powertrain Division Formed and Headquartered in Hagerstown

Throughout its history in Hagerstown, the Hagerstown plant facility had housed Powertrain Engineering, Purchasing and Manufacturing. However, while these functions were in the same building, they each reported to Mack Headquarters in Allentown, Pennsylvania. This reporting relationship made cooperation among and between the three units much more difficult than it needed to be. It contributed to slow decision making as well as conflicts between the functions regarding responsibility. When problems with an engine were uncovered by the warranty group, it was necessary to determine if the problem was an engineering problem, a manufacturing problem or a problem with a supplier's component. That information then had to travel up the line to Headquarters and then back down to Hagerstown to make changes. This structure slowed down decision making and reduced the organization's ability to satisfy customers in a timely manner. When,

---

[116] Personal interview with Roger Johnston, March 18, 2020.

in the tear down audit of an engine that occurred monthly, a defect was discovered there were often contentious battles between manufacturing and engineering staff regarding who was at fault for the defect. The finger-pointing not only impacted cooperation between the units, but it also negatively impacted delivery, quality and cost.

When Volvo acquired Mack and RVI, one of the early changes was the creation of the North American Power Train Division with a Senior Vice President located in Hagerstown. This Senior VP had total responsibility for Powertrain Manufacturing, Engineering, Purchasing as well as the support functions for those functional areas. This significantly streamlined the powertrain operations and helped foster greater cooperation between the functions that had always operated side by side in the same building in Hagerstown. But because they each reported to different "bosses", cooperation was impaired.

The Senior VP assigned to lead the North American Powertrain Division was Denis LeBlond. Once he assessed what was going on in Hagerstown Manufacturing, he was impressed with the way the Total Quality Process had been organized there. He requested a proposal from the Maryland Center for Quality and Productivity to facilitate a similar process to help him assimilate these previously separate functions into a world-class Division.

Volvo formed a Global Power Train business unit with operations in France, Sweden, Brazil and the United States. Each of those units had the challenge to achieve and sustain world class performance as well as to bring to market those products that meet the needs of customers in their respective market areas. Compared to the European Power Train business units, the North American Powertrain Division had all of its component business units in the same facility. However, LeBlond realized that to take advantage of the co-location, the Hagerstown operations must operate more effectively as a single aligned business rather than as three loosely connected separate functions reporting to corporate offices located elsewhere.

More specifically, he knew that by December 2002, the Division must show significant cost improvements, an increase in "speed," continued labor-management collaboration in all facets of the business, improved synergy and collaboration. The Division must move toward becoming a team-based organization where cross-functional teams operated like business units.

To help create this new culture, the guidance team structure and the values mentoring process utilized in Manufacturing were also set up in Purchasing and in Engineering facilitated by the Maryland Center for Quality and Productivity. The intent of this transitional structure is to accelerate the cultural change in these business units and align the culture with the tenets of the Volvo Way and be based on shared values that will enhance trust, information sharing and continuously improving business results. In the North American Powertrain Executive Guidance Team meeting, Chuck Salter GM of Engineering said that the process in Engineering is focused on engaging all the people to focus on customer's needs and to work with purchasing and manufacturing to enhance the process. Tony Lopes, GM of Purchasing stated that his primary objective of the Guidance Team in Purchasing was to create a partnership with other functions that has the same dedication, focus and concerns related to business goals.

By creating the position of North American Powertrain Senior VP, Volvo made a very important step toward creating a future for the Hagerstown Plant. However, simply having the office located there did not guarantee that this would be the site chosen to manufacture the next generation of diesel engines. That decision would come later based on the performance of the plant and based on Volvo's satisfaction that a new labor agreement could be negotiated that would create the work rule flexibility needed to enable the plant to become a world-class producer.

The "Red Thread" Approach to Managing Change

Becoming part of Volvo was a blessing for Hagerstown for the reasons previously cited. However, culturally, it was not an easy change. The "Mack Bulldog" culture was deeply ingrained in the workforce, especially the long timers. They had been through a lot of ups and downs over the years, but the Bulldog pride was very strong. The shift in culture that began when

Ross Rhoads and Jim Stewart launched the Total Quality Management process had begun to chip away at the old top-down autocratic management system, but the "macho- Harley riding" image was still very strong among members of the workforce.

This culture clash became obvious when there was a lively discussion in the plant over what to do with the main symbol of the plant to the Hagerstown community. This was a water tower that sat on a hill overlooking the plant. On this water tower was the Mack Bulldog logo. I can never recall any discussion when Renault RVI purchased Mack about replacing the Mack logo on the water tower with a Renault logo. However, soon after the Volvo purchase the issue was raised about what to do about the Water Tower. In this discussion, which was quite lively, feelings of the plant about the Volvo image surfaced. While the plant population respected Volvo's reputation as a successful global enterprise, it carried the "image" to many of the Mack employees of the "yuppie, soccer mom" had resulted from the image of Volvo cars used by Moms to transport their sons and daughters to sports practices and school. That was quite a contrasting image to the Mack Bulldog culture. Some suggested that the water tower be repainted with just the Volvo Logo displayed. After a lively debate, the decision was made to have both logos displayed on the water tower since the plant still produced products for both brands. In some ways, this debate was trivial, however it surfaced some of the feelings in the workforce that caused them to be skeptical of some of the cultural changes Volvo would introduce as part of the corporate philosophy statement – The Volvo Way.

Roger Johnston had an innovative way to guide the plant through this shift in thinking that made it more acceptable to the Bulldog people. Here is how Roger outlined his approach.

> *"Volvo had a document that described their philosophy and values called "The Volvo Way." If you boiled it down, it was essentially the golden rule. You treat people as you would like to be treated.... Generally, the Swedes tended to practice the Volvo Way behaviors and values.*

I had the advantage as the guy in the corner office to transition through a number of phases in the evolution of the organization. But from the point of view of the guys on the shop floor, if you don't watch it, and over time you have various people tugging you in different directions what is the "soup du jour" – we are going to do this now, while three years ago you said we were going to do that. If you could not show them the "red thread" to show how this was connected, that was a challenge. We went from (Mack to) the Renault organization – whatever that meant – including the vestiges of Olivier's time here, and we had the memories of what had been done with Ross, for the people who had been here then. We had the people rejoin us in 1998-1999 who had been out for as long as 9 years, so they had not even been here in the time period doing those things (i.e., The team activities that were part of the Total Quality Process). They had to be brought on board because they had been laid off when a bunch of work went out of the plant. They had been singed and were a little unhappy. Work was given up to the outside and they lost their jobs for 8-10 years. So, we had a lot of homage in the work force, but not entirely. We had different groups that were impacted in different ways. You had to recognize that and bring them in to a group of people and how do you get them to feel like they are pulling together. One group explains it one way with one set of words then Volvo uses a different set of words. How do you help people to see the translation and yet the commonality between the different approaches? We needed to figure out the ways to do that. So, it did not look like we were just changing directions the next time the wind blew. We had to show it was related and not altogether that different.

So, the teamwork, the team formation, the change in assignment of responsibility between the organization management and the shop people that began in the 90's _began to chip away at this huge block of granite like the people who carved Mt. Rushmore. When you go out there and see all the "tailings" on the ground you realize that that had to be worked on. People got a taste of it; I had that sense. That is what motivated me when Andre Morel offered me that role there. I often commented on that in the plant. I had been impressed in the 90's when I saw these guys that were well into their careers, probably been used to doing certain things a certain way all along, become willing to try something new. I would not have expected it. And I told them that. That had been encouragement for me. So, this was an organization that may look on the surface that they were going to do things the way they had always done it and I'll get in your face and tell you that if you want to hear it. There were a few people who did, but most did not. Quite the contrary, they were on the track to do something new. So, they had a taste of working in teams in the Total Quality effort that was here. They were willing to restart that because we had gotten far enough in the evolution to have some trust there._

Then we became part of Volvo and how was Volvo's team concept similar to where we had been. We had been in the forming stage with company and union talking about roles and responsibilities. How do we structure it? So that we have the best luck and chance of success when we kick it off. ..We did not want it to be thrown by the wayside when we became part of Volvo so how did we shape it so that our new owner could say "Ah, we see our identity in that. And we could see how from our view it connects to the work we have been doing at this site for the past 15 years. I felt very fortunate that the Volvo organization gave us room to do that."[117]

---

[117] Personal interview with Roger Johnston, March 18, 2020

After hearing Roger describe his approach to helping members of the workforce see the continuity across the time periods, language and different owner, I asked Roger to talk more about his "red thread" metaphor.

> *"I'm not sure where it came from, it used to be on the back of a tie. If you pull on the red thread it runs through everything. The red thread is the "constants", the "givens", it is those things that that are immutable that you never change. For us, it came into play with regard to our teamwork activities. Whether you call it a "basic work unit", a quality circle, at the end of the day it is a group of people that are engaged to do the work with greater responsibility on how it is done, how well it is done, how it is trained, how you deal with absenteeism, how you deal with discipline. It is the philosophy that that responsibility should be pushed to the lowest level in the organization because it will be more effective there. That is an objective that was established in Hagerstown as early as the early 1990's. It was a mindset that if we keep working on it, we will get there. We are fortunate that we expected that to happen, and Volvo expected it to happen, and both are willing to go through the stages necessary to achieve that objective. Our workforce and our union were willing to say during my time that "yeah we are going to take another swing at it. Because we stepped away from it for a period, we did not like it, management did not seem to like it either, but that has changed so let's get back at it. And I was fortunate to come in at that time."[118]*

Certainly, it was fortunate for the Mack/Volvo plant in Hagerstown that Roger came in at the time he did as well. His background, intellect and modesty were the right fit for the situation at the time Volvo acquired Renault/Mack. His "red thread"" metaphor served well to enable him to lead a culture change that was quite complex and necessary.

---

[118] Ibid.

Volvo Plays Hardball

In 2003, following Volvo's insistence that before they could commit to Hagerstown as the site to build the next diesel engine, they needed greater flexibility in the way the plant operates. This was translated into changes in the work rules specified in the labor agreement between the company and the UAW in Hagerstown. This led, as stated earlier, to management and the UAW reopening negotiations to consider modifications to the contract. After that was accomplished in the early part of 2003, the company and the union felt they had lived up to their part of the agreement and had, through tough bargaining, provided Volvo the flexibility that was needed.

One of the things that allowed management of the Hagerstown plant to be able to respond to Volvo's demands for flexibility was due to the investment that Roger and the UAW had each made in building a partnership following the departure of Olivier Vidal. This began with the unilateral act by Jim Stewart to introduce Roger as the new plant manager to key union officers and workers in the plant. It continued after Jim Stewart retired as UAW Local 171 President at the end of May 2000. At that time, Maurice "Mo" Kaiser, the Local 171 Vice President, took over as President June 1, 2000. Mo described how Roger built a strong, trusting relationship with the union.

> *"Roger had been there about a year and a half before I became President. People had already learned to trust him. Shortly after I took over, Volvo bought us. Roger told us that the Swedes are people of their word. When they tell you something, you can believe that it will happen. We found out that that was not entirely true. Roger would come over to the union hall every other Thursday morning to meet with the committee body. He would bring Danny Stoner (Director of Manufacturing) with him or someone else. He would tell us what they saw coming up and how we could work together the right way to make things happen. Roger was the only one who would come over and talk to us like that all the time. Roger was always upfront with us. He could walk up to*

someone on the shop floor and start talking to someone and they really appreciated his method. The process in the Thursday meetings would be that Roger would tell us what they hoped to do. But also, he would listen as each member of the committee body would share information about problems they had. Sometimes, Roger would say this is what we are planning do you think this will work or he would ask how can we make it work better. With this management style our grievances fell almost to zero. That is a good measure of the relationship".

"We never had a relationship like that before and I know it is not like that now. Roger would say people ask him "How can you work with the union." His answer was "How could you not work with the union. They have a contract, they abide by it, and we know what the rules are, and we work together to get things done. We all get up in the morning and put our clothes on and we all want to go into the plant and enjoy what we are doing there."

"When Roger first came in it took a while for the foremen and general foremen to learn Roger's way. We would say to Roger we are having this or that problem and Roger would say "I'll take care of it." And then he would get his (management) people squared away. The Foremen and General Foremen had gotten used to having their own way with things and Roger made sure they got in line with his thinking."[119]

Roger described the process they went through to create more flexibility and respond to the challenge or ultimatum from Volvo. Volvo may have viewed it as a challenge, however given the bargaining power Volvo had over the future of Hagerstown, to many in the plant it felt like an ultimatum and what made it worse was that it was vague.

---

[119] Telephone interview with Maurice Kaiser, May 6, 2020.

"In 2003, we worked through what we felt was the necessary level of change to the contract. Our owner (Volvo) did not tell us what they wanted. They said they wanted "more flexibility." Can you help us understand what you mean? And they said we want more flexibility. So, we took a run at it. We talked to the State of Maryland. We got the local people tied in – got the Governor's office tied in and made good progress. Not phenomenal but good progress. Progress that we were satisfied with. And so, we took that back to the company after we took it to our people. They voted in the changes at a high rate. I think it was about 94%. It changed responsibilities of individuals, changes some things about overtime, it made significant changes and reduced the cost for us at Hagerstown. And we presented that to Volvo, and they came back with the decision that Hagerstown would be the site for Powertrain for its operations here in North America."[120]

However, Volvo was not satisfied. Later in 2003, they raised the ante. It was not clear to the Hagerstown management what caused them to come back again and ask for "more flexibility." This is how Roger Johnston described that dialog that ensued.

"Then they came back at the end of the year, and they said, you know, we really need more flexibility. We said, this seems like a discussion we have already had. We have already re-negotiated the contract, and you have already announced that this will be the place. Volvo responded, we need you to reopen the discussion and we need more. Are you saying that the decision is really not made for Hagerstown? Volvo responded, you need to understand that that was a decision for direction. A decision for direction means that we plan to do that, but until it is done, it is not done."[121]

---

[120] Interview with Roger Johnston, March 18, 2020.
[121] Ibid

Roger's reaction to the new request was "This discouraged us." Mo Kaiser's response was a little stronger.

> *"We had reopened the contract to try to give more flexibility. We finally dealt with their issues regarding flexibility and then Volvo said it is still not a "done deal." They said we need more tax relief from the State. I called the Governor's Office and Senator Paul Sarbanes' office to tell them what was going on. They contacted the Governor's office and I think the state came up with about 3 million more dollars. This was to get the commitment (for Volvo) to invest about 150 million to build the new diesel engine in Hagerstown. We gave them a lot of concessions. As far as Volvo, my feeling was that they never would be satisfied. As far as Roger, he was caught in the middle and tried to make sure we were taken care of as far as keeping Hagerstown in Hagerstown and that we had good working conditions. Roger's wife told us that he lost a lot of sleep as we were going through these discussions regarding concessions – but it had to happen to assure our future.[122]*

Roger elaborated further about this process and the impact it had on the plant workforce when they had to go through this uncertainty about their future one more time.

> *"Upset as we were, we-company and union- sat back down. We got over our anger about that and we worked through that and had the necessary discussions with the State and eked out some more support from the State of Maryland. They also were unhappy this was a revisit of an issue where they also felt that they had satisfied our requests. All around, everyone found a way to kick some more in. And we did. The training support was picked up by Washington County. I can't remember if the support from the State was capital or tax relief, but it was real*

---

[122] Telephone interview with Maurice Kaiser, May 6, 2020.

money. It was several million dollars. It was tied to jobs – the normal kind of thing you would expect.

Ultimately, in 2004 it was decided definitively that yes, we will invest the money in Hagerstown. At that time, we initially said it would be $175 million, and we knocked that down to $145 including the Engineering Test Lab upgrade. So, they approved it and began to invest the money.

That was a huge challenge. We had to get that behind us- that we were going to be here. But that threw some sand in the gears for a while as people said "Again!?" When during all the years that Renault was the owner, we kept hearing about the threat to close the plant......Now they were saying you don't like the transmission. They want us to get rid of the transmission. They want to take down a building. They wanted to take 40% of the plant away. They said the plant is too big. You don't need all of that. Let's stop making the T-300 transmission (the Mack transmission.) We did not have anything to replace it with. They said, "We will." We said, let's see what that will be before we shut it down. It turned out that there really was not a product to replace it. We resisted- once it is gone it is gone. To this day (2020 – 16 years later) the building is the same dimensions that it was then. A decision was made recently that we would make gears for the automated manual transmission that is used both in Volvo and Mack trucks. The T-300 is just about done with its life now (early 2020). This is a product we did not have in 2007 when Mr. Moberg wanted that building down."[123]

Mo Kaiser, retired as President of the UAW Local 171 at the end of May 2004. He described his feeling upon retiring after what he and the Union had just gone through.

[123] Personal interview with Roger Johnston, March 18, 2020.

"My first concern was getting a good contract. After we had a good contract, Volvo was not satisfied and asked us to reopen it. That took its toll on me, too. The last thing I wanted to see was the plant die because of a decision I helped make. When we ratified the agreement, we told our people that we were between a rock and a hard place, and this was the best that we could do. Here we are 16 years later, and they are still working. It's tough when you have the weight of all those working and their families."[124]

I asked Mo how he would like to be remembered as President of 171. He responded:

"..that we made it a better place to work and that we had a job to do, and we did it to make a good product and keep everything going." [125]

Earlier, I had asked Mo's predecessor as President – Jim Stewart, how he wanted to be remembered as President. Jim had served as several threats to close the plant were avoided and just after it was announced that Volvo would purchase the plant and that Roger Johnston would become the new General Manager.

"The only thing I want to be remembered for is that we did what we believed in doing. It wasn't me who saved the plant – it was the officers, Bill Nutter (former Shop Chairman), Bobby Shoop (Shop Chairman}, the Executive Board, all of us who stood down there and had a stake in everything that was happening. "We", literally not "I" along with management and the University of Maryland saved that plant. And they are in there working right now (16 years later.")[126]

---

[124] Telephone interview with Maurice Kaiser, May 6, 2020
[125] Telephone interview with Maurice Kaiser, May 6, 2020.
[126] Telephone interview with Jim Stewart, April 27, 2020.

CHAPTER 5

Transformation to World Class – Roger Johnston and the UAW Partnership (Phase 2)

The reality of Volvo ownership became fully felt in 2004. The year began with a visit by Lars-Goran Moberg, President of Volvo Powertrain to tour the plant and introduce the 2004-2007 transformational business plan for the global powertrain business. The plan defined the "wanted position" for Powertrain by 2007 to have moved from three different brand divisions – Renault, Volvo and Mack to a single global organization based in different geographical locations – Sweden, France, Brazil and the US (Hagerstown, Maryland.) By 2007 the single organization will have undergone a "competence shift" with respect to product development and purchasing. *"The new global product platforms for engines, transmissions and axles will be in place and the legacy products will have been phased out. The supplier base will have been reduced from 800 to 300 and the new global purchasing concept implemented. IT tools and processes will also have been unified and the global industrial footprint put in place with new industrial facilities up and running."*[127]

---

[127] Volvo Powertrain Corporation, Volvo Powertrain Execution and Delivery, Business Plan 2004-2007.

In explaining the rationale for this plan, Moberg focused appropriately on the message they have heard from customers. As truck markets in Europe and the US have de-regulated, mergers have led to fewer but larger customer fleets. The customer's main requests are for satisfactory productivity and low cost of ownership. Legal requirements on engines have continuously become more demanding with respect to emission levels and these requirements are converging with respect to on-road and off-road vehicles. However, despite this convergence, there are enough differences geographically in test procedures, in-use requirements and diesel fuel quality standards that a single global technology is not feasible. This fact drives increased cost and complexity for engine product development. While the demand for new technologies increases, the product life cycle for the technologies continues to shorten. All these factors require heavy duty truck makers to move to increase volumes and move toward industrial consolidation and restructuring. However, in order to satisfy customers who, have somewhat different needs, the products must allow for "optimized customer need adaptation" of the common base products.

Two other aspects of the business plan emphasized by Moberg were the financial and human resource expectations. He pointed out that Heavy Duty Truck manufacturing is a capital-intensive business. As a result of the investments required, the business plan includes an expectation of a 20% return on the capital assets invested and a continuing positive cash flow. With regard to human resources, Volvo refers to its strategies as The Volvo Way. The Volvo Way derives from the core values of the Volvo Groups Founders who had a concern for people and ingrained this philosophy into the management of the company. Since the beginning of the company, it has built a reputation for safety, quality, reliability, and responsibility. The two elements of the Volvo Way are the company's values – *What we stand for,* and its culture – *Who we are.* Since the company believes that any organization tends to get what it measures, Moberg emphasized that the Volvo Attitude Survey would be the way that he will monitor whether the Volvo Way is being practiced within Powertrain. This survey is administered company-wide periodically and is basically a measurement of whether management within the company is living up to the promises made in the Volvo Way documents.

In Hagerstown, this new business plan required nothing less than a total transformation at the same time that the growing economy was driving increased demand for legacy products. The "old saw" about rebuilding the airplane while it is flying in the air was an apt description of the challenge facing Denis Leblond, Roger Johnston, his team and the leaders of the UAW. More specifically, the challenges for Hagerstown were: (1) make Manufacturing, Engineering, and Purchasing act as one team to align their efforts toward the Powertrain Goals and Culture; (2) Create a "plant within a plant" to launch the new MD engine production with new manufacturing methods and technology and a new culture and work rules required to move toward "world class performance; (3) continue production of the legacy product at quality levels and volumes that met the needs of the assembly plants and most importantly, the needs of the end customers through 2006.

Following Moberg's visit and meeting with the management of the Hagerstown plant, Denis Leblond, Senior VP of North American Powertrain, held two town hall meetings in an effort to explain the business plan to the entire plant population. These meetings were held on March 2, 2004. He also announced that demolition had begun in an area of the plant that came to be called "The MD area". This would be the area of the plant where the new assembly line would be installed for manufacturing the dual brand, global product line. The ability to announce the beginning of the installation of the new assembly line provided tangible evidence that a transformation was happening in Hagerstown.

The effort to communicate to employees the reasons for the transformation and to begin to engage them in this effort continued in the April-May 2004 issue of the ***Powertrain Press.*** Roger Johnston wrote the editorial for this issue, and it focused on the change that will be needed within the Hagerstown Plant. Roger's editorial stated:

> *As I write the editorial comments for this month's Powertrain Press, I find that once again we are confronted with change all around us- some of a good nature and some which most definitely falls into a category I've termed in the past as "good problems." The Town Hall meetings of a few weeks ago, speaking*

to the business plan for 2004 to 2007, have begun the sharing of information as we move forward with the transformation of our site as a part of the global Powertrain Business Unit. We are already working in the Engineering group on future products; we're contributing to the global Purchasing sourcing activity for the future products; and in Manufacturing while we have been building prototypes for a number of months, we now begin the physical changes to our shop. The first activity, now underway is centered on creating the new assembly area to be used for the MD 16 and D12 one-quarter assembly, followed by the MD 11 and MD 13 full assembly. The area will encompass transmission assembly as well.

We have a huge job ahead of us; and if we look to the manufacturing and site work alone, we have the need to essentially reconfigure the building, the manufacturing and business processes, the information systems, the products and to a certain extent, ourselves. While today our manufactured products are supporting only the Mack brand in North America and to a lesser extent Renault V.I. in Europe, the world which we are entering requires us to carry the enthusiasm, pride and customer focus we have for the Mack brand into the Volvo brand for our North American customers. As we all know, this is not an easy transition. We have to continue to show our existing customers that we understand their needs and expectations, as well as to begin to prove the same to our new customer base. We can expect some customers of both brands to be skeptical and rightfully so. Meeting their needs and exceeding their expectations from the first day onward will go a long way toward earning the trust which forms the foundation of a solid future.

Earlier, I mentioned "good problems." We're entering a time period in our market where we see signs of increasing demand – an order backlog exceeding 10,000 units and growing. Meeting this demand here in the States means we've had to increase our build rates and bring in more material and people. At the same time, we're operating in an improving national economy and a global economy with emerging new sets of conditions. Even a year ago, we would not have predicted that demand in China for steel, concrete and oil would have dramatic influences not only on the prices of these commodities, but just as importantly on their availability. One of the challenges going forward is to work through the material availability and pricing issues. In parallel with this we have training of new people, control and improvement of quality, constant focus on improving our costs, and the preparations for our future.

In short, these are exciting times. Welcome to the challenges ahead![128]

David Perkins Elected as the New President of UAW Local 171

At the end of May 2004 Mo Kaiser retired as President of Local 171. It had been the tradition within the Union, that the Vice President would typically run and be elected as the new President. Given the momentous change going on following the Volvo purchase of RVI and Mack another major change was introduced following Mo's retirement. The assumption that Greg Murray, Mo's Vice President, would be elected and would assume the presidency did not happen.

The surprise winner of a very close election was David Perkins. David entered the plant on July 9, 1973, as an assembly line worker on the carrier assembly line. The carrier was a truck component that had been outsourced from Mack just before Renault bought the plant from Mack. David had been steadily moving up the UAW hierarchy and taking his "lumps" in a number of union elections where he had been unsuccessful, often running as an outsider against the "hierarchy." To his credit, David had taken his losses in elections as a challenge. He described what happened when he was talked into running for a "Committeeman" position:

---

[128] A Message from Roger Johnston, *Powertrain Press*, April-May 2004, p.3.

"From a personal perspective, I was feeling that we need change...So a lot of guys said, 'You need to run for the Union Committee.' I said, I love what I am doing, and I am a relatively shy person. I don't know if I want to go out and run for election. But they talked me into it. So, I went out and talked to all the "skillies" (i.e., skilled trades employees – since he was running for the skilled trades position on the Committee). But "long story short" I heard a couple of people say "it is just a two-year degree" when I said that I had an Associates Degree. The guy I was running against had no degrees, but he beat me soundly. Later, he became one of my great supporters. But when I heard the comments "it's just a 2-year degree" I said, "to heck with it", so I went to night school and got my bachelor's degree."[129]

This constructive response to a disappointment became a pattern during David's career. Whenever, he encountered an obstacle, he did not brood or make excuses. He took charge of his life and took steps to remove the obstacle whenever he could do so. He also did not hold grudges against people that beat him in an election. Describing this dynamic he shared these thoughts about getting his bachelor's degree and his relationship with the winner of the election.

"So, I said, if I ever run again, although I don't think I will, I now have my bachelor's degree and they can't say it is just a 2-year degree. Al Huston was the committeeman who ran against me and beat me, but we became very close friends. He was a great supporter. They formed a skilled trades committee and Al appointed me to chair that committee which took me into the bargaining sessions. It was not an elected position, but it carried a lot of weight. Looking back, I don't think he appointed me because he was worried that I would run against him again, I think he did it because we became friends. "[130]

---

[129] David Perkins, Telephone interview, July 26, 2021.
[130] Ibid.

This pattern of taking action to overcome obstacles repeated itself and that spurred David to push himself even harder. He had also discovered from his first effort to pursue the Associates Degree that he really liked education and was inspired by it.

> *At this point I felt good about myself. I had my 4-year degree, I was working as chair of this committee for Al Huston, I was happy. Then Al told me they had created a new position called Sourcing Representative. It was a full-time position. What you did was work with the company to try to insource work and keep from outsourcing it. I said that is perfect Al. I would love that. So, I applied for the job. I did not get it. They gave it to a former committeeman named John Svoboda. My philosophy is that things always happen for a reason. For the next couple of years, I started thinking, I know John is probably going to retire in a couple of years, so what could I do to make myself more competitive to apply for this position. That job would be the pinnacle, the ultimate position. So, I took the LSAT (Law School Admissions Test). I applied to two law schools and was accepted by both.... I enrolled at Dickinson Law School. When John Svoboda retired, I was going to Dickinson at night, and I did get the Sourcing Rep position. It was like a three-year blur, but I just took it one day at a time. The job got me back into working with management.*[131]

Again, David Perkins responded to disappointment by taking steps to improve his "game" and make himself more competitive. Even though he felt the sourcing representative position would be the pinnacle of his career, he had more mountains to climb. However, the next mountain would also present challenges.

> *"When I had obtained my law degree, the plant newspaper ran a graduation issue and they put my announcement in it. I remember that Roger Johnston came down to my*

---

[131] Telephone interview with David Perkins, July 26, 2021

office and said, 'Well I guess you will be going to the International.' I said, Roger, if you cut my arm right now, I would bleed Mack Trucks red. This place has been my life. I don't plan on leaving it." [132]

Not only did David with his new law degree not leave the plant he chose to run for President of the UAW following Mo Kaiser's retirement. David described what happened following his decision to run."

"Basically, my running split the union in two. Half the current officials backed me. The other half backed Mo's VP... You are expected to support the hierarchy. You don't come in and upset the applecart. Bobby Shoop (UAW Shop Chairman at the time) came in and asked me to run for VP. He said Greg (Mo's VP and the expected next President) will retire in 8 years and you can run then. I said Bobby, I like you, I respect you, but at this point in my life I want to make change. I'm not going to sit back and watch someone else do something that I disagree with. The union officials who did not support me were people who felt their way of life was going to disappear... The election got really nasty as there were anonymous letters attacking my girlfriend (now my wife), etc. I ended up winning by 17 votes.

The election was challenged. The international union sent someone down to do the investigation. They then overturned the election. They ordered a new election. They ordered it because one of my supporters had mailed back a couple of letters from people and on the letters, he wrote "Vote for Dave". The company had paid for the stamps used to send the letters. They used that as the reason to invalidate the election. I remained President during the investigation, but they ordered a new election. We were in bargaining then at the time of the new election and I figured there was no chance I could win. I'm up here in

---

[132] Telephone interview with David Perkins, July 26, 2021

King of Prussia (where the bargaining sessions were held) and the "machine" is down in the plant moving against me. But I beat him by over 600 votes in the new election. It looked to the membership that my opponent was trying to reverse the will of the people, so we need to "drain the swamp." We need to change what was going on is how the people felt. They came down on the "good ol' boy system. They decided they needed someone who will break this thing up. So, I won by 600 votes. [133]

The outcome of this election delivered to Roger Johnston a partner in the UAW president's role who was a strong supporter of change. In addition, the relationship between David Perkins and his Shop Chairman, Bobby Shoop, which was initially strained after the election became a very close working relationship. This was enabled in part, due to some unfortunate medical difficulties that Bobby endured which led him to become largely confined to the office. However, as a result Dave assumed a larger role as President than he might otherwise have had. This positioned him to be a very strong President and that aided him in his efforts to bring change within the union and to be an effective and strong partner with Roger. Roger and David led the effort to make the changes required to execute the mandates of the 2004-2007 Business Plan. Doing this and at the same time meeting the demands of the production schedule was a very "heavy lift" indeed.

The Transformation Project in 2004 launched a great deal of activity. In this document, it is not possible to describe everything that went on between 2004 and 2007. However, I will provide an overview of the Transformation efforts under three categories. The first category will be the overall leadership activities focusing on the North American Powertrain Division as the unit of analysis. The second category will focus on the Manufacturing efforts to transform the thinking of the unit from business as usual to a new definition of "world class" as the performance standard. Third, we will summarize some of the transformation activity in the new production area that was called the MD area. This is the new assembly line installations to produce the global brands MD 16 and D12 and the MD

[133] Ibid

11 and MD 13 diesel engines. It also involved the new assembly line in the transmission area to produce the new MD transmission. Finally, the paint and test areas as well as the maintenance, materials and quality groups serving the new global engine and transmission assembly platforms were also part of the new MD area.

Transformation of the North American Powertrain Group (NAPG)

The North American Powertrain Group was initially formed following the purchase of RVI and Mack by Volvo in 2000. When Denis LeBlond became the General Manager of the Division in 2001, this was when the organizational change became a reality.

The development of the 2004-2007 business plan obviously required a great deal of strategy analysis and development before it was announced in January 2004. Much of this preliminary work involved product planning which required the Hagerstown Engineering Group to be engaged in design work well before 2004. In order to be able to launch a new engine product in 2005, there was at least a three-year lead time requirement. So as early as 2002, the Hagerstown Engineering Group was engaged in this preparatory work.

For example, in 2002, when the Engineering Guidance Team was formed it consisted of the General Manager, the Engineering and Administrative Union President and the heads of each of the key Engineering functional groups. Tony Grezler, the General Manager, stated that it was his hope that the Guidance Team would help the Engineering Group focus on "how we do things in the 'longer term' and help balance the current focus on the "short term urgencies of the day". Dale Williams, the Engineering and Administrative Bargaining Unit President who had participated in the Manufacturing Guidance Team for several years, shared "how this team has led to significant improvements in how manufacturing operates." Dale had for a long-time advocated creating a similar Guidance Team in Engineering. With the creation of the North American Powertrain group led by Denis LeBlond, the time was now right to do so.

In an article for the Powertrain Press in mid 2002, Tony Grezler described some of this preliminary work that had begun in 2002.

> *...... With the announcement of the Industrial Footprint decision, we in Product Engineering are also defining our role within Powertrain. It has been decided that we will not develop the ETECH/ASET engine for the next major emissions change in 2007 but will introduce the new engine family for Mack and VTNA (Volvo Trucks North America) trucks. We are positioning ourselves to lead development for North American performance, emissions and application requirements, to support the new engineering plan for Volvo engines at Hagerstown, and to provide field support needed by our customers. Since North American diesel emission requirements are the toughest in the world and market demands are diverse, we envision this role to be challenging.*
>
> *We have initiatives in all three of these areas. Our new engineering quality system will soon be employed. We have initiated an Engineering Guidance Team to find better ways to work. We have a $17 million test lab improvement project which is just beginning to address both tools and facilities. All three areas need careful attention and our full support. Our challenges are immense, but so are our opportunities. It really is the time for the entire plant to work together towards a successful future.* [134]

By 2004, when the Transformation Project in Powertrain was launched, the Engineering Guidance Team, which Tony referenced, had become a reasonably mature team that had already dealt with some of its more basic issues and was better prepared to focus on its vital role in the new business strategy. As an example, the Engineering Guidance Team had developed and launched an extensive 3-day training program for members of the Department on Project Management as their key mechanism for "Driving Change." This program focused on the elements of the Volvo Global

[134] Tony Grezler, *Powertrain Press*, July/August 2002, p.1.

Development Process as well as the Hagerstown Part Change Request process as the two primary contexts for applying Project Management skills. In addition to core project management skills and tools, the program also included modules focused on group process skills and how Engineering could operate more effectively as a member of the Powertrain Team. Also, quite importantly, the management style of the leadership team in Engineering, like that of Manufacturing, was operating in a mode that closely resembled the Volvo Way. This prework enabled the Engineering Group to "hit the ground running" in 2004.

In Hagerstown, despite the fact that Manufacturing, Purchasing and Engineering were all located in the same building, they had tended to operate as somewhat separate fiefdoms, each reporting to their respective functional organizations at Mack-RVI Headquarters in Allentown, Pa. By creating the Powertrain group, each of these operational groups would report to the Powertrain Group with a dotted line relationship to their functional group in Allentown. This created a matrix organization structure that was a major change from the past. The former organizational structure made communication and decision making cumbersome and slow. It also made teamwork between the three functional units in Hagerstown -i.e., Engineering, Manufacturing and Purchasing much more difficult because each function reported to a different functional head in Allentown. As a result, while the new matrix structure looks good on paper, the reality is much more complicated. By 2004, these relationships were still being sorted out and some people were still asking "Who do I really work for?" "Who is my boss?"

This issue of role definition and role clarity was one of the key issues for the NAPG as Dennis LeBlond and the executive team worked to execute and deliver the performance called for in the 2004-2007 Powertrain Business Plan. A major focus of this business plan was to take advantage of the economies of scale available to Volvo if the fragmented industrial structure could be simplified and consolidated without sacrificing value to customers. For Hagerstown engine manufacturing, what this meant was that the number of engine platforms would be reduced from 18 company-wide to 2 global platforms. As a result of this consolidation, the number of parts used in the new engine range will be reduced to 35% of the number of parts in the 2001 product inventory. This consolidation offered major cost, quality and speed advantages. However, it placed a greater emphasis on engine software to enable the two engine platforms to be adapted to customer requirements in different countries, different climates, and different trucking applications. Thus, the global platform engines were simpler in terms of the number of parts, however, they were more complex in terms of the engine control systems driven by the more complex engine software.

Another challenge for NAPG was to take advantage of the new organizational structure to create greater cohesion and alignment of the different functions located in Hagerstown. We can illustrate this challenge by showing how the company used the Volvo Global Attitude Survey (VGAS) as a way to surface opportunities and challenges.

The VGAS included items that measured the following attitudes of employees focused largely on their perceptions of how they are managed:

- Respect
- Co-operation
- Delegation/Influence
- Performance feedback
- Internal information/communication
- Overall understanding
- Goals
- Individual development
- Easy to implement
- Planning/Follow up
- Personnel and environmental issues
- Attitude to change

Basically, the VGAS is designed to assess the extent to which the organizational units are living by the Volvo Way. Out of all the questions in the survey, through research with the instrument, 11 items have been deemed to be critical questions that have an impact on profitability of the organizational unit. Managers receive feedback on their Employee

Satisfaction Index which represents the percentage of crucial questions that are on or above the norm.

The VGAS feedback process makes use of individuals in the company trained as facilitators to help recipients interpret the feedback and develop action plans to address areas in need of improvement.

The feedback report to the Senior VP of NAPG highlighted that his workgroup was rated as not being free from conflict that negatively impacts the operation of the group. Many of these conflicts resulted from the remnants of the old organization structure through which functional leaders of the 3 major functions reported to bosses in the Allentown corporate headquarters. The decision regarding how to deal with this issue led to the formation of a Conflict Management Team consisting of the leaders of the major units within NAPG that were now the direct reports of the NAPG VP. Following several meetings and a root cause analysis the group found that the major causes of the conflict included the following:

- Lack of trust and respect among the players;
- Lack of clear ownership of the problem/and lack of clear understanding of the functional responsibilities in the materials, logistics and purchasing areas;
- Decision making by players not based on facts;
- Inadequate systems to support materials managements ramp-up and ramp-down decision making;
- Certain business processes are not "capable" of meeting their customer requirements – e.g. the engineering change process, rapid prototyping process and materials management process.
- Insufficient goal clarity and goal conflict;
- Staffing levels that do not permit adequate involvement of key people in decision making regarding process improvement;
- Insufficient understanding and appreciation of the requirements of other functions;
- Differences in management style and philosophy among key players;
- Rather than resolve the conflict, the Senior VP reinforces the conflict that one of the team members introduces into the system

through distorted information, lack of respect for a peer, personal attacks, etc.

Following receipt of this information, the facilitator then worked with the recipient – the Senior VP of NAPG to develop a plan to improve the situation. Without a process such as the VGAS to surface and identify such management problems, there would have been no systematic way to assure that managers are adhering to the values and the Volvo Way. Furthermore, failure to address issues such as dysfunctional conflict among key functional business unit leaders makes it impossible for NAPG to totally align its efforts in support of the Volvo Powertrain strategic objectives. This helps explain why research underlying the VGAS has proven that the issues being measured are related to business unit profitability. Failure to detect and address these critical management issues would significantly reduce bottom line performance.

In addition to aligning management of the major functions around the strategic objectives NAPG also had to be concerned with assuring that business processes in each functional area were able to meet the 2004-2007 desired performance levels. The global Powertrain objectives were organized under three key strategies – profitable growth, product cycle management, and operational excellence. North American Powertrain had responsibilities in all three of these areas. However, the major responsibilities of the North American group were in the product cycle management and in operational excellence.

Denis LeBlond, the first Senior V.P. of NAPG, was not able to follow-through on these plans as he was replaced in 2004. His successor, Sten-Åke Aronsson brought a different and more appropriate skill set to the task of transforming NAPG. His knowledge of the three key functional areas within NAPG, his experience in a variety of global general management roles, and his personality were perfectly suited to the challenges in Hagerstown. In addition, Sten-Åke had played a key role in Volvo's decision to locate production of the next generation diesel engine in Hagerstown. For all of these reasons, Sten-Åke seemed to be the ideal new leader of NAPG.

The remainder of this discussion will focus on the efforts in Hagerstown manufacturing to (1) build and deploy a culture in manufacturing that supported and enabled achievement of world class performance as the essential performance standard for the plant, and (2) executing the strategy to produce and deliver Mack and Volvo engines using the same new, global, heavy duty engine platform and the T-300 transmission. This was referred to as Implementing the MD process.

Moving to a World Class Performance Standard –The Performance Matrix Process

It is quite easy to say that our goal is to achieve "world class" performance. It is much more difficult to define what that means in reality. This was one of the challenges given to the Manufacturing Guidance Team in Hagerstown. Several things were clear. Even if the manufacturing management were able to define world class for the various dimensions of performance, i.e., cost, quality, delivery, etc. this standard could not be imposed by giving an order. To achieve world class, the standard must be understood and accepted by each person on an assembly line, each maintenance mechanic, each materials handler and each quality technician in the gage lab. This meant that the move to world class is an educational process that requires new learning and acceptance of significant change on the part of every person in the plant. Because of the interdependence of functions in a manufacturing organization, world class for the plant cannot be achieved until all functions are performing at world class levels.

Another complexity with regard to moving to a world class performance standard is that world class is a moving target. What may be considered "best-in-class" today is not static. Every organization seeks to achieve competitive advantage so the desire for continuous improvement is a never-ending goal. This means that it is necessary to continually monitor the performance of others in order to determine how the definition of "best in class" is changing. The process to study others in terms of performance level and in terms of understanding business processes that produce the performance level is called "benchmarking." Performance benchmarking is the effort to determine the best-in-class performance level. Process benchmarking is the effort to determine the process or the "means used" to achieve the best-in-class performance level.

Another approach to determining "world-class" is to adopt the performance criteria of a generally recognized "world class" award system. An example of this in the U. S. is the Malcolm Baldrige National Performance Excellence Award. The criteria for this award include descriptions of world class management systems with respect to a number of categories e.g., Leadership, Strategy, Customer Focus, Measurement and Analysis Systems, Human Resource Management, Results, etc. These elements of the world class management system criteria can be used to assess the comparable systems of an organization to identify strengths and opportunities for improvement.

The approach chosen to define world class by the Manufacturing Guidance Team in Hagerstown was a combination of benchmarking and utilization of award criteria. This led to the creation of the High-Performance Matrix that was developed and deployed within the manufacturing and support systems in Hagerstown. The focus of the High-Performance Matrix was on the performance of Employee Work Units or (EWUs). Employee Work Units were teams of people at the workplace level who were formed to improve the performance of the team. EWUs were formed in manufacturing as well as in the support functions e.g., materials, maintenance, quality, etc.

The Matrix was created by a development group chartered by the Manufacturing Guidance Team. This team defined 7 dimensions of performance that applied to each Employee Work Unit in the plant. These 7 performance dimensions were aligned with the Volvo Powertrain Business Plan in terms of how the business plan performance dimensions were translated to the shop floor level. The 7 performance dimensions which define the vertical columns of the matrix were:

Dimension 1 – Quality
Dimension 2- Skill Development
Dimension 3 – Empowerment
Dimension 4 – Safety, Health and Work Environment
Dimension 5 – Cost

Dimension 6 – Delivery
Dimension 7 – Environmental

The rows of the Matrix corresponded to performance levels on this dimension. The performance level corresponded to the percentage of the world class standard the EWU had attained. 6 levels were defined corresponding to 0%, 20%, 40%, 60%, 80% and 100%. Under each performance dimension the matrix cell corresponding to each performance level was defined by verbal benchmarks describing the objective evidence required to demonstrate that the team had achieved this level of performance. An example of a completed High-Performance Matrix for the Quality performance dimension is shown in Figure 4 below. The matrices for all 7 performance dimensions are shown in Appendix B.

	QUALITY (V2)
100 %	The team meets all internal customer requirements. Team quality performance shows no negative trends in any area related to internal customer requirements. A systematic process is in place to anticipate changes in customer requirements and take action to maintain process capability. Team has gone a minimum of 1 year without scrap/rework (other than by tool breakage or power outages). Team makes an *annual* minimum of 4 significant process improvements (as judged by Plant Manager and Staff).
80%	The team meets most internal customer requirements. Positive trends exist in most metrics related to internal customer requirements. All Key Control Characteristics are under statistical process control and demonstrate process capability of 1.33 or greater.
60%	A process is in place to measure internal customer satisfaction. A systematic process is in place to take action to improve internal customer satisfaction based on the data. Analytical tools and processes are used by operators to insure consistent product quality. A preventive approach to problems is evident. All Key Control Characteristics are in-spec. Some evidence of the use of design of experiments for process improvement is available.
40%	Key Control Characteristics have been identified for all processes. Key Control Characteristics have been validated (substantiated) in relation to external customer requirements. A plan/do/study/act problem solving methodology is in place.
20%	Team has defined its internal customers and their requirements. Team members understand work instructions.
0%	Team has not identified its internal customers and has little understanding of their requirements.

Figure 4. Performance Matrix for Quality Performance Dimension

Deployment of the matrix to Employee Work Units was done by trained coaches who acted as facilitators for the matrix deployment. "Coaches" were hourly employees who were specially trained for the coach and facilitator role. In working with an EWU, the coach would do the following:

a. Issue an invitation to each team member to attend a team meeting at a specified time;

b. Invite a member of senior management to open the meeting with a discussion of the business challenges and how the matrix process will assist the company to better engage its employees in meeting the competitive challenge and the needs of Volvo and Mack customers;

c. Provide an overview of the matrix and how it will be used to enable teams to conduct a performance assessment and set improvement goals for the team;

d. Lead the team through a force-field analysis of the matrix deployment to identify the "headwinds" and "tailwinds" that will impact matrix deployment;

e. Conduct a discussion to address ways to take advantage of the tailwinds and minimize the headwind forces;

f. Lead the members of the EWU to conduct a team self-assessment to determine group consensus regarding their present performance level on each of the 7 matrix dimensions and have their current performance levels validated by the UAW Performance Excellence Coordinator;

g. Using the next 6 months as the planning horizon, lead the team members to establish the targeted performance level they will work to achieve by the end of 6 months;

h. Lead a planning discussion to create the action plan to move the team's performance from the current levels to the target levels;

i. Assist the team to clarify and define additional training or resources the team will need to achieve the targeted performance levels.

j. Assure that a connection is made through the Performance Excellence Coordinator with the trainer or trainers and make sure the training is budgeted;

k. Monitor during the next 6 months that team meetings are held, and minutes are kept and that the team is moving toward its targeted performance levels;

l. Provide consulting assistance to the team as requested or required. As consultants to the team, the coach should not just answer the question or solve the problem, they should use the issue to help the team learn and build their own increased capability.

Figure 4 provides an overview of how the matrix was used in a process to help EWU's move to world class performance. In this diagram the ovals in each column represent the beginning or current performance level for a team. By definition, Level 10 is defined as world class. The difference between the current performance and world class is depicted by the red arrow. Although not depicted in this diagram, there is a "red arrow" on each of the 7 columns of the matrix unless current performance on a particular dimension is world class so there is no performance gap. These "performance gaps" represent the challenge for each EWU to close through their action plans and team meetings. The guidance given to Coaches and by Coaches to teams is that the EWUs are not expected to close the gaps "overnight." Improving performance levels is a long-term process that is aligned with the Volvo Powertrain Business Plan. Even though it is a "long term process" there needs to be a sense of urgency

OVERVIEW OF THE MATRIX

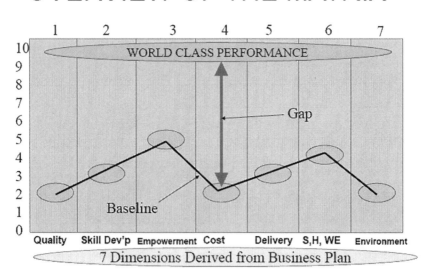

Figure 5

Use of the Performance Matrix to Monitor and Guide the Move to World Class for a Team

The gap that exists today is not a "theoretical" gap it is a real gap between Volvo and its most advanced competitors. And, since competitors are "not standing still", this gap will increase in size if Volvo is not improving at least as fast as competitors. However, if we, Volvo Powertrain, desire to be number 1 in the industry and assure our security, we must improve at a faster rate than our competitors. Because our customers' requirements keep changing, "world class" is also a moving target. Over time, this world class bar will be raised as customer requirements change and as our competitors improve.

The guidance to EWU's is that it is not expected that you will choose to work on all 7 dimensions at the same time. Initially, the teams should prioritize a subset of the dimensions where improvement is most urgent.

In addition to the matrix as a performance improvement tool, the process that it enables supports the culture change that is part of the move to world class. When Roger Johnston stated that one of his challenges, after being named General Manager, was to find a way to "take the collective intelligence of the work force and move it like the Queen Mary so it could be brought to bear on the challenges of the business.....", he was describing the need for a major culture shift. Goal setting and decision making in the plant had typically been a top-down process. Through the matrix process, the EWU has more input into the choice of team performance targets as well as the steps that need to be taken to achieve the targets. As the teams assume more responsibility for their performance, the role of management also must change dramatically. Their role shifts from top-down goal setting to communicating broad business plan objectives and supporting the EWU in translating these objectives into EWU goals and action plans. Management's role is to support the team's improvement efforts and to identify and remove roadblocks to their sustained performance improvement. Roadblocks can include lack of resources, lack of training, lack of support from other functions, etc. The need for behavior changes on the part of teams as well as managers represented a major culture change for Hagerstown which did not always occur smoothly. However, over time, the realization grew that these changes were necessary for the plant to move to world class performance. And the performance matrix was a tool to enable and guide these changes.

As we move to the next part of the transformation of Hagerstown, implementing the MD process, we will discuss some of the approaches used to help management with the behavior changes needed on their part as well as the behavior changes required on the part of the front-line work force.

Moving to the World Class Work Environment – Implementing the MD Manufacturing Process

By the time that Volvo acquired the Renault truck business (RVI) including Mack Trucks, Hagerstown had transformed significantly from what it was in 1990 under Mack Trucks management. However, the next phase of the transformation of Hagerstown was enabled and made necessary by the Volvo Powertrain decision to manufacture the "next generation" of diesel engines for North America in Hagerstown. In my conversation with Volvo North American Powertrain's Senior Vice President Sten-Åke Aronsson, who was involved in the decision to locate North American Powertrain in Hagerstown, there were a number of factors involved in the decision. However, two major factors were the skills of the workforce in building engines and transmissions, and the fact that both management and the UAW in Hagerstown had developed a partnership and had demonstrated their ability and willingness to change.[135] This ability to change was significantly tested by Volvo in the negotiations prior to their decision to invest in Hagerstown by their demand for "more flexibility." It was tested further by additional demands for "more flexibility" even after the decision had been made. However, Roger Johnston and the UAW leadership in Hagerstown, passed the test.

As described in the 2004-2007 Powertrain business plan, moving to "the next generation engine" represented a major shift within Volvo Powertrain from having three separate industrial systems to manage three different product programs in Europe, Brazil and North America to a single global industrial system managing a single global product program.[136] This new engine platform was designed to create and produce an engine that complied

---

[135] Personal conversation with Sten-Åke Aronsson, 2007.
[136] Volvo Powertrain, *Volvo powertrain execution and delivery: Business plan 2004-2007.*

with emission levels that would have been viewed as virtually impossible to achieve in the past. While having a single global engine platform allows Volvo Powertrain to spread its extensive product development costs across a larger number of engines and achieve economies of scale, it was still necessary for the products to be able to meet the different needs of customers in each of the geographical markets it served. This ability to customize a single product platform to meet differing customer needs had to be achieved largely through the programmable software systems that control engine performance.

This shift to "One Team-Three Sites" had significant implications for the entire Powertrain Organization. It entailed major changes in product development, purchasing and vendor selection and management, and information systems which also moved to consolidate legacy software systems across the company to a single platform.

In parts one and two of this chapter we discussed some of the changes at the level of Powertrain North America and we discussed the efforts to move the culture of the plant to a "world-class" performance standard. This previous discussion was driven by the need to prepare for the implementation of the MD manufacturing system in Hagerstown which is the focus of this third section of the chapter.

The MD implementation in Hagerstown involved building a "plant within the plant" that operated with a different set of manufacturing technologies and a different organizational culture. It was literally a plant within the plant with walls separating it from the traditional factory, different air handling and heating and cooling systems, different lighting, etc. It consisted of a different assembly line with state-of-the-art information technology for guiding the assembly process and for materials handling. It involved new processes for materials management, maintenance and supporting functions, e.g., paint shop and engine test, etc. Managers had to learn to manage differently, and assembly line workers had to learn to work differently. For everyone, the performance standards for cost, quality and delivery were significantly raised. The plan for 2004-2007 was to launch this new culture and process initially in a designated "new plant within the plant". Over time, it would be spread to the entire plant as the transformation proceeds and as legacy products were phased out along with the "legacy culture." We will refer to this initial MD launch as the pilot MD initiative in the "plant within the plant".

The physical infrastructure for the pilot MD product assembly was a major project that required demolition of a large portion of the manufacturing shop floor and the installation of the new assembly line workstations, computer terminals for assemblers, robotics for material handling, etc. The major roles for Hagerstown management were to implement the product and technology plan developed by Volvo Powertrain and to develop and implement the strategy for deploying the culture that would support this new way of working. Therefore, our discussion will focus primarily on the "human infrastructure" and the processes involved to "hire" and train managers and workers for this new way of working.

In Chapter 4 we quoted Roger Johnston on his effort to explain the need for change in Hagerstown by using what he called the "red thread" metaphor. Basically the "red thread" referred to the commonalities that connect key concepts and practices as the plant has evolved through different phases and changes. This was his way of helping people accept new ideas by connecting them through the "red thread" with things that had been done before. The "new idea" did not mean that we are rejecting what was done in the past but that we are really building on the past as the current situation (e.g., new owner) and its demands continue to shift.

This "red-thread" philosophy was built into the deployment of the MD training process for management and non-management employees. One of the helpful tools in describing the "red thread" was the chart in Figure 5. This chart lists in the left column, the key issues addressed by the three improvement strategies deployed in Hagerstown. This refers to the Total Quality Process initiated in the Ross Rhoads period. The Mission Driven program implemented in 2004 – 2006 was followed by the Volvo Production System fully introduced in 2007 and integrated with the MD initiative. The X's indicate whether the issue was addressed by the improvement strategy. As this chart depicts, there was a great deal of commonality and overlap across the three major improvement strategies. The chart clearly points out that the "red thread" runs across these improvement initiatives as each one builds on the previous strategy and does not, in any way, represent a rejection of the previous improvement approaches. It is also a way of validating the notion that "world class", as we conceive it, is a moving target requiring continuous improvement and change.

Evolution to the Volvo Production System (VPS)			
ISSUE	TOTAL QUALITY	MD	VPS
Safety is No.1	X	X	X
Performance = QDC Quality, Delivery and Cost Deployment	X	X	X
Requires Training (Competence Management)	X	X	X
Self-Managed Work Teams		X	X
PDSA (e.g. TPM)	X	X	X
Process Improvement (Continuous Improvement)	X	X	X
External Customer Focus (Customer Service)	X	X	X
Emphasis on Culture Change	X	X	X
Lean Philosophy		X	X
5-S Focus			X
Suggestion Program	X		X
Standardized Work			X
Poke Yoke (Error Proofing)	X	X	X
Kaizen (Continuous Improvement)	X	X	X
Kan Ban (Visual Material Management)		X	X
Environmental		X	X

Figure 6
Evolution to the Volvo Production System (VPS)

MD Workplace Structure

Following a great deal of planning and research on how other organizations have moved to a team-based structure, the Hagerstown MD workplace structure was designed as a three-tier structure. Individual hourly employees were formed into teams which represented sections of the assembly line process. Each team would select one of their members to serve in a temporary rotating role as "Coordinator" to provide guidance and assistance to the team members. The first level of management within the MD production areas were called Advisors. Compared to the traditional structure, the ratio of Advisors to assembly technicians would be significantly reduced with the "coordinator" role essentially replacing the first level of management.

This new structure is very consistent with the objective that Roger Johnston had described when he assumed the role of General Manager of manufacturing in Hagerstown. He stated that for survival of the plant, it would be necessary to harness the intelligence of shop floor employees and guide that intelligence toward meeting the business challenges of the plant. This MD structure is a major step toward fulfilling that purpose.

The second part of fulfilling that purpose involves building a culture within the MD organization that would support that purpose as well. Creation of this culture was done by building on the Total Quality culture and strengthening its implementation through additional training and decision support tools. Several critical components of the culture building process were designed into the MD environment launch process. These included the following:

- Integrating the values that had been defined for the Hagerstown Plant to underlie the partnership between the Hagerstown management and the UAW with the elements of the Volvo Way;
- Developing and deploying the process to recruit and select existing employees and management from other departments from the traditional factory into the MD workplace;
- Creating a prerequisites agreement for employees and management that defined the new behaviors expected in the MD work area. Management and UAW members entering the MD

area had to sign these agreements and commit to uphold these new behaviors;

- Development and deployment of a comprehensive training process covering team success factors and team decision making strategies as well as technical training on assembly technology and processes;
- Definition of team ground rules based on the key principles and values of the MD culture;
- Development and implementation of the process to certify the technical competence of assembly technicians to perform error-free work on day 1 on the job;
- Designing and procuring uniforms for each person working in the MD area to signify their professionalism and competence to perform world class work.

The process for an existing employee to enter the MD area began with a canvassing presentation. Members of the UAW leadership and management leadership conducted a presentation explaining the rationale for establishing the MD area, a description of what the new area would contain and how it would operate, what would be required of workers in this new area in terms of work practices, hours, need to wear a uniform, etc. Following the presentation, which was designed to provide a "realistic preview" of work in the MD area, individuals were asked to indicate if they would like to join this new area. Those who volunteered were then asked to sign a Prerequisite Agreement which was a commitment to follow and support the elements of the MD culture. The prerequisite agreement is presented in Figure 6.

Pre-requisite Agreement

- Participate in a skill needs assessment
- Demonstrate qualifications before being assigned to a work group
- Participate as a work team member in a team environment
- Recognize the authority of the bargaining unit coordinator role
- Take direction from multiple sources of leadership and supervision
- Wear a uniform – union made in the USA, with a joint company and union logo
- Comply with the "How we will work" practices

- Accept the team coordinator role if selected
- Meet customer requirements daily
- Waive bid rights for 6 months
- Compulsory job rotation within the team

Failure to live up to this agreement could result in disqualification for the MD area.

Figure 7
Bargaining Unit Pre-Requisite Agreement Items

Employees who volunteered to join the MD Area and who signed the Pre-requisite agreement were then scheduled to participate in an extensive four-week training program. The content of the training covered both team dynamics training and technical skills training. Figure 7 lists the Objectives of the 4-week training program.

The Team Dynamics portion of the MD training covered many of the MD "culture building" approaches and processes. This training began with some basic assumptions underlying the training content which were:

1. Everyone in this training wants to be here since you are volunteers, and you want to be able to perform your work error-free on day 1;
2. The MD production area is not only a new manufacturing facility with a new technology, but it is a beginning of a new culture and a new way of working in Hagerstown;
3. The training you will receive will be done for all subsequent people entering the MD area. However, like everything done in this area, there will be an effort to improve the training efficiency and effectiveness over time. So some changes are likely in content and delivery mode following this initial training implementation.
4. Collaboration in the learning process is required to model the way that work will be carried out in this area.

MD Training Objectives

Trainees who complete the 4-week training program should be able to:

1. be an effective team member;
2. explain the expectations regarding safety, ergonomics, environment, work systems, and goals;
3. demonstrate pride in building both Mack and Volvo engines and convey a world class attitude as an ambassador for visitors to the plant;
4. perform the prescribed duties of at least three work stations in an error-free manner;
5. take individual responsibility for decision making regarding quality and delivery for their work station;
6. participate as a team member to make decisions regarding planning, measuring and improving team performance in terms of safety, quality, cost, delivery and environmental performance;
7. demonstrate an understanding of the demand flow manufacturing approach;
8. be able to explain how the diesel engine they are building works;
9. be able to explain why we are doing things that we are doing with respect to the manufacturing process, the product plan, the culture, etc. from the perspective of the competitive situation, the business plan and world class benchmarks.

Figure 8
MD Training Objectives for the Initial 4-Week Training

Much of the content of the training program was guided by the "Ten Elements of Team Success". The content of the training provided specific guidance in translating these elements to the MD team environment with specific examples and a review of specific methodologies to implement the elements. These ten elements were defined as:

1. Clarity in team goals;
2. A plan for improving performance;
3. Clearly defined roles;

4. Clear communication within the team and between the team and its customers and suppliers within the building;
5. Beneficial team behaviors – i.e., behaviors that help build team spirit and performance;
6. Well defined decision rules with respect to decisions made within in the team;
7. Balanced participation – i.e., making sure everyone "pulls their load" within the team;
8. Agreed upon performance metrics;
9. Awareness of group process;
10. Use of the scientific process and use of facts to analyze and solve problems and develop action plans.

The issue of clearly defined roles became a critical factor in the implementation of the cultural transformation. While it is easy to say the words "clearly defined roles" it is much more difficult to put this into practice in multiple workplaces experiencing new technology and significant production pressures. It proved even more difficult as the MD culture was introduced into the areas of the traditional plant.

Within the MD culture there were four key hourly employee roles: (1) Assembly technician; (2) Assembly support technician; (3) Assembly coordinator; and (4) Assembly support coordinator. The exact number of people in a team varied but a typical team might have 6-10 Assembly technicians and one coordinator. The team could also have 2-3 Assembly support technicians and an Assembly Support Coordinator who served the Support technicians in 2 or more teams.

While the role of Assembly technician in the MD area was broader than the role of "assembler" in the traditional factory, it was the role of Coordinator that represented the greatest change from the past. The purpose of the coordinator in the MD culture was described in the original training as:

> *"...to guide the team in safely meeting daily production schedules and to improve the team's flexibility, capability (empowerment and training) and performance (cost, quality, delivery and environmental.)"*

The coordinator role is the interface between the first level of management (e.g., Manufacturing Advisor- the new term for the first level of management) and the front-line employees. In the new culture, the job demands the both the skills of the former first level manager/supervisor in the old culture as well as the technical knowledge of the most skilled production workers in the former culture. As the MD process was initially launched in Hagerstown manufacturing, the demands of the coordinator position as designed, and the criticality of the position were underestimated. A significant amount of preparation and planning went into the launch process in terms of defining the job and in terms of defining the selection criteria for the position. However, it was not until the Manufacturing Guidance Team began to receive feedback from the factory floor in the pilot MD area that reality struck. This feedback led to a recognition of the reality that the complexity of the coordinator role had not been fully appreciated and that not enough preparation was given to coordinators who initially were selected for the role. Some coordinators wanted to return to the floor as assembly technicians. There was variability from area to area regarding the extent to which the coordinator role was really being carried out. The original idea that coordinators would rotate out of the position after 6 months was questioned as being too short for coordinators to learn their role. In addition, the teams were struggling to meet their production goals.

This led the guidance team and the MD model team to take actions both to help the coordinators in the pilot areas and to rethink the approach for coordinator preparation as the MD culture was expanded beyond the pilot area to the remainder of the plant beginning in 2007. The Guidance Team members conducted interviews with the original group of coordinators to get more detail regarding their struggles. Another action was to begin a benchmarking effort with other sites within Volvo and with companies outside of Volvo.

One of the benchmarking sites was the GM-Allison Transmission Plant in Baltimore. Another benchmarking site was the Toyota Powertrain site in Georgetown, Kentucky. Allison is a UAW plant while Toyota is non-union.

REVISED COORDINATOR JOB DESCRIPTION

Coordinator and Team's Customer: Next production operation and Receiving Truck Plant

Coordinator Purpose: The coordinator position exists to guide the team in safely meeting daily production schedules and to improve the team's flexibility, capability (empowerment and training) and performance (cost, quality, delivery, and environmental)

Coordinator Duties/Tasks

1. **Monitor and assure safety of operations**
   a. **Assure that required safety training is provided to the team**
   b. **Assure that regular safety audits are conducted, and findings addressed**
   c. **Assure that the team has identified and prioritized ergonomic issues that serve to restrict team performance or job rotation possibilities and has provided written documentation to the ME and Advisor.**

2. Assure that team meets daily production schedule
   a. **Assure that all production workstations are filled by a trained technician.**
   b. **Fill in for technicians as a last resort.**
   c. **Relay instructions from advisor.**
   d. **Assist advisor in conducting daily startup meeting**
   e. **Assure co-workers have the proper line balance and are able to perform their job as the balance is written. Involve ME as required to correct problems.**
   f. **Assist team members in performing simple maintenance tasks or emergency stock handling as required.**
3. **Assure that team members are trained and certified to perform all workstations within the team.**
   a. **Assure that the team understands the certification process.**
   b. **Assure that each team member is certified to perform at least three adjacent workstations when the team initially starts its activity.**

    c.   Assure that the team has current and accurate work instructions for each workstation.

    d.   Determine who is the designated team trainer for each workstation.

    e.   Develop and maintain versatility diagram to monitor status of training.

    f.   Develop training plan that will achieve cross training/certification of all members on all workstations within a 6-month period.

4. Improve the performance of the team with respect to delivery, quality, cost, and environmental performance.

    a.   Assure that all members of the team understand the team KPI's.

    b.   Develop mechanism to track team KPI performance and communicate results weekly to the team.

    c.   Conduct performance matrix assessment of the team's baseline performance level and set improvement goals.

    d.   Utilize problem solving tools and data as required to achieve performance improvement goals.

    e.   Build team flexibility and knowledge through development and implementation of a job rotation plan that enables members to maintain their capability to perform each workstation.

    f.   Utilize 5-S process to improve cleanliness and orderliness of the workplace.

5. Assure that team activities are administered in accordance with plant guidelines, Federal and State regulations and plant certifications (e.g., ISO 9000, 14000, etc.).

    a.   Assure that overtime records are maintained and analyzed to assure equalization.

    b.   Assure that documentation required by ISO (e.g., training, work instructions, etc.) is maintained and utilized to guide teamwork.

Figure 9
Revised Coordinator Job Description.

One of the lessons learned from Toyota was the way they view the significance of the coordinator role which they call "team leader." The former GM and VP of Powertrain for the Toyota Georgetown plant said:

> *"If one were to use a sports metaphor, the coordinator is the most important person in the plant. The coordinator is similar to the point guard in basketball or the quarterback in football. The Advisor is the coach."*

The coordinator runs the plays that move the ball down the field and puts points on the board in the football metaphor. The analogy is similar in basketball. On the factory floor, the coordinator is responsible both for meeting production targets and improving the processes used to meet production targets. The Advisor role is to help train and develop the coordinator and to support their work. It is clear that the "pilot" implementation by Volvo did not place this degree of importance on the coordinator role in the initial launch.

However, based on the early experience in the initial MD assembly areas and the benchmarking effort, the Vision for the Coordinator position was considerably strengthened in importance. The revised coordinator job description is shown in Figure 8. This revised vision more closely reflects alignment of the coordinator job activities with the elements of the High-Performance Matrix – the Volvo North American Powertrain operational definition of World Class performance for a team.

Another lesson learned from the benchmarking effort was that it is not possible to conceive of the coordinator position apart from the total production system that supports it. This was another key factor that increased the degree of difficulty for VPTNA since it was transforming from a previous transformation. As was shown by the "red thread", Figure 5 above, Hagerstown had to move well beyond the culture that had enabled the plant to be chosen by Volvo to build the engines and transmissions for the global product platform. It had to fully implement the requirements of the global Volvo Production System (VPS). It had to do this at the same time it was meeting increasing customer orders for the legacy engine that was still being produced by the traditional areas of the plant. The manufacturing management had to manage this transformation at the same time it was attempting to achieve dramatically increased production levels for the legacy product. The fact that they were able to effectively build and launch the pilot MD initiative was a significant achievement. It simply was not possible to fully implement the transformation to the Volvo Production System in this environment given the resources available. As a result, the coordinators in the pilot areas were attempting to move to the new culture without all the supporting tools that would become available when the new Volvo Production System was fully installed. This required the vision for the coordinator position to continue to evolve as the VPS would be introduced plant wide in the later part of 2007 after the legacy engine manufacturing was being phased out.

David Perkins was the Union President and was a member of the Guidance Team in the 2004-2007 period when the MD rollout was being planned and implemented. With the benefit of hindsight, David shared his perspective on that rollout process quite a few years later. David also remained as union president after Roger Johnston left Hagerstown and was therefore able to watch the evolution of the transformation that began in 2004 but continued under new Volvo general managers. Here is what David had to say about that initial period:

> *"The transition to the MD process was initially very good. We pretty much hand-picked the people who were the initial participants in the MD rollout. There was no penalty for staying with the old process and not moving to the new one (MD production area.) Most people did not want to move over. It was basically the younger ones who really bought into this new concept.... So, the people who moved over were volunteers and were given intensive training. They were basically told they were special, they were the ground breakers, and they had a sense of importance.... That first group got four weeks of training and as for uniforms, at that time they were just wearing T-shirts and hats. I remember that after three weeks, we brought a tour through the plant. It was from AAA Trucking, a major buyer, not at the level of Fed*

EX or UPS, but a very nice customer. During the tour some of the assembly technicians walked up to the visitors and asked if they were from AAA Trucking. They said, we appreciate your business, and we know that you do this, and this, and this. After the tour, the head of AAA Trucking said: 'I have never been in a place where the person who was assembling my engine knew who I was and what my business was. That was impressive'. To me, that was the way that I had hoped that it would be with everything in the new MD area."[137]

When asked "What were the most significant changes for people who went into the MD process?" David had several insightful comments:

The most significant thing that had the most impact for us from the Union perspective was job rotation. 1 up, 1 down. (This meant that everyone on the assembly line must not only learn to perform the tasks on their assigned position, but also the tasks associated with the position following theirs and the position preceding their position on the line.) It made practical sense, and it was not something that was unheard of, but it did not happen in the old way of working. You worked your way into a job and that was what you did. So, job rotation was the major thing we had to face as we were bringing a lot more work into that MD process.

The resistance from the union was that people just did not want to change. Change is difficult. Especially in a union industrial environment. But the job we are talking about was not protected as individuals in the union contract. But the practice had been that if you have a job of putting on flywheels, and another job opens up and if you have the seniority, I will consider moving you up to that new job. But, until that, you will be putting on flywheels. You are not putting on flywheels today and dropping heads

[137] David Perkins, in-person interview, September 14, 2021.

tomorrow. So that is the way people got used to it and they resisted. They think "Why should I have to learn a new job? I did not sign up for this. Also, not all of the union representatives (committeemen) were supportive of the MD process. There had to be a cultural change among the elected union representatives to support this new process. So, job rotation was probably the biggest hurdle we had to overcome." [138]

Another challenge that we discussed earlier is that we underestimated the complexity of the coordinator role. Can you share your thoughts about that situation?

"The coordinator role was a huge issue. Even among the elected union officials it was a huge issue. Support for the position was about 50-50 (among union officials.) A lot of people looked at the coordinator role as a union protected, management puppet. So, we made a lot of mistakes. We put coordinators in there who were elected by the team members. What happened then was, if you wanted to be re-elected, you really could not do the role that coordinators were elected to do. If you did the role, you were not re-elected. That came out very quickly. Coordinators were something we were constantly changing and trying to get it right. I am not sure we ever got it right even to this day. Today (2021 – 17 years later) that position is called "Value team captain." We incorporated a lot of the philosophy of what coordinators should be. But value team captain role today: (1) is a well-defined position in the union contract. It is there, here are the duties and responsibilities, the person is selected (by management) through an interview process and the union does not grade you on the interview. The union does sit in on the interview process to make sure everybody is treated fairly. Management selects the coordinator based on specifically defined criteria. At first, we (the union) were

---

[138] David Perkins, in-person interview, September 14, 2021.

part of the scoring process. But then we got the union guy saying I'm not giving my guy anything but top points. So, we could not have that, but we just want to make sure that everyone is treated fairly. If I am interviewed by Manager X and Manager Y, then the next guy needs to be interviewed by the same interviewers. The union's role was to assure consistency of the process and application of the criteria. It is almost getting to the point of what we expected and wanted it to be when we launched the role of the coordinators.

Where we failed the most with coordinators as we were going into the MD system was, we tried to be too responsive to the criticisms we would get that (we were trying to turn union members into management team leaders) and we built in too many safeguards, e.g., they were elected, could only serve a 6-month tenure, etc. …. It was tough to be a coordinator (but it was much tougher) when you get this resentment – 'You are not my boss'. So, the coordinator probably thinks, I like the role, I like the responsibility, but if I do this, I will probably not be re-elected. We put them in an untenable position by having them be re-elected by the team. The union thought that was what we had to do to sell this to our membership. The mistake was on our part."[139]

Another requirement for people who chose to move into the MD areas was that they would wear a uniform. This became a very complicated issue to implement. From the Guidance Team's perspective this uniform was an important symbol that a new culture was being created with a new level of professionalism and it would signify to employees in the plant as well as visitors that this group of people were striving to attain the standard of world class performance. The reaction that David described from the visitors from AAA Trucking who entered the MD area was an example of this new standard of professionalism and customer focus. From his

---

perspective as Union President, David shared a variety of challenges that were faced in attempting to implement this MD policy.

> *"At first, the uniform only consisted of T-shirts and hats. It did not become a big issue until we went to a full uniform of pants and shirts. I was a supporter of the uniforms. To me the symbolism – and Roger Johnston lived this as well- meant that I would never go to work without my uniform shirt. Roger was the same way. I don't care if he was leaving the plant to go downtown to talk to the Chamber of Commerce, he would wear his uniform. He did not change to a suit and tie. Other people, when they left had a white shirt and tie because 'I am important' and I want them to know I am important.*
>
> *The uniform symbolized professionalism, but not for us, but for people coming into the plant. It impacted the way they (as customers) viewed us. The salespeople told us that they wanted to use Hagerstown to sell trucks. (In the past) We could never bring a customer to Hagerstown because it was a dump, it looked terrible, it was dirty. But (with the new MD plant) we wanted to use this new plant to say this is where your engines are coming from. The uniforms helped create the image for visitors that these people have it together. Also, for me it was important that the supervisor was not wearing a white shirt but that he was wearing the same shirt that the assemblers are wearing. It showed we are on an equal level. There was no hierarchy like the one that exists when a manager wears a shirt and tie to show that he is better than the person not wearing a white shirt and tie.[140]*

That was the rationale behind wearing uniforms. It made sense. However, putting this policy into practice became much more complicated than anyone anticipated. David talks about the struggle over more than a year to resolve the challenges:

---

[140] David Perkins, in-person interview, September 14, 2021.

We started off with T-shirts and they were a minor problem. [141]..But then we got into arguing what colors the uniforms could be. That is when Gothenburg got involved. (Gothenburg is the Swedish city where the Volvo Global Headquarters is located.) You can't have red, you can't have blue, you can't have green, so we came up with gray. Unfortunately, gray can be considered a drab color. We came up with uniform pants, and they had to be black. The fits for females were terrible. They were uncomfortable. It was a disaster. We tried to say just let them wear black pants but no, they have to wear uniform pants... Then they painted the floors gray. So now we are wearing gray shirts on gray floors. So, they did go to black. Black T-shirts but they were hot. Once the whole plant was air conditioned it was not so bad. Then it became a cost factor. The supply area looked like we were an Eddie Bauer store or something with all the shirts stacked up everywhere.

We, the union, demanded that the uniforms be American made and union made. Sounds like a wonderful concept. However, to find an American made, union made clothing manufacturer that could give you a diverse range of styles was almost impossible. We found one – Protexall. They worked with us as well as any company could, but they were just not in the business of making clothes for women. Had we not made the uniform requirement that they were American made /union made we would have been better off. Allison did not do that.[142] So they could go

---

[141] The original concept was to present the uniforms as a "graduation symbol" to employees who successfully completed the MD training prior to being assigned to work in this new area. Unfortunately, the factors discussed above prevented this idea from being implemented.

[142] Allison was a GM-UAW transmission manufacturing plant in Maryland that served as a "benchmark partner" for some of the MD transformation concepts adopted by the Hagerstown plant.

> *out to a wider range of manufacturers than we could....*
> *(The women there) were fine with the uniforms.*[143]

Choosing to move into the MD area not only required the bargaining unit employees to change how they worked, but managers were also required to engage in different behaviors than in the past. To assist managers in assuming their new roles they also participated in canvassing presentations that provided a realistic preview of the management work roles in the MD area. Like the bargaining unit employees, managers were given the option to opt into the MD area or not. However, the message to managers was a bit more coercive than with bargaining unit staff. Since the ratio of managers to hourly employees would be reduced, there were relatively few positions for managers who did not choose to move into the MD area. Clearly the message was, we are moving in this direction and you either "get on board" or you will be looking for work elsewhere in a year or less.

As with the bargaining unit employees, managers choosing to enter the MD area were required to sign a prerequisite agreement as well. Figure 10 lists the elements in the manager Prerequisite agreement.

I commit to leading and supporting the new manufacturing culture by:
• Participating in a training needs appraisal;
• Creating a positive work environment by living the manufacturing values and the Volvo way;
• Assuring that people in my department or area of responsibility demonstrate qualifications before being assigned to a workstation;
• Supporting the team environment by shifting my role from "boss" to coordinator and/or coach;
• Soliciting formal feedback on my performance semi-annually from my peers and my team and using that information to improve my performance as a leader;
• Developing the capabilities of the bargaining unit coordinator and the team members and empowering them to make increasingly responsible decisions and to utilize team planning, problem solving and process improvement tools (e.g., Performance Matrix, etc.) to improve performance;

---

[143] David Perkins, in-person interview, September 14, 2021

- Aligning the performance indicators in my area of responsibility with the goals of Volvo Powertrain and assuring that all people understand the goals and indicators;

- Providing regular and frequent performance feedback to the coordinator and teams regarding the performance of their area;

- Confronting in a positive manner, examples of behavior that do not conform to our values, our team ground-rules, and our business commitments to customers;

- Supporting the team(s) in meeting daily, customer requirements;

- Enabling the job rotation plan of teams through assuring required training is provided and resolving of ergonomic impediments;

- Wearing a uniform- union made in the USA, with a joint company union logo;

- Taking actions required as a last resort to meet the customer commitments of the department in the event that the teams are unable to do so;

- Capturing and share knowledge with my peers and colleagues throughout the plant regarding lessons learned in phasing in the new manufacturing culture and use this knowledge to improve and accelerate the phase-in process;

- Being a role model for the "how we will work practices" and assure that the practices are implemented and followed in my department or area of responsibility;

- Support my team's ability to meet customer requirements by holding accountable those other functions in the company that support our ability to do our job including suppliers of parts, services, and information.

Figure 10
Prerequisite Document for Managers/Supervisors in MD Area

To assist managers in making the transformation into the MD area, a training program was developed. The objectives for this management training are displayed in Figure 11.

At the end of this training, management participants will be able to:
1. Create a positive work environment by living the manufacturing values and the Volvo way;
2. Assure that people in my department or area of responsibility demonstrate qualifications before being assigned to a workstation;

3. Support the team environment by shifting my role from "boss" to coordinator and/or coach;

4. Solicit formal feedback on my performance semi-annually from my peers and my team and using that information to improve my performance as a leader;

5. Develop the capabilities of the bargaining unit coordinator and the team members and empowering them to make increasingly responsible decisions and to utilize team planning, problem solving and process improvement tools (e.g., Performance Matrix, etc.) to improve performance;

6. Align the performance indicators in my area of responsibility with the goals of Volvo Powertrain and assuring that all people understand the goals and indicators;

7. Provide regular and frequent performance feedback to the coordinator and teams regarding the performance of their area;

8. Confront in a positive manner, examples of behavior that do not conform to our values, our team ground-rules, and our business commitments to customers;

9. Support the team(s) in meeting daily, customer requirements;

10. Enable the job rotation plan of teams through assuring required training is provided and resolving of ergonomic impediments;

11. Wear a uniform- union made in the USA, with a joint company union logo;

12. Take actions required as a last resort to meet the customer commitments of the department in the event that the teams are unable to do so;

13. Capture and share knowledge with my peers and colleagues throughout the plant regarding lessons learned in phasing in the new manufacturing culture and use this knowledge to improve and accelerate the phase-in process;

14. Be a role model for the "how we will work practices" and assure that the practices are implemented and followed in my department or area of responsibility;

15. Support my team's ability to meet customer requirements by holding accountable those other functions in the company that support our ability to do our job including suppliers of parts, services, and information.

Figure 11

Objectives for the MD Management Training Program

Both the bargaining unit training and the management training provided an introduction to the Volvo Production System (VPS) that was being phased in gradually. VPS was defined as follows:

VPS is a methodology that combines lean manufacturing and six sigma to maximize shareholder value by achieving the fastest rate of improvement in customer satisfaction, cost, quality, process speed and invested capital.

The VPS methodologies are organized into 10 Pillars (as in the pillars that support a building). These pillars each contain improvement tools and techniques that are applied as appropriate in the manufacturing organization. Each of the 10 pillars has an assigned Pillar "owner" who is responsible for assuring effective deployment of the pillar methodologies across the organization. The 10 pillars are viewed as the elements of World Class Manufacturing. They are:

1. Safety and Work Environment
2. Customer Service
3. Cost Deployment
4. Continuous Improvement
5. Quality Improvement
6. Operators Maintenance
7. Specialist Maintenance
8. Initial Phase Management
9. Competence Development
10. Environment

As we have pointed out above, these Pillars build on and extend many of the concepts contained in the previous Total Quality initiative and the MD initiatives in Hagerstown. They add rigor, more emphasis on scientific management and scientific problem solving. Full implementation of the VPS began with an audit of Hagerstown manufacturing by a consultant from Japan who rated the manufacturing operation on each of these Pillars and compared the site with other sites within Volvo Powertrain. The initial audit was conducted before the plant had attempted a full launch of the VPS for the reasons previously stated. One person described the audit as analogous to taking a test on material when you have not yet received the textbook. Nevertheless, the audit provided a baseline for Hagerstown and pointed out many opportunities for improvement. This helped launch Hagerstown manufacturing into the next phase of its transformation.

In retrospect, it is easy to realize that in an ideal world the full-blown VPS would have been put in place at the same time that the initial pilot MD launch occurred. However, it is rare that we can ever live in an "ideal world."

In Hagerstown and with Volvo North American Powertrain, the end of 2007 represented the end of the first phase of the Hagerstown transformation under Volvo ownership. By the end of 2007 Roger Johnston who had led manufacturing since 1999, much longer than the tenure of a typical Manufacturing VP, moved from Hagerstown to a new role in Greensboro, N.C. with Volvo's North American Headquarters. Hagerstown also had a new VP for Engineering and a new head of Purchasing. Very importantly also, the man who had played a key role in choosing Hagerstown as the site for the new engine platform, the Senior VP for Volvo North American Powertrain, Sten-Åke Aronsson, also left Hagerstown to return to his native Sweden and retirement. Sten-Åke had been the ideal Senior VP to lead the transformation. He was very smart and experienced, he was strong but modest, he was focused on the task but understanding with respect to the fact that change takes time. He was very respectful of the people in the plant at all levels, but he was persistent in moving the plant in the direction it needed to go. He also was quite effective in improving teamwork between the major functional areas in Hagerstown that had experienced internal conflict with the previous Senior VP.

Shortly before Roger left Hagerstown, his colleagues held a "going-away" ceremony to pay tribute to him for what he had done to assure a future for the Hagerstown plant. Even though Sten-Åke had already returned to Sweden, when he learned of the celebration for Roger, he asked that the words below be read to the group. [144]

---

[144] Message emailed to Thomas C. Tuttle, November 27, 2007, from Sten-Åke Aronsson.

"Dear Roger:

Firstly, I wish you all success, happiness and joy in your new challenge, but I'm of the opinion that it's a vast misuse of your skills!

During our years together, I always respected your way of managing your troops. Especially, I liked the way you involved all of your co-workers!

I sincerely hope that what you started in this way of working will for years to come heavily contribute to the future success for Mack, VTNA and other Volvo-products on your side of the ocean. I regret that I can't be with you personally tonight, but I'm with you in my thoughts.

May the Lord bless you and support you in your coming years and thank you for all your help to me!

Best personal regards,

Sten-Åke

The author was also asked by Denny Hollinger, who organized the event for Roger, to share some thoughts as well. These were my comments:

"It is an honor to be with this group of people who have meant so much to me over the last 18 years. I would like to provide my tribute to Roger by focusing on two defining themes that I have observed in working with Roger while he has been here.

I vividly remember our first breakfast meeting shortly after you arrived. The collaboration "train" between Mack and the UAW had jumped the tracks and a tentative approach had been developed to get the train running again. The strategy depended on how you would respond and what management style this "engineer" would bring to the job as the new GM. Little did we know at the time, that you would be the consummate "values-driven" leader that you have been. A leader who realized that the path to sustained performance improvement involved building a shared, compelling vision, earning trust, open and honest communication and creating a collaborative approach with the UAW to move toward the vision. Under stress, when less principled leaders might have reverted to the old autocratic style, you lived the principles you had helped define – Individual dignity, continuous improvement, mutual responsibility and collaboration, performance excellence. Walking the talk is the definition of integrity and you exemplified it consistently.

Whenever Roger would lay out the challenges to his leadership team – and during his tenure there have been plenty – he would end the sentence by saying in various ways – "what we have to remember in the midst of all this is that getting the job done comes down to people, their choices, their abilities and their values." You put your trust in your people to deliver the results and they gave it their all because you had earned their respect.

Theme 2 is that for Roger, what he was about here was always more than just a job. It was a "cause". The cause was demonstrating that management working with a group of represented employees could keep manufacturing work and manufacturing jobs in the United States. Nothing demonstrated this more vividly than a report he made to the Manufacturing Guidance Team (a joint leadership team) following his trip in July 2005 to Flint, Michigan.

Roger had roots in Michigan as he was an engineering graduate of the General Motors Institute (GMI)- now Kettering University. GM was born in Flint. While at GMI, Roger lived in Flint. Flint had been the site of a 44-day sit-down strike in GM in 1937 that established the UAW as the bargaining agent for employees of General Motors. So, it is fair to say that both GM, the UAW and the history of the unionized auto industry began in Flint.

What Roger reported to the Guidance Team that day was how a vibrant industrial city, once the showplace of America's world-leading auto manufacturing industry, had become virtually an industrial wasteland. Roger saw manufacturing plants where he had worked and studied reduced to rubble. Houses, buildings and businesses were shuttered. The city had fallen into receivership. The city, whose population peaked at 200,000 was now just over 120,000. Auto employment that had been 80,000 in 1978 was under 20,000 by 2000. A city that had built all the Buicks and Chevrolets in the country, now built no Buicks and Chevrolets.

Roger ended that story with the conclusion that what happened to Flint did not have to happen. It was the result of a long series of bad decisions by both management and the UAW. Both groups took their eyes off the factors that make a company competitive and successful. Focus on the customer. Control of costs. Listening to the ideas of people. The point he made to the Guidance Team was that what he saw in Flint reinforced his determination to make sure these things did not happen in Hagerstown. He told this story with sadness, passion and determination.

Roger, let me say on behalf of the State of Maryland – which I no longer represent officially – that while Volvo Powertrain North America's manufacturing operations have been under your watch – you have lived up to that promise. You are leaving behind an organization and a facility that is more competitive and that has a greater opportunity to succeed than what you found when you arrived. The core of this competitive strength is not the technology, but the relationships and the people that will put Volvo's 150 million investment to work.

Yes Roger, even though you are an engineer, you truly get it!! It's ultimately about the people, their values and choices and work is more than a job. These are the themes that for me have characterized an exceptional leader.

I am very sorry you are leaving Maryland. But I am happy you are going to my hometown. I know you will leave Greensboro in better shape than you find it – just as you did here in Hagerstown."[145]

---

[145] Comments by Thomas C. Tuttle on the occasion of the Going-Away Tribute to Roger Johnston, November 28, 2007.

Chapter 6

Lessons For Today's Leaders

*Someone's sitting in the shade today because
someone planted a tree long ago.*

-Warren Buffett

Close to 2000 people are employed today at the Volvo Powertrain Plant in Hagerstown, Maryland because of the "trees planted" in the plant between 1991 and 2007. We have attempted to tell the story of the people responsible for much of the tree planting that laid the foundation enabling this plant to remain one of the largest employers in Washington County, Maryland. Without the efforts of the people described in this book and many others, it seems certain that this plant would have suffered the fate of other well -known plants which have not survived such as GM-Flint, Lordstown Ohio, the GM-Toyota Nummi plant, the Allison Transmission plant in Baltimore, and the Navistar Engine Plant to name a few. These were manufacturing plants whose leaders were unable to create sufficient change to remain competitive.

What made the former Mack Trucks Hagerstown plant different?

This Chapter distills some of the lessons learned from this 16- year journey that enabled Hagerstown to escape the fate of these other plants. These thoughts emerged primarily from the interviews with key management and union leaders from the Mack-Volvo plant. The interviews were supplemented by the author's documents and notes. Those interviewed between 2020 and 2022 included, from management: Ross Rhoads, Roger Johnston, and email interviews with Sten-Åke Aronsson, former Volvo Powertrain Senior Vice-President, and CEO of Volvo North American Powertrain. Interviews from the UAW included former Presidents of Local 171 Jim Stewart, Maurice Kaiser and David Perkins and Bobby Shoop former Shop Chairman of Local 171. In the interviews, each of these individuals was asked to reflect on the question "What are the key lessons learned from the transformation of Hagerstown that would have relevance for leaders today concerned with organizational transformation?"

Of those interviewed, David Perkins had the unique ability to reflect on the cause and effect of the efforts during this 1991-2007 period in terms of the performance of the plant following 2007. David was an employee of the plant from the mid 70's until he left the plant to join the UAW Regional Office in Baltimore in 2016, except for a 3-year period when he worked for G-M Baltimore during a temporary layoff from Mack. His roles in the plant were assembler, skilled trades mechanic, union sourcing representative and local union President. In his capacity with the regional UAW office after leaving the plant, Dave still had oversight responsibility for the Hagerstown plant from the UAW Regional Office perspective. So, as this is written in 2022, Dave is still closely connected to the plant and is in a position to see how the "trees planted" earlier and the lessons learned from those experiences continue to influence actions and decisions in the plant today. He is also able to contrast that set of experiences with other plants he deals directly with in the Southeastern Region of the U.S. represented by the United Auto Workers.

A Unionized Plant Can Change

Perhaps the overriding lesson learned from the Hagerstown experience was, in David Perkins words, *"We proved that we could change in a union environment."*[146]

This statement could have also been made by Jim Stewart, and Maurice Kaiser who were the Presidents of UAW Local 171 prior to David. It could have also been made by Ross Rhoads and Roger Johnston the two of the three plant managers between 1991 and 2007. It could have been cited by Sten-Åke Aronsson as one of the key reasons that Volvo chose to locate its North American Power Train operation in Hagerstown rather than build a new plant somewhere else in North America. Each one of the plant leaders, demonstrated the willingness to move away from traditional relationships, to modify union contracts, and take a "leap of faith" that working together in new ways could enable the plant to survive in the globalized, competitive heavy duty truck market.

Why were they willing to do this? The simple answer from the union perspective, is that they had been able to create relationships with the senior plant managers based on trust and honest dialog. The other part of the answer from both union and management is they did it because they felt they had to. The leaders in both management and the union realized that "business as usual" would not enable the plant to survive.

Back in the late 1970's competition from Japan began to invade many of the markets in the United States from cameras to office equipment to automobiles and more. Company after company was losing major market share. One of the companies that was hit very hard by this new competition was Motorola. As a result, it was one of the first U.S. companies to adopt Total Quality Management to compete with this Japanese invasion. In a Conference with other major U.S. executives, a Motorola speaker, explaining their strategy, was asked "What enabled your change process to gain traction and succeed?" The Motorola executive responded that: *"Our change process gained traction when we realized that our survival was at stake."*

---

[146] David Perkins, September 14, 2021, in-person interview, St. Petersburg, Florida.

The situation was similar in Hagerstown. In 1971, when Mack Trucks was losing almost a million dollars a day, and when Renault was moving to acquire Mack, the union and management leaders in Hagerstown felt that "survival was at stake in Hagerstown." However, as Bill Nutter stated clearly, and as quoted at the beginning of this book, trust between the union and management had been destroyed. This realization led the State of Maryland, its governor and its chief economic development leader, Randy Evans to offer a package of economic incentives to Mack/Renault. In addition, Evans was smart enough to realize that economic incentives alone were not enough to save the plant. This led him to also offer the services of the University of Maryland, Center for Quality and Productivity (UMCQP) to serve as "third party neutral consultants" for the union and management to help them find a joint path to save the plant. In the absence of trust, a third party is essential to facilitating the change needed to survive.

From a "big picture view", change in Hagerstown came from a recognition by both union and management that survival was at stake. However, the ability to implement the necessary strategies and activities required the establishment of honest dialog and building of trust between management and the union. Because of the past "wars" between the UAW and Mack management at the corporate level, which spilled over to the Hagerstown plant, the involvement of a "third-party" from the University of Maryland was an essential element of the ability to drive the necessary changes.

David Perkins summarized the importance of a neutral third party in the process:

> *"Bill Nutter was right. Had this been a program run by Mack, it would have failed. They could have run it, maybe just as good as you did, but it would have still failed because we (the UAW) would not have bought into it. From the union perspective, it was not just any third party. If you had been the third party as "Tuttle National Corporation", it would not have worked. But Dr. Tuttle, from the University of Maryland carries a tremendous amount of weight. From the union member's viewpoint, they say I can buy into that. It is not just some*

*company they (Mack) hired who will just preach the party line.
They look at you as a truly independent source of information
and thought process. It did not matter that you were housed in
a Business School, you were still perceived as independent. I will
tell you that every UAW member, when we talked about this,
everybody was fine with it because it was from the University
of Maryland and that made it legitimate. This is not something
they (management) are trying to push on us. They are not going
to get the University of Maryland to bend their way, because
the University of Maryland is powerful enough to maintain its
independence. So, they trusted you.*[147]

From my perspective as the project leader, I think David Perkins is right
that the primary benefit I brought to the situation was that I was wearing
the "uniform" of the University of Maryland. However, in performing
that role I also had the benefit of several things that helped me prepare
for my role as a facilitator of this change process. First, I was not just
representing the University of Maryland. I was Director of an organization
jointly created by the University of Maryland Business School and the
Maryland Department of Economic and Employment Development.[148]
Fortunately, I had considerable mentoring from several leaders, both
union and management. One of my Board Members was the UAW Local
Union President from the Baltimore Broening Highway General Motors
Assembly Plant named Rodney Trump. My Board Vice-Chair, Dominic
Fornaro, was the President of the Maryland AFL-CIO. These relationships
gave the Center credibility with the UAW regionally and both labor leaders
were mentors to me. Another key mentor that helped prepare me for this

---

[147] David Perkins, September 14, 2021, in-person interview, St. Petersburg, Florida.

[148] Three visionary leaders, Rudy Lamone, Dean of the Business School, Jay Jacobs VP
of Human Resources at Black and Decker and Chair of the Maryland Economic
Development Advisory Council, and Leonard Elenowitz of the Maryland Department
of Economic and Employment Development were the three people most responsible
for the creation of the UMCQP. Like the leaders in Hagerstown, these three men
were also "tree planters". The UMCQP was created in 1978 to promote union-
management collaboration and improve productivity and quality of working life as
a way of protecting and growing jobs in the State. The Center was founded as the
Maryland Center for Productivity and Quality of Working Life and its name was later
changed to the University of Maryland Center for Quality and Productivity UMCQP.
The Center existed in the University from 1978 – 2004.

role was Forrest Behm. "Forry" as he was known, was the former President of International Operations for Corning Glass. Before his retirement from Corning, he was tasked by Corning CEO Jamie Houghton to lead Corning's Total Quality Management Process.[149] Much of the change methodology that we implemented with Mack Hagerstown at the beginning of our process drew extensively on coaching from Forry Behm. As my involvement with Mack continued, I became a member of a Quality Council of the U.S. Conference Board. This Group provided a window on over 30 U.S. Corporations that were involved in similar change processes within their industries. It was through the U.S. Conference Board Quality Council that I met Tom Carter from Alcoa. Tom introduced the group to a consultant named Brian Hall who had helped Alcoa with its focus on Values Management. Brian and his colleague Benjamin Tonna developed the Hall-Tonna theory and framework that we described in Chapter 4. Both Tom Carter and Brian Hall became mentors for my work with Mack on values management. So, while the University connection gave me the perceived independence, the "expertise" to guide the change process drew on my opportunities to learn from many experienced leaders from both labor and management.

Lessons Learned from the Ross Rhoads Period – 1991-1997

Once management and the union committed to launching the change process in 1991, the UMCQP facilitator outlined the elements of the change process in a proposal as described in Chapter 2. Reflecting on the key elements of the change process, three were most important. First, there was a comprehensive assessment of the "present state" within the plant. Second, the change process established a "change structure" in parallel to the formal organizational structure to manage and enable the change

---

[149] Forry told a story that taught me a key lesson. He said that when CEO Houghton asked him to lead Corning's change effort he did not respond immediately. He thought it over for a day. Then when he met with Houghton the next day he told his CEO, "I cannot lead this effort. You must lead it. If you do that, I will be happy to assist you." The key lesson to me was that as a consultant, I could not lead the change effort at Mack. It must be led by Ross Rhoads and Jim Stewart the top management and union leaders in the plant. My job was to assist them in that effort.

process. The third key element was developing and conducting a plant-wide training program.

The assessment provided key data that enabled the UMCQP and the management and union leaders to base the change process on facts and to integrate local examples into the plant-wide training material. It also provided data regarding needs for improvement that the Guidance Team could address as the change program proceeded.

The change structure consisted of the Guidance Team[150] co-chaired by the Plant Manager and the Union President. Members were the management people who were heads of the key manufacturing organizational units that reported to the Plant Manager. Union members in addition to the Local President were the union shop chairman and union committeemen. The Guidance Team was facilitated by the author serving as the external, third-party facilitator from the UMCQP. In addition to guiding the process, this change structure and its regular mandatory meetings served as an accountability mechanism to force the change process onto the calendars of a group of very busy people. There is a tendency for managers in a survival mode, facing the pressures of daily work, to focus on the "urgent and important" issues. The change process was "important" but not as urgent as shipping engines and transmissions every day to the assembly plants. It was not a trivial issue to force these busy managers and union leaders to pay attention also to changing the organizational culture. Largely, that was the role of the facilitator and the change process led by the plant manager and the union president.

In addition to the Guidance Team, the change structure included Performance Improvement Teams. These teams were principally focused on building important aspects of the culture for performance improvement. Initially, three improvement teams were established. They were the vision and mission team, the employee involvement team, and

[150] Initially this leadership group was called the "Steering committee" and later in the process the title was changed to "Guidance Team" which was a more accurate title for the functions of the group. This Guidance Team structure remained in place from 1991 until 2007. Its role was diminished during Olivier Vidal's tenure as plant manager and re-established in its initial form under Roger Johnston's leadership in 1999. For most of that time the author served as an external facilitator for this Team.

the third was the training development team. Each of these teams was given a "charter" by the Guidance Team. The charter outlined the purpose of the team, the members, the expected results, the time frame for results and the team's boundaries with respect to budget, authority, etc. The use of "charters" to guide performance improvement teams was designed to avoid misconceptions by the Guidance Team and the improvement team members regarding what was expected from the teams.

In retrospect, it is evident that this culture change structure was an essential element of the plant's survival strategy. It was necessary to force the management of the plant to pay attention to the need to change the culture as well as respond to the daily performance pressures from the owners regarding to cost reduction and quality improvement. At the time this process began, the philosophy of many managers in the plant was reflected in this anecdote shared by Arnie Gozora, one of the reviewers of an early draft of this book. Arnie was a senior manager in the transmission manufacturing department when the change process was launched. He later became co-facilitator of the change process with the author during the Roger Johnston era. Arnie provided this view of how he was taught to manage as a new supervisor at Mack-Hagerstown:

> *I was given a task by the Engine Department Superintendent. I accomplished it, much to his surprise. He asked me how I accomplished it so quickly. I told him that at the beginning of the shift, I introduced myself to the key union person that performed this work and shared with him what we wanted to accomplish. He said, I will try. I checked with him around lunch time, and I said we are looking good, and I asked him if he needed anything to allow him to finish the job. He said, I think we will make it. The Superintendent's reply was "so you were collaborating with the enemy. Gozora, you are going to have to learn to give orders!"*

This was the culture that had to change in Hagerstown. Unless the change process consciously focused on creating a new organizational culture, there was no way this plant could survive.

In addition to strong, consistently supportive leadership from Ross Rhoads and Jim Stewart, a key to the Guidance Team success was having "rigor" in the ground rules that the members developed and accepted. The ground rules for the Team were that the team would meet every other week for at least one hour. If members were physically in the plant when the bi-weekly team meeting occurred, they were expected to attend the meeting. Members themselves were expected to attend and they could not send a substitute. Every meeting had a written agenda, distributed in advance, and minutes were kept and distributed. Members were expected to come to the meeting prepared and every meeting ended with a meeting evaluation. These ground rules sent the message that the meeting process, like every "process" within the plant should be continuously improved. The expectation was that the rigor of meeting behavior in this Guidance Team would also cascade down the organization to improve meeting behavior throughout the plant.

Another key lesson learned from the implementation of this "change structure", especially in an environment where "trust" between the union and management was lacking, was that the structure forced dialog between the Plant Manager and the Union President as they had to work together to lead this change process. Much of this dialog occurred outside of Guidance Team meetings. However, forging a trusting relationship between Ross Rhoads and Jim Stewart was clearly an outcome of the structure. In addition, there were many other elements of the change process as it evolved that enabled their relationship to grow. For example, it became stronger as Ross and Jim jointly "kicked off" each of the 40 5-day training sessions as the plant-wide training proceeded over the two-year period of the training implementation. By publicly serving as role models during the training implementation Ross and Jim sent a strong message to both the management and union work force that senior management and the senior union leadership were united in the effort to save Hagerstown. The importance of this message to the plant population cannot be overstated. However, it was also an important message to the broader Hagerstown community, and perhaps most importantly, to the owners of the plant – Mack and RVI.

The third key element of the change process was the plant-wide training. There were several lessons learned from the plant wide training process implementation beyond its value in helping develop and display the trust that was developing between Ross Rhoads and Jim Stewart. The author, working with the training development team, was aware of the limitations of "consultant driven" training in terms of enabling client organizations to fully integrate the training into their operations. In developing the training approach, the guidance team considered several different models. One was the model used by Xerox to deploy total quality training. Their approach enabled each level of management to "cascade" the training down the organization starting with the Chairman training his direct reports, the VP's training their direct reports and so on down the organization. By forcing each level of management to become trainers, they had to become quite knowledgeable with the training content. This model also enables "bottoms-up" accountability. If employees see their bosses behaving in ways inconsistent with the message, they communicated in training they could point this out. This can be a healthy, if sometimes painful, organizational process. However, following discussion, this model was not chosen by the training development team as the model to be used in Hagerstown because the guidance team members did not feel that the managers and supervisors were able to credibly serve as trainers. Also, given the production pressure they were under to meet delivery goals, there was not time to fully train all of them to be trainers. [151]

The approach chosen was for the UMCQP consultants to develop the training content and then have the proposed training modules reviewed by the Training Development Team and the Guidance Team. However, rather than have managers cascade the training through the organization, the Hagerstown model chosen was to identify teams of potential trainers – one manager and one union member- who would be trained as "trainers" and then have these training teams deliver the training to the organization. The training development team put out a call to the entire plant organization to ask members to volunteer to serve as trainers. As Ross is quoted in Chapter two, management was surprised to find **"there were more volunteers than**

---

[151] Arnie Gozora (Jan. 23, 2022, memo to the author) pointed out that "to make a change especially cultural change it takes an investment in a person's competencies and an investment in a person's values development (e.g., self-worth and dignity). For several reasons, Mack had not made those types of investments in its people prior to 1991.)

we needed, and they were all good." This led to the decision to expand each training team to include three members.

A key lesson learned from this experience is that there is a tendency for management to underestimate the capability of members of the workforce and their willingness to become involved. Certainly, this was true at the beginning of this process. The other part of this lesson learned is that while there are many members of the workforce who desire more responsibility and challenge, that desire is not universal. There are significant individual differences in the extent to which members of the Hagerstown work force desired more challenge and opportunities to learn new skills.

Another lesson learned from the initial Total Quality Training for the entire workforce was the unintended consequence that the training helped increase the perceived "gap" between what was taught in the classroom and what was practiced in "actual daily work." This gap reflected the fact that the training effectively described the desired workplace behaviors in order to improve both performance and job engagement among members of the workforce. However, it made evident the fact that what was being described was not what was being practiced consistently in many of the work areas of the plant. This "gap" resulted in large part between the extreme pressure from the owners of the plant for performance improvement with respect to cost, quality, and delivery of the required number of engines and transmissions per day to the assembly plants. The Guidance Team forced the senior management to also pay attention to culture change along with achieving these demanding and essential performance results. Middle management, however, was torn between these two sets of seemingly conflicting requirements. Because pressure on them for performance results was more visible than the pressure for culture change, the gap between daily work behavior and and the Total Quality training message grew. It was difficult for middle managers to believe that the techniques delivered in the total quality training would produce the performance results that were essential. So, under stress, they often reverted to the old management style that the anecdote from Arnie Gozora depicted. While, following the training, few managers believed that the union was the enemy, they did not yet trust their union employees to deliver the results required without management pressure. The reality, which became obvious later in the change process, was not that the union employees could not deliver the results, it was that many managers simply lacked the skills to manage in the new way due to the lack of investment that had been made in their skill development. Despite this situation, and the fact that the implementation of the new culture, while improved, was not perfect, enough changes were made that the plant still had significant performance improvements during and following the TQ-1 training between 1991 and 1994.

Much of the performance improvement during this period resulted from the improved trust between union and management, increased understanding by management and employees of the urgency and the means to improve quality, cost and delivery performance, and a significant organization change. The plant reorganization moved the plant from a "vertical" departmental structure to a more "horizontal" business team structure. The business team structure created much better alignment of the functions that supported the production departments (e.g., quality, manufacturing engineering, maintenance, materials management, etc.) with the actual production departments and increased their accountability.

The significant performance improvements achieved between 1991 and 1994 were accompanied by considerable external recognition in the press and they enabled the plant to receive the U.S. Senate Productivity Award, Maryland's version of the Baldrige Award. These accolades led the Hagerstown plant to take a pause to celebrate what they had accomplished. It had been so difficult to maintain the pace of change in the race to survive that there was a feeling that we need a chance to catch our breath. In any sustained change process where people feel like they are climbing a mountain that keeps growing taller, it is essential at various points in the process to pause, look down the mountain to see how far we have climbed and celebrate our progress. This celebration then helps create the renewed energy to sustain the climb.

Unfortunately for Hagerstown, this "pause" was short lived and the celebration was short. Renault had assumed greater control of Mack and the performance targets were continually adjusted upward. Under this pressure from Renault, there was a brief reversion to "old school" management by Ross Rhoads. He was pressured by his Mack Corporate bosses to bring in an outside contingency consulting group to utilize classic industrial engineering time and motion study methods in the effort to reduce costs while increasing output. In the Total Quality "change process" launched in 1991, the implicit agreement was for decisions such as this to be made jointly by the union and management. That principle had been a key to creating trust between the UAW and Mack management. However, given the external pressure, Ross felt that he had to act unilaterally to meet the goals he had been given which were to increase output without capital investment. This decision backfired. It knocked the joint union management process that had produced significant performance gains between 1991 to 1994 off the improvement track.

The lesson learned from this experience is that trust established between the union and management that takes a long time to create can be lost virtually in an instant by unilateral action by either party.

In the attempt to rebuild the trust relationship, the UMCQP, which had not been actively involved in a facilitation role for the past, roughly two years, was asked to come back and help launch Total Quality 2. Events had changed the situation somewhat since the UMCQP had departed. Renault was now firmly in charge as the owner of Mack and Hagerstown, as well as other sites of Mack Trucks had been assigned a Deputy General Manager from France. After a brief "assessment" the UMCQP became re-involved as a facilitator for the Guidance Team and work began to develop a new plant-wide training program to deal with some of the identified needs from TQ-1 as well as the new realities with the new owner. The main focus of TQ-2 was to reduce the "gap" between the behavior practiced in the plant's daily work and the TQ philosophy and improvement strategies taught in the training sessions.

Several changes were made in the training development process in TQ-2 as result of lessons learned from TQ-1 and the assessment prior to TQ-2. One lesson learned was that the knowledge level of the management and union employees with respect to Total Quality implementation had progressed substantially from the situation in 1991. As a result, the training development process was largely done by Mack union and management employees with the UMCQP's role being that of a facilitator of the training development process. The second lesson learned was that the training development process must have as one of its objectives to fully integrate the Total Quality content into the planning and management systems that guided daily work in the plant. In TQ-1, the responsibility to make that integration of the TQ content with daily job content was largely left up to the trainees.

The title of the TQ-2 training was "Creating the Future Through Total Quality Planning". The key purpose of this training was to build greater understanding among management and the union employees of the business and to integrate the TQ process with the way we run the business. However, before the TQ-2 process could be launched, Renault changed top management at Mack Headquarters and an assistant plant manager was installed in Hagerstown and one other Mack plant. The assistant plant manager in Hagerstown came from Renault's operations in France. In 1997, the assistant GM became the plant manager. He attempted to follow the example that Ross and Jim had set with TQ-1 by kicking off each of the training sessions with Jim Stewart. However, the new GM was not able to recreate the trust between the Union and Management.

The major lesson learned from this experience was that this training process and the roll-out were the victim of another type of gap. The training material emphasized the TQ philosophy of collaboration based on trust between the union and management. However, the gap this time was that the "control" philosophy exhibited by the new General Manager conflicted with the collaboration philosophy presented in the training material. The General Manager's "my way or the highway" leadership style destroyed the trust. No training program could overcome the loss of trust between management and the UAW in Hagerstown by the autocratic style exhibited by the General Manager.

Lessons Learned from the Olivier Vidal Period – 1997-1999

A number of lessons were learned from this period 1997-1999. First of all, the business context Mack was operating in had changed. To compete successfully, the plant had to obtain more output from the existing resources. Renault was either unable or unwilling to invest a significant amount of new capital in Hagerstown. The new GM had strong technical expertise and he initiated changes that, as Roger Johnston stated, were "directionally correct." However, his process for introducing these changes ignored the human element. Just as Ross Rhoads acted unilaterally to bring in the consulting firm, Olivier Vidal did not involve the union leadership in his efforts to change Hagerstown. This unilateral decision style caused the relationship with the UAW leadership to deteriorate to the point that the UAW pulled out of the joint union-management Guidance Team. This "team" had been the key "change structure" mechanism that guided the successful transformation of the plant for the past 7 years. The loss of the union's involvement and support led to a decline in the output of the plant despite the unilateral efforts of management to produce 200 engines per day. Output dropped to less than 100 engines per day. The output declines left Renault with no option other than to replace Olivier Vidal as plant manager. The adversarial relationship that had produced such poor results in the late 1980's when there was a war between the International UAW and Mack corporate management, returned in the form of the conflict between Olivier Vidal and Jim Stewart. This conflict produced performance results that threatened the survival of the plant again.

Once the UAW withdrew support for the joint process and withdrew from the Guidance Team, the UMCQP was brought back into the plant to salvage the "sinking ship". However, the relationship could not be salvaged if Olivier Vidal remained at the helm.

Lessons Learned from the Roger Johnston Period - Phase 1 - 1999-2003

Process to Rebuild Trust Between Union and Management – The process to rebuild trust between the UAW and Management started immediately when Roger Johnston arrived as GM in Hagerstown. This effort had several elements.

    a. **Unilateral Act by Jim Stewart President of UAW Local 171** – Immediately upon Roger's arrival in Hagerstown, Jim took it upon himself to escort Roger on a tour of the plant during which he introduced Roger to key union officials and many of the plant employees. They also visited a number of offices and met key people in the Engineering Division. This tour sent a very strong signal to the plant population that there was a "new management style" in Hagerstown and that the UAW was ready to re-engage with the transformation process. Through his actions, Jim Stewart staked his reputation on collaboration with the new plant leadership. This meant that the UAW chose to work with and support the new management style in manufacturing and to improve the relationship between Engineering and Manufacturing in the Plant. These relationships were essential for the plant to succeed.

b. **Restart of Guidance Team and Improvement Teams** – Further evidence of the renewed management-union collaboration was the restarting of UAW participation in the Guidance Team that Roger Johnston restored as the vehicle to guide the continuing transformation of the plant. These moves signaled the re-establishment of a joint union-management transformation process that also included third party facilitation by the University of Maryland Center for Quality and Productivity (UMCQP). The label given to the renewed transformation effort was "Partnership for the Future."

c. **Values Management Process** – One of the key initiatives of the Guidance Team facilitated by the UMCQP was the effort to build a common set of explicitly shared values to serve as the conceptual foundation for the Partnership for the Future. Reflecting back on this period during his interview, Roger Johnston stated that the values management process produced "**a different kind of communication (between the union and management.) It came through working with the values side of the equation. That was the new language that was created, and we needed that. You know, you have your position, I have my position and we are all human beings on this planet. Well, we are all the same.**"[152] A major lesson learned from the Values Management Process was that the values of management and the values of

---

[152] In-person interview with Roger Johnston, October 29, 2019.

union members had much in common and that the power of the joint set of shared values provided a more balanced foundation than either the values of management or the values of the union acting alone.

d. **Partnership for the Future Training** – The Guidance Team chartered a team to develop and plan the delivery of a new plant wide training process that shared with the entire plant population several key messages. These were: (1) A review of the accomplishments of the plant especially when the union and management were working together in a joint improvement process; (2) Explaining the financial basics of the business and what needed to be improved to enable the plant to be globally competitive financially and how employees can through their behavior impact the financial performance; (3) Providing a realistic explanation of the market forces in the heavy truck market and the requirements to be competitive in that market; (4) Presentation of the shared values resulting from the measured value priorities of the union and management that would serve as the foundation of the Partnership for the Future. The emphasis in this module was to help participants understand how they could put the values into practice in their daily work; (5) A description of the joint Leadership System that would guide the continuing transformation process and how all members of the plant population can be involved in that system through improvement efforts within their Employee Work Units (EWUs); (6) Presentation of a competitive analysis of the manufacturing operation emphasizing its strengths and needs for improvement.

e. **Contracting out Engine Block Manufacturing** – In the effort to produce 200 engines per day and deliver them to the truck assembly plant, Roger Johnston hit a major bottleneck. To produce 200 engines per day, the plant needed to produce at least 200 engine blocks. However, despite many efforts, the engine block line could not meet this goal. This produced a major dilemma for Roger. Here is how he described the situation:

"It was paramount that we found a way to take the collective intelligence of the workforce and move it like

> *the Queen Mary so it could be brought to bear on the challenges of the business to deliver that many engines per day.... We remember that the cylinder block line was a quarter of a mile long. There was a transfer system that was aged, and sometimes a bit recalcitrant. Most of the knowledge of how to keep that series of machines running resided in the heads of the people who were there all day long. That group of people had the ability to get us there. But we were not, as an organization, yet to the point where they felt the responsibility to do that. They hadn't worked at that level before. And the division of work concepts that existed dictated that if a machine stopped then a maintenance person was the person to take care of that. Not the operator. That was counter to the concepts that we wanted to have in place. We did not want to diminish the maintenance crew. We wanted them to work on the things they were good at, but we wanted the operators to do the things that were most effective in getting where we needed to go. We had not yet crossed that bridge".[153]*

Roger knew that the one taboo that a supplier to an assembly plant could not break was failure to provide delivery that stopped the assembly line. He had to find a way to get enough blocks per day to meet the needs of the assembly plant. So, Roger had no other option than to contract out the production of blocks beyond the number that Hagerstown could produce which was approximately 160.

In the interview, I asked Roger to reflect on the messages that his decision to contract out this block production sent to people in the plant.

> *"The message that it sent was probably two or three-fold depending on where one stood. For me, it was a message that we are serious about this because we don't have a choice. I explained it at the time. I want us to get out the maximum we can as long as we produce it with quality. But until we know we can do it, we cannot jeopardize the*

[153]   In-person interview with Roger Johnston, October 29, 2019.

*ability of the company to sell trucks. We haven't a choice.
If I had been on the other side of the discussion (the union
side) it probably sent the message "you don't trust me." I
was in the camp that said, "I want to believe you can do
it, but you have to show me!"*[154]

This decision by Roger to contract out engine blocks led to a dramatic
frenzy of activity that proved to be a catalyst for the changes the plant
needed to make in preparation for the challenges ahead. Roger described
what happened and why it was significant.

*"For the union, this represented a challenge. The Shop
Chairman Bobby Shoop came to me and said, 'Can we
try to get the maximum that we can get?' So, they took
it as a challenge and said in effect 'we will show you
what we can do! And we will show it to you in spades!
And they did, they made wonderful things happen with
that equipment, they made it 'sing'. But it wasn't easy. It
wasn't like they just said from one day to the next 'Well,
we will just give you the number you want.' There was
a lot of hard work. It became a challenge between shifts,
and then it was competition between shifts – which shift
will get the number before the next. Then they had to
cooperate between shifts for the benefit of the total plant.
They said to each other 'Wait a minute, you are leaving
my shift in bad shape when I come in because you did not
leave the buffers full. We leave them full for the next shift.
What kind of deal is that? I am sure there were some
spirited conversations between the operators and their
committee persons shift by shift to work out the details.
But as management we stood back and said, look, let's
give them some room to work here. Let's not get in their
way. We want them to be able to have an effect without
our interference. And it wasn't, let them fail, instead it
was let them succeed. And they did succeed.*

---

[154] Ibid.

This was a beginning of the acceptance of taking responsibility that had been management's responsibility. They said to themselves "Wait a minute. I know how to do that, why should I not do that. Sure, I can do that -I'll show you. There was a pride element that was triggered. The reality was that they did know what to do, they had always known what to do. It established that when there is a willingness and a capacity it is fulfilling – and there was some money in it for them as well... That a good beginning for the challenges that were ahead.[155]

The outcome was that once the union employees accepted the challenge, they were able to raise their output of blocks from 160 per day to 225, largely through improvements they were able to carry out themselves. Roger was able to cancel the contract to outsource blocks and all block production was returned to the Hagerstown plant.

f. **Management Communication Training** – A key lesson learned was the need for stronger management skills that enabled them to manage differently in a joint management system compared to the more autocratic-top-down system. Fundamental to this new way of managing was improved communication skills and processes. The UMCQP conducted an analysis of the communication skills and practices of individual managers in the plant who were viewed as exemplary communicators to determine what made them exemplary. These principles, techniques and skills were then built into a training program for managers.

g. **Re-launch Employee Involvement Process** – The employee involvement mechanism chosen for the re-launch was not problem-solving teams, fast-teams, or any other ad hoc teams. Instead, it was to reconceive each work group as a team in a structure called Employee Work Units. The approach recognized that moving from the beginning of an employee involvement process to the point that intact work teams can assume up to 80% of the decision making in a work group is a developmental process that may require several years. However, the target is to

---

[155] In-person interview with Roger Johnston, October 29, 2019.

enable each EWU to move through these developmental stages so that over time the group assumes more and more of the decision-making responsibility. The benefits of this evolutionary process will be lower costs, better decisions and quicker decision making.

h. **Symbolic Acts Support Trust Building** – When Jim Stewart took the new General Manager Roger Johnston on a trip through the plant to meet union leaders and union members across the plant this was both a symbolic act as well as a practical 2-way learning activity for both Roger and the people he met. Roger heard first-hand some of the concerns and hopes of the people on the shop floor and at the same time they got a chance to "size-up" their new leader. There were a few other key symbolic acts that also turned out to be very significant in helping return trust to the union management relationship.

When Roger arrived, the shop floor had never had air-conditioning. During a particularly hot spell early in Roger's first year, the plant temperature rose to over 90 degrees. Roger instructed some of his managers to bring in buckets of ice and fill them with water bottles to enable people on the shop floor to get some ice water to help them cope with the heat. No one in the plant had ever done that before and it sent a very strong message that Roger had empathy for the working conditions of the men and women in the plant.

Earlier, in the Ross Rhoads era, several symbolic gestures had been made to reduce the status differences between union and management. Changes included eliminating management parking spaces, changing the color of shirts worn (managers used to wear white, non-management wore blue), eliminating the different color badges for union and management and eliminating the management-only dining room for lunch. These changes had been implemented soon after the Total Quality Initiative was first launched by Ross Rhoads, Bill Nutter and Jim Stewart and they were helpful in sending the message that we "are one organization" and that we will sink or swim together. Another symbolic act by Ross was to send two union skilled tradesmen to Chicago to make a machine purchase decision normally made by management. This act was so significant that received it was given considerable publicity in the plant and in a local newspaper article discussing the Total Quality Process at Mack Trucks.

During the Roger Johnston era another key important symbolic gesture was for Roger to meet with Union Committeemen in the Union Hall outside the plant rather than meet with them on the plant premises. By meeting with union members on "their turf" rather than in his office was another way to level the status differences. However, while this was helpful in building trust with the union, there was a downside.

> *"..trust is earned, you don't get it overnight. You must show it by your actions, on and on and on... It took the collective efforts of meeting with the Committee and giving them the understanding of where we are headed...I could talk with the Committee, the President, the Shop Chairman and all the Committeemen on Thursday morning when they met (in the Union Hall). They would have the second and third shift committeemen there along with the first shift when they came to work. They would know what was going on. Sometimes it was unfair for the supervisors because the committeemen would know what was going on and the supervisors did not. That was a failing. I needed to do that differently."*[156]

Another symbolic act that acknowledged the importance of everyone in the plant was a change in language. It had always been the case in the plant that the terms "management team" and "leadership team" were virtually synonymous. Roger Johnston changed that. He kept the traditional meaning for the management team. However, in talking about the "leadership team" he emphasized that the leadership team for the plant included both the management leadership and the UAW leadership. This was an extension of some changes begun under Ross Rhoads but this change in terminology made explicit what was implicit in the way the Guidance Team was structured and the way leadership was practiced in Hagerstown by Ross Rhoads and Roger Johnston.

---

[156] In-person interview with Roger Johnston, October 29, 2019. n

Lessons Learned from Volvo's Behavior When the Company Took Control of Mack Hagerstown and RVI

In Chapter 4 we described how Volvo played hardball with Hagerstown to extract additional incentives and greater flexibility from the Hagerstown operation. Volvo leaders knew they had maximum leverage in seeking changes before consummating the deal to make Hagerstown the chosen site for locating its North American Powertrain Headquarters. Their demand for "flexibility" – a term that was never defined- was a two-edged sword. The ambiguity of the term and the stakes involved likely caused the Hagerstown team to seek more incentives than would have been required if Volvo had been more specific in its demands. It led the Hagerstown management and union to reopen the local union contract twice in a period of several months and remove language and practices that they felt limited "Volvo's flexibility." It also led them to go back to the State of Maryland and local political leaders in Washington County Maryland who had offered a package of financial incentives to Volvo to save the plant. Once the first offer had been made, the political leaders thought the deal was done. However, when Volvo negotiators said that the deal was not done, they needed "more flexibility" a second time, this did "sweeten the financial package" but left some "singed feathers" not only among Hagerstown management and union officials and the plant workforce but also the state and local politicians. The anxiety and pain felt by the union and management in the Hagerstown Plant from this decision process meant that Volvo had a great deal of work to do to win the hearts of the employees in Hagerstown. Roger Johnston and the union leaders had to quickly get over their anger and hurt feelings and begin to lead the process to move the plant forward under the new owner.

A very helpful "metaphor" Roger used to lead this transformation was his "red thread" concept. His use of the term was to help people in the plant interpret the new language used by Volvo to describe needed changes and link them to similar ideas that people in the plant had experienced in its past years. For example, Volvo packaged much of its philosophy regarding managing people and management by values under the concept of "The Volvo Way." Roger was able to show people the "red thread" that connected what Hagerstown had done in the past in the Total Quality

Process, employee teams, and values management to the Volvo Way. This was a very helpful approach to gaining understanding, acceptance, and trust of their new owners.

If an objective outsider assessed this negotiation, what were the gains and costs for Volvo? Their persistent and ambiguous demand for more flexibility helped the plant move away from many non-competitive practices that had been negotiated in the union contract over a number of years much more quickly than the two parties to the local agreement could have done so without the external pressure from Volvo. It certainly created pain, but the plant was better off after the changes were made. Necessary change can be painful. Was it necessary for the plant leadership to seek additional financial incentives from the Maryland politicians? Certainly, Volvo welcomed the additional State and local contributions. Were the financial incentives critical to the deal? We cannot know for sure, but this author doubts it. However, when your back is against the wall, it is hard not to seek every possible resource to make the deal. That is what the Hagerstown leadership did, and it worked!

Lessons Learned from the Roger Johnston Period - Phase 2- 2004-2007

a. **Volvo Assumes Control and Raises the Bar** – As a global company, Volvo's performance standard was by necessity nothing less than world class performance. It is easy to say the word "world-class". However, translating that standard into daily work processes across the plant does not happen overnight. We learned that lesson the hard way. One method used to operationally define world-class performance for each person working in the new MD production area was the Performance Matrix. The design of the Matrix, described in some detail in Chapter 5 defined levels of performance for each of the 7 major performance criteria in the manufacturing organization. This was an ambitious undertaking that had value in the training in explaining operationally what the "journey to world class" looked like for each work group. However, it also was planned to be used as a tool in the workplace for coordinators and work teams to support the transition from management goal setting to goal setting and planning by teams. As is described later, this only happened in machining areas and not on the assembly line.

b. **New Organization Structure of Volvo North America Powertrain-** The organizational structure change creating North America Powertrain made all the key organizational units in Hagerstown report to a Division Senior VP instead of functional unit heads in the headquarters organization in Allentown. This structure, especially when Sten-Åke Arronson came to Hagerstown created much greater collaboration and alignment between Engineering, Purchasing and Manufacturing.

c. **Global Business Plan-** When Volvo Powertrain launched its 2004-2007 Business Plan and communicated it effectively to all levels of the organization in Hagerstown it gave the people within the North American Powertrain organization a better understanding of how they fit into the global organization, a clearer sense of direction and a better sense of security that they have a future.

d. **Launch of MD manufacturing "plant within a plant"** – When demolition and new construction of the new assembly line (called the MD assembly line) appeared in the Hagerstown plant, spirits in the plant really began to improve as people could more clearly see the future. This future took on even greater clarity as volunteers were solicited to move into the new "plant within the plant" and as the first group of employees were trained in the elements of the new culture. Managers and employees were required to sign their respective pre-requisites document that was a commitment to support and live the new MD Culture.

The first group of employees received approximately 4 weeks of training and orientation to the new production area. This extensive training really helped them have a successful launch of the production of new product and success in building the new culture. As new groups of employees were brought into the MD area, the training became more streamlined as the training process improved and as production pressures for both the legacy engine that was still being produced and the MD product increased. After the legacy engine that was still being produced in the old part of the plant was phased out and people were forced to either enter the MD culture or leave the plant some problems surfaced. Two things produced them. One was that the last group of people to enter the MD area were more resistant to the culture change than the earlier groups who volunteered for the change. Second, by the time these more resistant people entered the MD area, the amount of training had been cut extensively from the 4 weeks for group 1. Basically, it became on-the-job training which eliminated virtually all of the cultural change content. Because of this, the relatively "pure" MD culture that group 1 experienced had become much less rigorous and departed significantly from the originally envisioned MD culture. The gap between the envisioned culture described in the training and the behaviors in practice on the shop floor grew.

It is easy to criticize the fact that the training program content was reduced for those individuals needed more training for them in order for them to accept the changes and function well in the new culture. However, the pressures for meeting engine delivery schedules were real. As production pressures grew, managers and committeemen tended to fall back into their old ways of working. It was difficult for management to justify taking people off the line for training that did not seem essential to their immediate task of assembling engines. The lesson learned was these decisions really were an indicator of the fact that manufacturing management and union committeemen on the shop floor had not fully accepted the new culture and that they lacked the skills to meet production goals in the new way.

e. **Difficulties in deploying the "coordinator" position** – One illustration of how the reality of the culture change departed from the vision was in the problems associated with establishing the role of "coordinator". Both the union and management underestimated the difficulty in performing the coordinator role as originally envisioned. This difficulty was increased as the amount of training given to the new entrants to the MD area was reduced. The key lessons learned with respect to coordinators were that in a union environment you cannot have coordinators elected by the work teams. Second, the original term for a coordinator was approximately 6 months. This was much too short as there is considerable difficulty in learning the skills to perform the coordinator role. We also overestimated the extent to which the union committeemen supported the creation of the coordinator role. Looking back to this period, Dave Perkins, who had been the union President at the time stated:

> *Even among elected union officials support for the position (i.e., coordinator) was about 50-50. A lot of people looked at the position as a union protected, management puppet...We put coordinators in there and who were elected by the team members. What happened then was, if you wanted to be re-elected, you could not really do the job that coordinators were elected to do. If you did the role, you were not re-elected...Coordinators were something we were constantly changing and trying to get right. I'm not sure we ever got it right. Even to this day.*[157]

f. ***Other Lessons Learned from the MD cultural transformation***
In addition to the lessons learned about training and difficulties with the coordinator function deployment, there were several lessons learned about the move to require uniforms in the MD production area. The rationale for uniforms were that (1) they reinforced the message of professionalism and world class performance; (2) they sent a strong message to customers and visitors to the plant that the culture and performance standards had been raised; and (3) the uniforms worn by union and management alike further reduced status differences in the plant and emphasized the message that "we are one team". There was definitely symbolic value in deploying the uniforms, but it is fair to say that the difficulties of launching this "symbol" were underestimated. Difficulties included finding U.S. suppliers (a requirement of the UAW when the UAW logo is displayed on the shirts) with an acceptable range of products. The lack of flexibility within available suppliers made it very difficult to find garments that fit both men and women and were also attractive

---

[157] In-person interview with David Perkins, September 14, 2021.

and comfortable. Even the decision regarding uniform color that was appropriate for a plant that manufactured products for two brands that each had their own color differentiation for products. Mack was red and Volvo was blue. Finding a color that did not signify either Mack or Volvo and that was attractive and practical created difficulties. David Perkins, to his credit, addressed a "root cause" for some of these difficulties. His comment was specifically referring to the coordinator position, however I believe his analysis could also be applied to some of the other decisions such as uniforms.

> *"The coordinators were where we failed the most going into the MD System. We tried to be too responsive to the criticism we knew we would get to try to create team leaders – we built in too many safeguards- elected, 6-month tenure, etc. ...we put them in an untenable position by having them be elected by the team. The union thought that was what we had to do to sell this to our membership. The mistake was on our part."*[158]

As David Perkins made this analysis, he did it with approximately 17 years of hindsight, having had time to watch how the position of coordinator, which is now called "Value Team Captain," has continued to evolve in the Volvo Hagerstown Plant. He was also speaking about decisions made at a time as he, as a relatively new Union President, was chosen in a very contentious election.

Another well-meaning effort, that had limited value at the time, was the effort to integrate the Performance Matrix into the role of the coordinator. The purpose of the Matrix was to enable employee teams to operationally define the meaning of world class performance for their team for each of their key performance dimensions (e.g., Cost, Quality, Delivery, Safety Health and Work Environment, Environmental Performance, etc.). It was also an effort to shift from top-down goal setting by management to more bottom's up goal setting by teams that were fully knowledgeable about the plant's business strategy and their responsibility to perform. Placing

[158] Ibid.

the requirement on well-trained, skilled coordinators would have been a challenge. But to expect new coordinators trying to find their way in navigating this new MD Culture was too ambitious. As the facilitator of this effort, I was a strong advocate for the development and use of the matrix. However, in retrospect, it was overly ambitious.

When I asked Dave Perkins if there was any evidence that the matrix concept helped promote goal setting by teams he said:

> *"Not in the assembly area. I saw that happen and we had more success in the crankshaft/camshaft machining areas than we did in the assembly areas. But that is because of the nature of those jobs, and they were much smaller departments. It was easier when you have just one small group of 6-10 people. It is not like an assembly area where you must complete your work every 3 minutes. You must keep the assembly line supplied with cams and cranks, but the time pressure is not quite as strong as the assembly line. In the cam and crank areas they set a lot of their goals."*[159]

g. **Bringing Experienced Global Leader to Hagerstown** – An excellent decision made by Senior Volvo Powertrain leaders was to send an experienced, global leader to be the Senior VP for Volvo North American Powertrain. This man was Sten-Åke Aronsson. Sten-Åke seemed to have the perfect blend of experience, wisdom, strength, humility, and cultural sensitivity to lead North American Powertrain through its continued transformation under the Volvo and Mack brands.

In writing this book, I asked Sten-Åke, who had returned to his native Sweden following his three-year assignment in Hagerstown, if he would share some of his lessons learned from this experience. He was graciously agreed, and his memory was keen enough to provide some very thoughtful advice to anyone who might be in a similar cross-cultural senior leadership position. Before coming to Volvo Trucks, Sten-Åke had been Managing

[159] In-person interview with David Perkins, September 14, 2021.

Director and CEO at SKF both in Sweden and in South Africa. After coming to Volvo Trucks, he had responsibility for R&D, Purchasing and Manufacturing. These were the three major organizations in Volvo Powertrain located in Hagerstown. So Sten-Åke was very knowledgeable in all three of these functional areas and had experience in creating synergy among these three key organizations. Mainly due to history, getting close collaboration among these three functional areas in Hagerstown was a continuing challenge. Even though they were co-located in the plant, they had historically each reported to separate functional areas at Mack Headquarters in Allentown, Pennsylvania.

Before being assigned to Hagerstown, Sten-Åke led a group of Volvo leaders and consultants who had to recommend to Volvo Powertrain Headquarters the most appropriate location for North America Powertrain. One can only imagine the conversation that might have gone on between Sten-Åke and Lars-Goran Moberg, President of Volvo Powertrain after Sten-Åke came back from his site selection travels. It might have gone like this:

> *Moberg; "Well Sten-Åke, what is your recommendation for the location of North American Powertrain?"*
>
> *Aronsson: "Sir, after considering all our options, we recommend locating the North American Powertrain Headquarters in the Hagerstown, Maryland plant.*
>
> *Moberg: Are you confident this is the best option?*
>
> *Aronsson: Yes sir. We believe this choice presents the minimum risk due to knowledgeable people in both the R&D and manufacturing organizations. We believe it is less risky also compared to building at a new location where we will have to continue to produce today's products and then close part of the plant after the legacy product expires. We also found the management and the union in Hagerstown to be supportive and we found that the Mack management in Allentown also would support this decision.*

Moberg: Well Aronsson, if you are so sure this is the right decision, I think you should move to Hagerstown and run this operation and prove to us that your recommendation is correct!

My attempt to imagine this dialog is purely hypothetical. However, it was fortuitous for both Hagerstown and Volvo Powertrain that Sten-Åke Aronsson came to Hagerstown.

What did Sten-Åke learn from this experience that would be useful to another CEO coming to a new situation in a country that was not his own. These are some thoughts that Sten-Åke shared with me after reflecting on his experiences that occurred more than 15 years prior to our communication. [160]. These thoughts from a very wise leader can be seen as timeless lessons learned.

(1). **You must live at the place and not visit the place some hours now and then** – Effective leadership of a transformation cannot be performed by so-called "helicopter management" in which the leader flies in and out every so often. An example of why this is important is described in an anecdote from Sten-Åke. This occurred shortly after his arrival in Hagerstown when many members of the workforce were still upset about the anxiety that the "hardball" negotiations produced before the Hagerstown site was announced as the location for North American Powertrain.

I happened to hear rumors saying that Volvo will "kill the bulldog"! We had bought our first bulldog when living in South Africa. However, working at Mack it became natural to buy a Bulldog puppy. We named it Max. To prove that I was not a Bulldog killer I brought Max into the plant. I know that made some impressions. In the plant magazine we also had a photo of me with Mack President Paul Vikner and Max in the middle between

---

[160] Email correspondence with Sten-Åke Aronsson, January 10, 2022. In the correspondence, Sten-Åke shared the comments in bold italics numbered 1-5. The elaboration on those points came from the author and were not reviewed by Sten-Åke.

> *us. After that, I never heard any more rumors about me being there to kill the bulldog![161]*

It is unlikely that a "helicopter manager" would have been as sensitive to plant rumors as a leader who lived on-site. Sten-Åke, with his experience, understood the importance of putting an end to this rumor and understood what a powerful message it would send for him to walk into the plant during the third shift with Max his bulldog. However, even more importantly, by living on site the leader becomes part of the community and gains an understanding of the local culture. It also enables members of the community to get to know the leader as a human being. Because of Sten-Åke's experience and personality this enabled him to be seen as a "real person" not an elitist from a different culture. His personal interactions in the plant and the community earned him enormous respect.

(2). **You must love to work with all people involved, including union members and leaders, and be a good listener.** Sten-Åke's interactions with management and union leaders in the plant authentically demonstrated this principle by his behavior. It took a while for members of the plant community who had been conditioned by Volvo's strong insistence of "more flexibility" which was interpreted as an owner that could never be satisfied to believe that Sten-Åke's empathy and sincerity was real. However, in a short while he overcame the plant members feelings about Volvo leadership being unreasonably demanding.

(3). **It is an advantage if you know the products and processes.** One of the means that Sten-Åke utilized to quickly win the respect of all levels of people in the plant was his demonstrated knowledge and understanding of the total range of work in the plant. He was able to knowledgeably converse with people on the shop floor regarding manufacturing processes, with engineering managers about engine design and testing methods, and with purchasing managers about vendor management. He was also able to lead the executive team through his knowledge regarding the processes of creating and implementing global business strategy. In these conversations, he was not giving orders, he was

---

[161] Sten-Åke Aronsson, January 10, 2022, email correspondence.

engaging in a two-way dialog and always respecting the others involved.

(4). ***You must communicate what you want to achieve and when it should be done.*** No one would come away from a conversation with Sten-Åke with uncertainty regarding his desired outcome. He exuded strength and competence. However, he understood that there could be roadblocks and that everything he wanted could not happen immediately. He had a realistic understanding of the pace of change; however, it was also clear that he would persistently pursue the goal. The pressure to change and the need to change to continue the transformation would not go away.

(5). ***Finally, it's like riding a bicycle. When you can ride, you don't consider why it was difficult to learn. Some people, regardless of education will never succeed, while others will just do it.*** With Sten-Åke in charge of North America Powertrain, the conditions for success for the Manufacturing Division of Powertrain led by VP Roger Johnston and Union President David Perkins were greatly enhanced. The initial period of Volvo ownership was painful for Hagerstown. However, the conditions to enable its survival could not have been more perfectly created by the leadership team Volvo had in place in 2004.

Conclusion

My motive in writing this book was to tell a story that was lived by an exemplary group of people. As a participant in the story, I cannot be totally objective because I was not only engaged in the story as a paid consultant, but I also became quite emotionally engaged in the story because it dealt with many fundamental truths. My consulting involvement ended 15 years ago as this is being written. In retrospect, what really stands out in my mind are those fundamental truths. In my final interview with Roger Johnston, conducted as he was in the late stages of his struggle with ALS, the fundamental truths took on even more poignancy.

In my final interaction with Roger, I asked him: "Why should anyone else care about this story?" Here is his response:

"What I believe, fundamentally, is that wherever operations exist that are part of an economic structure in a community… there is a dependence on that community and there surprisingly, usually, are a limited number of people who can either make or break those entities. A small group can determine not only that they can survive or thrive or that they atrophy and disappear. The influence of a business of any kind on a community is amazingly high through the taxes paid, income provided and the purchases they make, etc. If you take that on as a business leader, you have a responsibility to the community in which you operate. Remember, I had been to Flint. I have lived there. I have seen the devastation that can be the consequence of that limited group of people who have it in their hands to affect the outcome of many and failed to do so. If that small group of people fail to recognize their responsibility, then many people suffer. How best do you maximize the opportunity to secure the future of that operation? How do you marshal the resources that are at your disposal for the benefit of the greater good? That is the challenge. That is a huge motivation for me."[162]

What a different world it would be if every business leader, every government official, every elected official, even every parent asked themselves daily "How do I marshal the resources that are at my disposal for the benefit of the greater good?"

Roger went on to describe how he as a capitalist, a believer in capitalism, felt that a focus on the "greater good" should be the objective of a capitalist.

"I am a capitalist by nature, and if you ask me why a business exists – I will tell you it exists to make money. How do you make money – you must satisfy customers. So, how do you satisfy customers? Now we are getting down to the nut that must be cracked. How do you help everybody (within the business) understand what that looks like? I

---

[162] In-person interview with Roger Johnston, October 29, 2019.

love to speak to the new employees. I told them that I will tell you a lot of things and you may forget some of them, but there are two things that I don't want you to forget. 1. Change is constant. You will find yourself asking 'why are we changing that again'? Well, think about the world we live in. It is changing around us all the time. And we are in a race. If we are walking, and our competitors are running, we are not going to win. Change is constant and that is not a bad thing. 2. The second issue is 'Who do we work for?' In this organization this is a complicated question. Some will say 'I work for Mack'. Some will say, 'I work for Volvo'. In the Renault days, some would say they own us so I must work for Renault. Ultimately, we work for the customer. Think about that. Think about that guy driving across Kansas in the middle of snowstorm. Think about that guy driving into New York with a load of chickens. Think about those guys. They are the customer. Also, think about the guy who owns the trucking company. Or the independent owner who has taken out a note and mortgaged his house and is trying to make a go of it with that truck. Think about that person. That is who we work for. Somebody else will put the numbers on the paycheck. That is fine, but we work for the customer. If we satisfy the customer, that other person who puts the name on the paycheck -there is a pretty good chance they will be satisfied too."[163]

A final comment from Roger regarding why someone should be interested in this story provides a lesson learned from the Mack, Renault, Volvo story that could be applied to the political division that is threatening the democracy of the U.S. as well as other nations.

"There are so many things today – such as the expectations of the new work force who do want to be intellectually challenged and want to be involved and engaged in the business, but they do not want to be consumed by it. One

[163] In-person interview with Roger Johnston, October 29, 2019.

*of the ways to avoid being consumed by the business....
is to spread the load, spread the tasks and have more
people capable of fulfilling them. Inherently, most people
are able to do more than physical work. They have the
intellect in their daily lives to do things so why not allow
them to use that intellectual horsepower in their working
time? Getting more people involved in the activity of
the enterprise is an important aspect of what happened
here. But how do you get there? What is the "bridge"
that made so much of this possible? It was breaking
down the barriers of "us" and "them." "You believe
that!" so surely, "I can't agree with you on this". When
you think about society today, we have so much of this
identity politics, and it pushes people into corners. If we
as a company stayed there, we would have died. So, as a
nation can we find a way to get away from the "poles"
that the magnetism draws us to and take advantage of the
collective intelligence we have as a nation? We need to use
that collective intelligence for our competitive benefit. If
we don't, others will.*[164]

Roger's challenge to us, and the challenge presented by this story is whether we will, in whatever roles we occupy, answer the call posed by his question. "How do I marshal the resources at my disposal for the benefit of the greater good?" To use the metaphor from Warren Buffet at the beginning of this chapter, if we respond positively to this challenge, we will be remembered as "tree planters." Fortunately, in Hagerstown, Maryland today, some people are enjoying the shade from the trees planted by the exemplary leaders whose story we have told.

---

[164] Ibid.

Epilogue

In the years following Roger Johnston's and Sten-Åke Aronssen's departure from Hagerstown, David Perkins remained in his role as President of the local union. Dave had two priorities that he wanted to leave behind when the time came for him to move to his next role. One of these priorities was to bring into the plant a benefit of company sponsored health care for employees and their families. The second was to find a way to bring back into the plant production of the "carrier" production that was outsourced shortly after Dave was hired in Hagerstown. His challenge was to find a way to convince the new management team that it was in their interest to implement these two initiatives.

After working with the new leaders, Dave developed his strategy. He quickly realized that these two leaders were primarily concerned with being viewed as successful and climbing the corporate ladder. The new management team for the plant brought in a different management style that Dave described as being the antithesis of Roger Johnston. Dave, very astutely, had to frame the two priorities as being instrumental to the new managers career aspirations.

In order to have success, it was essential that Dave be willing to show how the two initiatives could make these two new leaders look good in the eyes of their bosses. Even though these were Dave's ideas, he had to be willing to let these new leaders take the credit if they were successful.

The way Dave managed to work with the plant manager to enable this work to return to Hagerstown was to recognize that the plant manager needed to find a way to fill up vacant space in the plant with work that would improve the utilization of plant facilities. However, he was not willing to pay more to have this work done in-house than he was paying to have it done outside the plant. So Dave Perkins and the union were presented with the challenge to bring work back but to only pay workers doing this work approximately $8 less per hour than regular engine assemblers. In order to sell this idea to his members Dave had to be very creative. He described the solution as follows:

> *"We setup the rules. No one would be forced to take it, you have the right to say I would rather be laid off rather than take a $16 per hour job. You could never force anyone who was already there to take these jobs. But there are people in the community who wanted a $16 an hour job with the benefits we offered. It worked so well that there was no issue when we asked management to raise them up to full rate because we got rid of the guys sweeping the floor making $24 per hour. These were trade-offs that you have to make. The plant manager did that not because it would be the greatest thing for the union. He was actually looking at it for himself. But that is fine. When he laid everything out, there was no subterfuge on his part or mine. We sat there together to work to bring this work in. "*[165]

The second priority for David was providing company sponsored health care for employees and their families. Again, he worked with management and built a hard-nose, rigorous business case for the idea.

"We brought in a full scale doctor's office- like urgent care on steroids. We have physical therapy, we have multiple physicians, they treat you and your family, the only stipulation is that the children have to be over 1 year old because we could not get the pediatrician to treat infants. The Clinic is called "Family First Health Care Center." It treats employees, treats their families, it is free to employees and free to families with no co-pays. We even started to draw blood and send it out to an outside lab so you don't

---

[165] Personal interview with David Perkins, September 14, 2021.

have to go to an outside lab. The facility is located in the plant. It is at the main entrance so families do not have to go into the plant.

The business model said you can now control many of the medical costs that the company had been paying. For example, if every employee went out for a physical, here is the cost to the company. If they took that physical in an in-house clinic the cost was 40% of what it would be on the outside. If we had 40-50% of our employees participating in the clinic it would represent several million dollars in savings.

Not only that, you also have convenience. A guy has a chest cold and before he would say I'm not going to leave work just for that. Then the chest cold proceeds to bronchitis and he would miss 4-5 days of work. So lost work time savings by getting that chest cold treated at the early stages was another major source of savings, not to mention the lack of spreading the cold to others in the plant. We put a Walgreens pharmacy in where people could pick up everything except specialty medication. And the medication could be obtained at a discount.

This clinic model has spread to two other Mack/Volvo facilities and it is a benchmark for other UAW sites. It is a huge attraction for employees and for employee retention.

I asked Dave if these innovations happened due to the honesty between union and management or was it that they had shared goals?

> *"I don't think it was shared goals. It was an alignment of different objectives. My objective was to get the carrier back (and the medical clinic.). It was not really my objective to have more dues paying members, but I wanted to have more work in the plant. That makes Hagerstown more stable and the more work we have the less likely it was to be shut down. The plant manager's goal was to make himself look good, show the money he saved and that he was a good thinker. Our objectives aligned with each other to get what we both wanted. But*

it was honesty with each other that allowed us to obtain that alignment. [166]

This honesty between the union and management leaders, enabled David, the leader of the UAW, and the plant leadership to leave a very positive legacy in Hagerstown.

---

[166] Personal interview with David Perkins, September 14, 2021.

APPENDICES

APPENDIX A

PARTNERSHIP FOR THE FUTURE TEAM CHARTERS

MACK-UAW GUIDANCE TEAM

CHARTER

Purpose - To develop and deploy a partnership that will allow us to become and prove every day we are the world's best with respect to quality, cost, delivery and plant cleanliness.

Membership -(alphabetical)

S. Broadwater
D. Hollinger
A. Gozora
R. Johnston
J. Leigh
B. Shoop
J. Stewart

D. Stoner
D. Williams
Union Committeeman - Production
Union Committeeman - Maintenance

If members are in the building, they are expected to attend the meeting. In the event that a member is not in the building, a substitute may be sent. However, it is expected that a regular substitute be named, and the member has the responsibility to assure that the substitute is fully briefed and able to participate.

Boundaries / Limitations

Team will work within the parameters of the national and local labor contracts. The contract will be considered a foundation for the partnership.

The Guidance Team will support and enable Department Leadership Teams. The Guidance Team will not micromanage the functional departments.

Meeting Schedule -

The guidance team will meet every other week - generally for 2 hours. Meeting dates through March are: 1/26; 2/10; 2/23; 3/2; 3/16; 3/30.

Magnitude of Improvement Expected

- The plant will meet business plan targets annually.
- Fast teams will be established as required to obtain breakthrough results on critical processes and bottlenecks.
- By 1/1/2000 there will be a significant improvement in the Human Synergistics Survey results.
- By 12/30/2000 Continuous Improvement process will be deployed to all basic work units.

- By 2001, Mack-Hagerstown will be chosen to not only assemble the next generation engine but to also produce major components of the next generation engine.

Customer / Approval Authority for the Guidance Team

- Customer is the people of the Hagerstown Plant
- Approval authority for expenditures follows spending authority guidelines in the Mack / RVI chain of command.

Reporting Requirements

- Regular reports of progress will be made to the people in the plant.
- The guidance team will review progress of the plant regularly and keep itself informed of progress against its performance expectations.

Meeting Groundrules

- Meetings will start and end on time.
- If a member is in the plant, he/she will attend the meeting. If member is not in the plant a designated alternate will attend. Member is responsible to assure that the alternate is fully briefed and able to participate fully.
- No character assassination will be allowed.
- All members will focus on the issues.
- There will be a specific agenda distributed one week in advance. Members will come to the meeting prepared. The agenda will be followed.
- Minutes will be taken at all meetings and distributed within Departments throughout the plant.

Communications Team Charter

1. **Purpose:** To improve communication effectiveness in the plant through assuring that appropriate communication processes are continuously improved.

2. **Members:**

Denny Hollinger
Warren Jeffries
Jim Leigh
Jim Stewart
Danny Stoner
Roy Tressler
Transmission Rep (TBD)

3. **Boundaries:** Team will work within the parameters of the national and local labor contracts. The contract will be considered a foundation for the partnership.

4. **Meeting Schedule** The team will meet weekly as indicated below:

Date	Time	Place
2/23	11:00	Customer Center
3/2	10:30	Exec. Conf. Room
3/9	10:30	Customer Center
3/16	10:30	Customer Center
3/30	10:30	Customer Center
4/6	10:30	Customer Center
4/13	10:30	TBD

5. **Improvement Expected** - The team will administer a baseline communication survey. Improvement targets will be defined in terms of this baseline survey results.

6. **Customer / Approval Authority** -. The customers for the team are everyone in the plant. A more precise definition of the customer is those people in the plant who have ownership of a particular communication media or communication process. The approval

authority for recommendations is the Plant Guidance Team. The final approval authority for the team rests with the Plant Manager.

Charter

Basic Work Unit Team

1. **Purpose** - Promote Continuous Improvement through basic work units, employee suggestions, and FAST teams.
2. **Membership -**

Arnie Gozora
Al Huston
Bobby Shoop
Dale Williams

3. **Boundaries / Limitations** - The team will work within the parameters of the national and local labor contracts. The basic work units and other employee involvement approaches must operate within in the constraints of existing budget and manpower levels.
4. **Meeting Schedule** - The Basic Work unit team will meet as follows:

Date	Time	Room
Feb. 24	11:00 - 12:00	Customer Center
March 3	2:30 - 3:30	Customer Center
March 16	2:30 - 3:30	TBD
March 30	2:30 - 3:30	Customer Center

5. Magnitude of Improvement Expected - The basic work unit team will judge its success in terms of the indicators tracked in the Mack Hagerstown business plan.

By December 30, 2000, Basic work units will be fully deployed and chartered in all appropriate areas across the plant.

6. **Customer / Approval Authority**- Customers for the team are the basic work units.

The Approval Authority for the team recommendations is the Guidance Team. Final approval authority rests with the plant manager.

Charter

Other Manufacturing Expenses (OME) Team

1. **Purpose** - To facilitate the OME cost reduction of 2 million by informing, tracking, publishing, and assuring that there is an effective system for continuous improvement of OME costs. The elements of the improvement system may include communication, performance feedback, individual and team problem solving, suggestions, FAST teams, and basic work units.
2. **Membership - (Alphabetical)**

Steve Broadwater
Arnie Gozora
Billy Rhodes
Dale Williams

3. **Boundaries / Limitations** - The team will work within the parameters of the national and local labor contracts. The OME team will operate within the parameters of existing vendor codes or seek change in these codes through formal channels.
4. **Meeting Schedule** - The OME team will meet as follows:

Date	Time	Room
Feb. 24	9:30-10:30	Customer Center
March 3	1:00-2:00	Customer Center
March 10	9:30-10:30	TBD

March 16	1:00-2:00	TBD
March 30	1:00-2:00	Customer Center

5. **Magnitude of Improvement Expected** - The OME team will produce and increase in awareness of the significance in OME costs as measured by an OME survey (or item in communication survey.)

   - There will be an increasing trend of OME awareness as measured by plant audits of bulletin boards and team meeting agendas.
   - OME cost trends will show a decrease toward the 2 million target.
   - The effectiveness of OME information transmittal will be measured by a survey or item in another survey.

6. **Customer / Approval Authority-** Customers for the team are the plant departments, communication team and basic work unit team.

The Approval Authority for the team recommendations is the Guidance Team. Final approval authority rests with the plant manager.

APPENDIX B

HIGH PERFORMANCE MATRICES

	QUALITY (V2)
100 %	The team meets all internal customer requirements. Team quality performance shows no negative trends in any area related to internal customer requirements. A systematic process is in place to anticipate changes in customer requirements and take action to maintain process capability. Team has gone a minimum of 1 year without scrap/rework (other than by tool breakage or power outages).Team makes an *annual* minimum of 4 significant process improvements (as judged by Plant Manager and Staff).
80%	The team meets most internal customer requirements. Positive trends exist in most metrics related to internal customer requirements. All Key Control Characteristics are under statistical process control and demonstrate process capability of 1.33 or greater.
60%	A process is in place to measure internal customer satisfaction. A systematic process is in place to take action to improve internal customer satisfaction based on the data. Analytical tools and processes are used by operators to insure consistent product quality. A preventive approach to problems is evident. All Key Control Characteristics are in-spec. Some evidence of the use of design of experiments for process improvement is available.
40%	Key Control Characteristics have been identified for all processes. Key Control Characteristics have been validated (substantiated) in relation to external customer requirements. A plan/do/study/act problem solving methodology is in place.
20%	Team has defined its internal customers and their requirements. Team members understand work instructions.
0%	Team has not identified its internal customers and has little understanding of their requirements.

	SKILL DEVELOPMENT (V2)[1]
100 %	Many team members have demonstrated competence in advanced financial analysis (e.g.cash flow analysis, etc.) . All team members have demonstrated knowledge pertaining to the department budget. Each team member has demonstrated competence in performing 100% of the jobs within the team. The team has at least four qualified trainers for each job on the team.
80%	Many team members have demonstrated competence in intermediate financial analysis (e.g. cost-benefit analysis, etc.) and advanced computer skills (e.g. word processing, power point and spreadsheet analysis, etc). Some members have demonstrated competence in advanced statistical analysis. Most team members have financial understanding of department budget. Each team member can perform 75% of the jobs in the team without supervision and the team has at least three qualified trainers for each job on the team.
60%	All team members have demonstrated competence in team problem solving, group process skills,meeting management, and group decision making. All team members have demonstrated financial understanding pertaining to costs within the team and some understand the department budget. Most have demonstrated competence in basic computer skills, and basic statistical analysis. Some have demonstrated competence in intermediate financial analysis (e.g. cost-benefit analysis). Each team member can perform at least half the jobs in the team without supervision and each team member can train others in at least 3 jobs. The team has at least two qualified trainers for each job on the team.
40%	The team has defined an annual training and development plan for each member which recognizes skill needs that are aligned with the Division business plan and as shown as the goal on the versatility diagram. Planned development milestones and targets have been met. Most team members have demonstrated competence in team problem solving skills (PDSA), group process skills, meeting management, and group decision making. Most team members have demonstrated financial knowledge pertaining to costs within the team and some team members have demonstrated competence in basic computer skills. Each team member can perform at least three jobs in the team without supervision and has familiarity of the functions of all jobs on the team. The team has a qualified trainer for each job on the team.
20%	The team has developed requirements for the versatility diagram. Some team members have demonstrated competence with team problem solving skills (PDSA), group process skills, meeting management, and group decision making. Some team members have demonstrated financial knowledge pertaining to costs within the team. Each team member is qualified to perform at least one job in the team without supervision and has familiarity with at least half the jobs in the team.
0%	Training is on-the-job, as needed. Some specialized formal training is provided in response to changes in the workplace (e.g. new equipment, tooling, personnel changes, new product changes, etc.)

[1]This matrix dimension is based on the assumption that the EWU consists of 6-12 members who perform a Meaningful "piece" of work (e.g. component, sub-process, maintenance of a defined area, etc.)

	EMPOWERMENT (V2)
100 %	The team establishes its own performance objectives and budget with knowledge of and in alignment with department and plant goals. It monitors performance in relation to these objectives and determines the gap between planned and actual results. The team adjusts resources (people, materials, etc.) within budgeted limits to achieve the goals. The team participates in capital project planning that relates to team activities.
80%	The team proposes its operational budget and business plan targets and manages its work within the assigned budget and business objectives. Team members evaluate performance of the team against the team performance metrics and targets. Team members develop work schedules to meet production requirements, address absenteeism or overtime requirements. Team members monitor team member performance and counsel employees as required. The team members participate in joint improvement efforts with other functions to prevent problems.
60%	The team implements and documents solutions to meet team goals for Quality, Cost, and Delivery and waste elimination. The team participates with other teams (e.g. support functions, production functions, etc.) to prevent problems and avoid waste. The team members plan and conduct celebrations in response to achieving performance milestones.
40%	The team formulates team performance goals that align with QDC goals for the Department/Plant. The team participates with support teams (e.g. maintenance, purchasing, etc.) to solve tooling/maintenance problems. The team utilizes a systematic, fact based process to identify "waste" (e.g. scrap, rework, delays, leaks, emissions, downtime, idle time, etc.) and utilizes a systematic process to reduce waste and the sources of waste.
20%	The team sets team rules within plant guidelines. Decide on leadership within the team. Reports tooling, maintenance, and process problems. The team understands QDC goals for the Division. The team fulfills requirements for certification as an EWU.
0%	Team is in the early forming stages. Little or no team leadership is in place. Team is relying on traditional supervision/management for guidance

	COST (V2)
100 %	**Team has met budget for each line item for the past 12 months.** Team drives efforts to find new sources of revenue.
80%	Team participates in business planning process and makes forecasts for cost reductions. Team has met its line item budget for 90% of the items for the past 12 months. Team evaluates impact of its budget changes on other operations.
60%	The team systematically reacts to budget line items that are trending negatively. Meets or exceeds budget for 75% of the line items in the team budget.
40%	The team participates in the development of the departmental and team budget. Team members monitor, document and review performance against the overall team budget on a monthly basis and make corrective action to address variances.
20%	Team understands its assigned budget and manages its expenses to be within 5% of the total budget target at the end of each quarter.
0%	The team is not aware of its budget and does not monitor costs at the team level.

	DELIVERY (V2)
100 %	Team has fully implemented Demand Flow Technology. Inventory is measured in hours. Kanbans are sized appropriately to meet needs of key customers. For maintenance organizations, the percent of maintenance hours devoted to preventive maintenance exceeds that of benchmark organizations. There is immediate response by maintenance to critical production machine problems.
80%	Team implements appropriate aspects of demand flow technology. Team participates in efforts to reduce lead time for its products or service. Service organizations have shown reductions in service lead times and cycle times.
60%	Team Understands cost of inventory for their piece of the operation. The team participates in training for and adoption of demand flow technology. Service organizations have shown reductions in backlog of service requests.
40%	Team members understand input material, work in process and output and its impact on inventory accuracy. Team members understand the manufacturing management system and its relationship to schedule and inventory accuracy. Service team tracks its performance in relation to its standards for responsiveness and delivery. The team demonstrates schedule accomplishment and conformity.
20%	Team understands internal and external customer schedule requirements, understands how requirements are translated to Departmental schedule, and understands how team schedule supports Departmental schedule. Service team develops standards for responsiveness and delivery.
0%	Team is not aware of the requirements of external and internal customers. Does not understand the relationship between team and departmental schedules.

	SAFETY, HEALTH AND WORK ENVIRONMENT (V2)
100 %	The EWU extends its prevention programs to include member's activities off the job and to member's families. Team has achieved a safety focus factor > 95% for the past 12 months. All team members participate in wellness, preventive health or fitness programs.
80%	Team works with Divisional Ergonomic Team in order to identify and remove potential ergonomic risks. The team proactively identifies hazards, near-misses, and ergonomic risks and takes action to remove potential problems. Team has obtained safety focus factor of > 95% for the past 6 months. Team members have not had a lost time accident for the past 12 months. Most team members participate in wellness, preventive health or fitness programs.
60%	Team has a current job safety analysis for each job in the team. Team participates in process safety analyses to identify and remove hazards. Team obtains safety focus factor of >90% for six consecutive months. Team members have had zero lost time accidents within the past 6 months. Some members participate in wellness, preventive health or fitness programs.
40%	EWU conducts safety and health audits and initiates corrective action. Team obtains safety focus factor > 90% for two consecutive months. Team members have had zero lost time accidents within the past quarter.
20%	Team incorporates safety and health issues into EWU meetings according to Plant Safety Office schedule. All team members have received basic safety training. Team either has one or more members on an active safety team, or is in regular contact with departmental safety team. Team reports demerit status within 30 days to the Safety Office.
0%	Team has not met safety training requirements as scheduled by safety office and is unable to demonstrate knowledge of basic regulatory guidelines. Department lacks an active safety team.

	ENVIRONMENT (V2)
100 %	The team has a documented and systematic process in place to reduce waste in all forms. The team produces zero hazardous waste and shows continuous reduction (per unit of production) in utility and raw material consumption. Long-term tracking is in place and well documented.
80%	Team members are actively involved in developing and implementing opportunities for improvement of environmental performance. The team identifies opportunities to reduce adverse environmental impact outside the factory, in the community and beyond.
60%	The team can show positive trends with respect to waste reduction and environmental impact. Team members understand how process changes can impact waste generation, utility or raw material consumption. The team assists the Department in improving environmental performance.
40%	All EWU members understand the environmental impact of their job and how his/her actions impact waste generation, environmental impact, and risk. The team is ISO 14001 compliant. Team members understand how they can impact energy, utility, and raw material consumption
20%	Team can identify waste streams, impacts, and risks, but has no clear ability to affect change. The department is ISO 14001 compliant.
0%	The team cannot identify all waste streams in their department. Team does not have a clear comprehension of environmental impacts and risk areas.

Appendix C

AGREEMENT ON UNIFORMS BETWEEN UAW LOCAL 171 AND VOLVO POWERTRAIN SEPTEMBER 19, 2006

1. Scope – This agreement applies to all Manufacturing employees in the MD work environment (Management and Non-Management) in Hagerstown and all others who choose to support the MD work environment.

2. Purpose of the Agreement - The UAW and Manufacturing Management have chosen to adopt a new way of working in order to meet the needs of our customers and enhance our future employment security. We have called this new culture "MD" for Mission Driven. This new way of working has been defined in the Union and Management prerequisite agreements and we have committed to these principles through signing these agreements and through participating in the MD training.

By committing to live the values and principles of this new MD work environment, the employees of Volvo Powertrain are demonstrating their professionalism, their pride in the products they make and their willingness to act as ambassadors to customers, community and visitors who come to the plant.

In order to symbolize these commitments, the employees of Volvo Powertrain have chosen to wear uniforms that demonstrate the joint commitment of Manufacturing Management and the UAW to meet and exceed customer requirements and to demonstrate their professionalism every day.

3. What We Expect of Each Other - Therefore, we will:

    a.   Wear the designated uniforms, as issued, when in the workplace;

    b.   Maintain and clean the uniforms in order to assure a professional appearance;

    c.   Practice the manufacturing values of Individual Dignity and Mutual Responsibility and Collaboration to ensure that we hold each other accountable for living this agreement and for practicing the professionalism that is essential to our mutual success.

INDEX

121, 122, 123, 124, 125, 126, 127, 128, 129, 130, 131, 132, 133, 134, 135, 136, 137, 138, 139, 140, 141, 142, 143, 144, 145, 146, 147, 148, 149, 150, 151, 152, 153, 154, 155, 157, 158, 159, 160, 161, 162, 163, 164, 165, 166, 167, 168, 169, 170, 171, 172, 173, 174, 175, 176, 177, 178, 179, 180, 181, 182, 183, 184, 185, 186, 187, 188, 189, 190, 191, 192, 193, 194, 195, 196, 197, 198, 199, 200, 201, 202, 203, 204, 205, 208, 209, 214, 221, 222, 223, 224, 226, 227, 228, 229, 230, 239, 240, 241, 243, 249
Juran, Joseph 33

K

Kaiser. Maurice (Mo) 123, 124, 138, 138, 150, 151, 153, 154, 155, 161, 208, 209
Kaizen 181
KPI 189
Kriner, Tom 40

L

Lamone, Rudy iii, 211
Lean 181, 200
LeBlond, Denis 144, 159, 166, 168
Lehigh Valley 19, 32
Leigh, Jim 87, 249, 252
Leopold, Les 18
Lewis, Bobby 41
Lopes, Tony 145

M

Mack vi, 1, 2, 3, 4, 5, 6, 7, 8, 9, 10, 11, 12, 13, 14, 15, 16, 17, 19, 20, 21, 23, 24, 25, 26, 27, 28, 29, 30, 31, 32, 33, 34, 35, 36, 38, 42, 43, 44, 45, 46, 51, 53, 56, 57, 58, 60, 62, 63, 65, 66, 71, 72, 73, 74, 78, 80, 85, 86, 89, 91, 92, 94, 95, 98, 101, 102, 105, 111, 112, 117, 120, 121, 128, 133, 136, 141, 142, 143, 144, 145, 146, 147, 149, 154, 157, 160, 161, 164, 166, 167, 172, 175, 178, 185, 202, 207, 208, 210, 211, 212, 215, 216, 218, 219, 220, 221, 228, 229, 234, 235, 236, 237, 241, 245, 251, 253
Mack,Jack 5, 9
Mangini, Bob 40

Made in the USA
Middletown, DE
28 September 2022